With the disappearance of the Habsburg empire after First World War, the imperial port of Trieste passed into Italian hands. During the Second World War, the Nazis reclaimed the city as part of the Reich. In 1945, Trieste slipped through Tito's fingers and was internationalised under Allied military government control. In 1954, it returned to Italian sovereignty.

This book examines Trieste's transformation from an imperial commercial centre at the crossroads of the Italian, German and Balkan worlds to an Italian border city on the southern fringe of the iron curtain. Concentrating on local sources, the book shows how Triestines, renowned for their cosmopolitan Central European affiliations, articulated an Italian civic identity after the First World War. Tracing the fitful process of affirming Trieste's Italianness over the course of nearly four decades of liberal, Fascist and international rule, it suggests that Italianisation resulted from complicated interactions with Rome and interference by international powers attempting to strengthen western Europe at the edge of the Balkans.

Essential reading for specialists in modern Italian history, this book offers a crucial perspective on the reshaping of Europe in the twentieth century, during the Cold War period and beyond.

ROYAL HISTORICAL SOCIETY

STUDIES IN HISTORY

New Series

MAKING TRIESTE ITALIAN, 1918–1954

MAKING TRIESTE ITALIAN
1918–1954

Maura Hametz

THE ROYAL HISTORICAL SOCIETY
THE BOYDELL PRESS

First published 2005

A Royal Historical Society publication
Published by The Boydell Press
an imprint of Boydell & Brewer Ltd
PO Box 9, Woodbridge, Suffolk IP12 3DF, UK
and of Boydell & Brewer Inc.
668 Mt Hope Avenue, Rochester, NY 14620, USA
website: www.boydellandbrewer.com

ISBN 0 86193 279 X

ISSN 0269–2244

A catalogue record for this book is available
from the British Library

This book is printed on acid-free paper

Printed in Great Britain by
Cromwell Press, Trowbridge, Wiltshire

Contents

FOR TODD
AND JONATHAN AND ZACHARY

Publication of this volume was aided by a generous grant from
the College of Arts and Letters, Old Dominion University

Acknowledgements

I am deeply indebted to a great many individuals and institutions for support in the preparation of this book. An Award for Advanced Research on Europe from the German Marshall Fund of the United States and the Council for the United States and Italy allowed me to spend a full year engaged in research and writing in 1999–2000. Old Dominion University provided a summer grant, support in aid of publication and allowed me leave to complete the project. Brandeis University and the Fondazione Giovanni Agnelli provided assistance at key junctures.

Archivists and librarians in the United States and Italy were helpful, exceedingly patient, and courteous in response to my inquiries, in person and in writing. In Trieste, I would like to thank the staff of the Archivio di stato, in particular Signora Carla Triadan and Director Ugo Cova for their encouragement and assistance. At Trieste's Archivio diplomatico, Signore Arcon offered help and suggestions. Signora Ninino guided me through the collections at the archives of the Civici Musei di storia ed arte. At Old Dominion University, Beverly Barco and Pamela Morgan acquired materials from near and far. Librarians at the New York Public Library fulfilled endless requests on hot summer days for books buried deep in the stacks.

Colleagues and friends have been extremely generous with their time and unflinching in their support for the project, even when they disagreed with my approach or as they offered apt criticisms. I owe special thanks to Mark Mazower who saw the essence of the book through the murkiness of a draft, was instrumental in the book's publication and even provided the title. Alice Kelikian has been a mentor and friend, offering valuable advice and guidance. I would like to express my gratitude to Alexander DeGrand, John Davis, Roland Sarti, Nancy Wingfield, Lucy Riall, Richard Jones, Aaron Gillette, Larry Wolff, Annette Finley-Croswhite, Ruth Ben-Ghiat, Lois Dubin, Giovanni Panjek, Pieter Judson, Giovanni Vianelli, Austin Jersild, Catherine Albrecht and the many anonymous readers who took the time to review or comment on my work at various stages. Marina Petronio, Lucio Marampon, Emidio Sussi, Pietro Covre, Paolo Marz, Lidia Mattichio Bastianich and Marina Hadziomerovic provided assistance along the way.

Research in Italy would have been impossible without the assistance and friendship of Michela Bassanese. The Bassanese and Pisani families were gracious hosts during stays in Trieste. Thanks to the many friends who shared their love for the Adriatic city and, in particular, to Riccardo Kriscjak who introduced me to the natural splendour of the Carso and Istria. The Piovan family offered warm hospitality and a perspective on national identity in the Veneto and Friuli. Sanja Juric and the Juric family introduced me to the

Italian traditions of Croatia from their home in Zagreb. All deserve my heart-felt thanks.

Sharon Hametz, Natalie Danner and Rosa Motta greatly improved the book with their editorial and stylistic suggestions. Christine Linehan and Joy McCarthy of the Royal Historical Society guided the manuscript through the editorial process with great patience. I alone take responsibility for the short-comings that remain. The jacket illustration is reproduced by kind permission of the Ministero per i Beni e le Attività Culturali, Soprintendenza PSAD del Veneto. The map was prepared by Donald K. Emminger, Graphic Designer, Old Dominion University, Norfolk, VA, to whom I am most grateful.

Finally, I wish to thank my family. My parents Marilyn and Ivan Hametz instilled in me a love for learning and a curiosity that sustained me through years of research and writing. Sharon Hametz, Patricia Hametz, Chris Berner and Audrey and Richard Webb helped me to keep a sense of humour and perspective. The book is dedicated to my husband and sons. Todd Webb, with good humour and grace, has stuck by with a love that has sustained me for years. Jonathan, who came along midway through the project, and Zachary, who arrived near its completion, have made it worthwhile.

Maura Hametz

Abbreviations

AdS	Archivio di stato, Trieste
BC, RP	Biblioteca civica, Trieste, raccolta patria
BCCI	*Bollettino della Camera di Commercio e Industria di Trieste*
BMLT	*Bollettino Mensile del Lloyd Triestino* later *Bollettino Mensile del Gruppo Armatoriali Italia-Cosulich-Lloyd Triestino*
CCIA	Camera di commercio, industria e artigianato, later Camera di commercio, industria, artigianato ed agricoltura
CGCVG (adg)	Commissariato generale civile per la Venezia Giulia, atti di gabinetto
CGCVG (ag)	Commissariato generale civile per la Venezia Giulia, atti generali
PPT (rc)	Prefettura della provincia di Trieste, divisione I: riduzione cognomi
RMCT	*Rivista Mensile della Città di Trieste*

Trieste and Italy's shifting eastern border, 1918–54

Introduction

One glance at a map begs the question, 'Why is Trieste in Italy?' The city is located on the eastern Adriatic shore opposite and a bit north of Venice. It is on the landmass contiguous with the Balkans. The simple answer is, 'Trieste is in Italy because the negotiators of the Paris Peace gave Italy sovereignty over the Habsburg port.' After the First World War, the former Habsburg commercial maritime capital, of approximately 200,000 inhabitants, stood on the Italian side of the new border between Italy and the Kingdom of Serbs, Croats and Slovenes.[1] The city called Triest by the Germans, Trst by the Slavs and Trieste by the Italians became the capital of the new north-eastern Italian territory of Venezia Giulia.[2] Political and juridical absorption did not equate to acceptance of intrinsic or incontrovertible Italianness. Over the nearly four decades, from 1918 to 1954, Italy fought to prove its rightful claim to Trieste and promote the Italianness of lands at the head of the Adriatic Sea.

In 1917 Triestine historian and Italian nationalist Attilio Tamaro asked, 'Of what is Trieste a part if not of Italy?'[3] The answer was not a simple one. Austro-Germans held the city that, for more than five hundred years, had been under the house of Habsburg. The South Slavs, in particular Croats and Slovenes, saw the lands on the eastern shore of the Adriatic as part of their patrimony. Abandoned by the defeated Austrians, interwar Trieste became an Italian border town where the interests of Italians and Slavs, or Italy and Yugoslavia collided.

The creation of the South Slav state and the eastward expansion of Italy established the geopolitical basis for diametric opposition between Slavic and Italian interests after the First World War. Most analyses of Trieste's fate in the twentieth century approach the history of Trieste with this contest in mind. Trieste perches precariously at the edge of Italy and western Europe. The 'problem', 'conflict', 'question' or 'struggle' relates to the establishment of the Free Territory of Trieste and the impact of the emerging Cold War on local political affairs in the wake of the Second World War.[4] The city's reas-

---

[1] This study refers to the South Slav State or the Kingdom of Serbs, Croats and Slovenes for the period prior to 1929, when it officially became the Kingdom of Yugoslavia.

[2] For the sake of clarity and consistency, throughout the study place names reflect Italian usage unless the specific context calls for use of a Slavic or Germanic name.

[3] A. Tamaro, *Trieste et son rôle antigermanique*, Paris 1917, 101.

[4] The best-known studies are D. De Castro, *Il problema di Trieste: genesi e sviluppi della questione giuliana in relazione agli avvenimenti internazionali*, Bologna 1952; J. Duroselle, *Le Conflit de Trieste, 1943–1954*, Brussels 1966; B. Novak, *Trieste, 1941–1954: the ethnic, polit-*

signment to Italy in 1954, after nine years of Allied military governance, appears as an early victory for the west, an indication of democratic supremacy over communism and, in retrospect, an affirmation of the justice of the extension of Italian sovereignty over the city.[5]

Historically, from the western point of view, the Adriatic had separated western Europeans from the 'less cultivated, less polite' parts of Europe.[6] The contest over territory in the upper Adriatic area is understood as a conflict between Italians and Slavs.[7] Slovenes, Croats and Serbs who appear in the generic category of 'uncultured' Slavs, are opposed to 'civilised' Italians. Historical literature and pamphlets produced for international consumption by Italians, South Slavs and emigrant groups engaged in projects of national construction in the era of the First World War reinforced notions of polar opposition or at least diametric difference.[8] For the South Slavs, this was part of the national building process. Glossing over ethnic and cultural differences among Slavs justified inclusion in a Slavic nation state. These bi-polar categorisations supported understandings of allegiance and identity that affected political and cultural developments in the region over the course of the twentieth century.

Recent studies of Trieste and surrounding areas, spurred by the breakdown of Yugoslavia, have begun to emphasise the multiple ethnic perspectives that informed Yugoslav and Italian relations.[9] This study injects an additional perspective by uncovering the enduring attachments to Central Europeanness and cosmopolitanness that remain relatively unexplored in works examining Trieste after the city's annexation to Italy. Nation-centred political alignments arising out of the First World War forced a choice between Italy and Yugoslavia, but did not erase underlying attachments to formerly Habsburg lands of Central Europe. In fact, Trieste's reputation as a commercial centre serving Danubian lands attracted Rome. After 1918 Rome promoted

---

ical, and ideological struggle, Chicago 1970; R. Rabel, Trieste, the United States and the Cold War, 1941–1954, Durham, NC 1988; G. Valdevit, La questione di Trieste 1941–1954: politica internazionale e contesto locale, Milan 1986; and G. Sluga, The problem of Trieste and the Italo-Yugoslav border: difference, identity, and sovereignty in twentieth-century Europe, Albany 2001.

[5] J. Campbell (ed.), Successful negotiation: Trieste, 1954: an appraisal by the five participants, Princeton 1976; B. Heuser, Western 'containment' policies in the Cold War: the Yugoslav case, 1948–1953, London 1989; R. Dinardo, 'Glimpse of an old world order? Reconsidering the Trieste crisis of 1945', Diplomatic History xxi (1997), 365–81.

[6] L. Wolff, Inventing eastern Europe, Berkeley 1994, 316.

[7] G. Sluga, 'Liberating Trieste, 1945–1954: nation, history and the Cold War', unpubl. PhD diss. Sussex 1993, 130.

[8] Distinctions between Slovenes, Croatians and Serbs are drawn and the more precise terms are employed only where the historical literature discriminates between ethnic groups or where references pertain to contemporary events.

[9] Sluga, The problem of Trieste, and P. Ballinger, History in exile: memory and identity at the borders of the Balkans, Princeton 2003, offer nuanced treatments of Italian and Slav relations in the area.

the city as a springboard for irredentist ventures and as a base for economic intervention in Central Europe. Italy pursued international economic ambitions and encouraged nationalist aims, perpetuating the 'antithesis between the economic element and the national one' that Triestine socialist and scholar Angelo Vivante identified in 1912 as 'the guiding thread of all Triestine history'.[10]

Implicit in Attilio Tamaro's question of 1917 regarding Trieste's rightful place in Italy was opposition to Austro-Germanic interests not to Slavic ambitions. Unlike the Germanic inhabitants of Italy's other new territory to the north, dubbed Venezia Tridentina by Italian nationalists, Italians and Slavs had shared the disadvantages of ethnic minorities in the Austrian empire.[11] Tensions no doubt existed and were increasing between those espousing pro-Italian and those promoting pro-Slavic political programmes before the war, but both recognised the potential for gain in the wake of the monarchy's demise.

After 1918 Italy aimed to assimilate the new eastern borderland, to make its capital Trieste subservient to the needs and desires of the central government. However, the Italian government's aspirations were unclear, and its goals were changeable. Trieste remained a city on the periphery – at the border of the Italian state in territorial or spatial terms, at the edge of the reach of the state's power, and often on the fringes of its interest. At the same time, the city's geographic and cultural distance from Rome afforded an 'opportunity structure', or a range of 'possibilities of action', tied to Rome's vacillating expectations.[12] After 1918, assimilation into the Italian state was complicated. Italy and Italian nationalists promoted the new territories of Venezia Giulia and Venezia Tridentina as integral to Venetian lands. Nationalists dubbed the Veneto, or Venezia Eugenea, and the two new territories the Three Venices or *Tre Venezie* to emphasise ties between the regions. Yet, Italianisation in the upper Adriatic took place in an area developed over five centuries to facilitate Austrian trade in the Balkans and the Mediterranean. For Italy, Trieste was both an international port and a border town.

Along the new northern border in Venezia Tridentina, Germanic influences posed a clear threat to the state's territorial integrity, and Italian politicians were forced to confront inhabitants' Germanic identity. In Trieste and the areas to the east, Germanic influences slipped into the background. With no state to champion their interests, those espousing pro-German sentiments quit the Adriatic territory or assimilated into the local population. Trieste's economic networks developed by the Habsburgs remained oriented toward

---

10 A. Vivante, *Irredentismo adriatico*, 1st edn Florence 1912, repr. Trieste 1984, 221.
11 The population of Venezia Tridentina included predominantly Italian areas (mainly in Trentino) and predominantly Germanic areas (mainly in South Tyrol).
12 S. Rokkan and D. Urwin, *Economy, territory, identity: politics of west European peripheries*, London 1983, 2–3, discusses the pitfalls and possibilities for border regions interacting with central governments.

Central Europe. The Paris Peace buried the Habsburg political entity; the influence of the empire endured.

The transfer to Italian sovereignty made Trieste's Italian residents part of the ruling ethno-nationalist group. Over the course of the decades following annexation, Rome pursued policies designed to reinforce cultural notions of *italianità* or 'Italianness' consistent with statehood. In the irredentist tradition, nationalists in Trieste and on the peninsula supported and facilitated assimilation, a goal of the programme favouring the 'redemption' of all ethnically Italian lands since nineteenth-century unification. However, the construction of national affiliation rather than the destruction of foreign ties (or inclusionary rather than exclusionary processes) guided development. The 'imagined' community of Italy proved sufficiently broad to tolerate aspects of Triestine communal and individual identity that reflected the city's history as an internationally oriented Habsburg port. The commercial elite, which enjoyed broad cultural and economic influence and even political power, albeit indirect, found Italian power networks particularly permeable.[13] Being accepted within the bounds of Italy did not require Triestines to mimic the Italianness of the peninsula because, even for those in Unification Italy, no clear standard for cultural Italianness was offered. Triestines joined others exhibiting a variety of characteristics that signalled meeting points rather than absolute convergence of elements constituting Italian identity. The Triestine perception of national belonging formed only one of myriad locally defined associations with the nation or homeland. As Peter Sahlins observed in the Pyrenees, the contours of national identity in the borderlands evolved 'less as a result of state intentions than from the local process of adopting and appropriating the nation without abandoning local interests, a local sense of place, or a local identity'.[14]

In some respects, Trieste showed its Italian face before 1918. A majority of Triestines considered themselves linked to Italy through ethnic origin, language, education or vaguely defined cultural affinities. The Habsburg era identification with the *Kulturnation* was not conceived as coincident with membership in the *Staatsnation* based on allegiance to the political entity and defined by internationally accepted borders and institutional political frameworks.[15] In the multi-national empire, where dynastic loyalty did not preclude allegiances to regionally or culturally based communities, Triestines' anational affiliations were understood as a commitment to a transnational identity or 'cosmopolitanness'. Local 'invented traditions' combined opposi-

---

[13] On the role of local elites and the permeability of the Italian state see C. Levy, 'Introduction', to C. Levy (ed.), *Italian regionalism*, Oxford 1996, 6ff.

[14] P. Sahlins, *Boundaries: the making of France and Spain in the Pyrenees*, Berkeley 1989, 9.

[15] G. Bosetti, 'La Jeune Nation italienne entre "ethnos" e "demos" ', in *Marginalités: frontières, nations et minorités*, Grenoble 1994, 48, discusses these competing frameworks for exploring the development of national identity.

tion to rural Slavs with attachments to urban Central Europe.[16] Internationalist commercial aspirations seemed at odds with Italian interests, but
Trieste's cosmopolitan reputation formed a vital component of the Triestine
relationship to the Italian state. Commercial leaders with international ties
played a vital role in facilitating absorption and promoting loyalty to the
Italian state. Working within the Italian political framework where possible,
but in private ventures as well, they delicately balanced cosmopolitan associations with institutional loyalties. Their overlapping loyalties guided
Triestines toward integration with Rome on paths paved with Central
European commercial stones.

Scholars of state nationalism might see Trieste's cosmopolitan orientation
as residual, anti-modern provincialism or traditionalism, but scholars of the
frontier have seen the 'ambivalent loyalties' of borderland peoples as 'conspicuous and historically important'.[17] In fact, local belief in the cosmopolitan orientation of the city did contribute to a form of myopic *municipalismo*
or municipalism, a tendency to exaggerate the international importance of
the city. After 1918 the regional or urban affiliation inspired confidence and
a sense of security, albeit misplaced, that Trieste could survive and prosper as
an autonomous entity should national alignments shift once again. Faith in
the natural or organic strength of the port city surfaced in recurring calls for
internationalisation or for the granting of free port status. Economic interests
and irredentists bent on repudiating the Germanic Habsburg influence
promoted the city's purported autonomy. By coincidence their stance was in
line with that of the socialists who pursued internationalism as a key element
of their ideological platform.

After the First World War Triestines, like other former imperial subjects
throughout Europe, struggled to be accepted as citizens of the national state.
In Rome, suspicions lingered that Triestine Italianness was compromised, but
Trieste, like Vienna, retained economic affinity to the west. Despite the unre-
lenting decline in the economic fortunes of the port city, promotion of
western-style capitalism remained a priority. Those committed to
western-based notions of democracy and freedom cast territorial issues in
black and white. However, the lack of clear natural boundaries separating
ethnic communities complicated the politics of sovereignty in the upper
Adriatic territory. Idealistic principles of ethnic national self-determination
could not adequately accommodate the population of mixed origins and the
complex web of allegiances. International mediators were not concerned
particularly with the exact position of the boundary line between Italy and
Yugoslavia or with the details of Italian or Slavic claims. They became
involved in local disputes because, in the western mind, the eastern border-

16 'Invented traditions' is derived from E. Hobsbawm, 'Introduction', to E. Hobsbawm and
T. Ranger (eds), *Inventing traditions*, Cambridge 1983, 2–3.
17 O. Lattimore, *Studies in frontier history: collected papers, 1928–1958*, London 1962, 470.

land of Italy formed the edge of 'civilised' Europe at the gate to the 'uncivilised' Balkans.

After 1918 Rome's policies induced members of minority populations to accept the trappings of locally defined allegiance to Italy and Italianness. The majority of Triestines, including many ethnic Slavs, collaborated in the formation of ties to Rome and the promotion of a local version of Italianness. Slavs, considered representatives of an assimilable inferior culture, and, at the same time, as agents of a dangerous and even primitive adversarial state, bore the brunt of xenophobic persecution, particularly under Fascism.[18]

After September 1943 Nazi occupation and brief Yugoslav rule compromised Triestine Italianness. The interruption of Italian sovereignty opened the door for international mediators after the Second World War who debated and reiterated various claims to Trieste and surrounding territories during the period of Allied military rule. Allied negotiators' internationalisation of Trieste was consistent with the notion of the city's commitment to and association with free trade in Central European networks, but this unaligned position proved untenable in the climate of bi-polar divisions emerging with the onset of the Cold War. The descent of the iron curtain from 'Stettin in the Baltic to Trieste in the Adriatic' did not simply define political spheres.[19] It drew sharp delineations between economic systems. Capitalist orientation based in liberal economic traditions helped to justify Italian claims to Trieste. When the western Allies grew weary of their role as overseers of the city they fell back on preferences for the 'western' Italians over the 'eastern' Slavs with the added element of support for democratic and capitalist Italy over communist Yugoslavia. In 1954 foreign interests hammered out a settlement of the territorial contest over the Free Territory of Trieste. The compromise imposed on Yugoslavia and Italy by international mediators assigned the city of Trieste to Italy and affirmed the coincidence of Triestine agendas with Italian national aims and international interests that had evolved since 1918.

Emphasis on the city's relationship to its Slavic neighbour, and Germanic domination of Central Europe, often read *Mitteleuropa*, contribute to a tendency to marginalise Trieste, the city at the eastern reaches of western Europe.[20] In 1986 Timothy Garton Ash noted that Prague and Budapest, rather than Berlin or Vienna, formed the loci of renascent Central Europe, coalescing in response to the desires of European intellectuals in the former

[18] Sluga, *The problem of Trieste*, 53, explores the importance of these visions of Slavs.
[19] D. Cannadine (ed.), *Blood, toil, tears, and sweat: the speeches of Winston Churchill*, Boston 1989, 303.
[20] E. Schwarz, 'What Central Europe is and what it is not', in G. Schöpflin and N. Wood (eds), *In search of Central Europe*, Cambridge 1989, 145–7, traces the contemporary intellectual focus on Germanic culture in central Europeanness to the influence of Friedrich Naumann's *Mitteleuropa* published in 1915.

satellite states to distance themselves from Moscow.[21] In the 1990s Slavic Central Europe re-emerged. The collapse of Yugoslavia contributed to the reconceptualisation of Central Europe. Slovenia and Croatia, subject to centuries of Habsburg control and tied to the Roman Catholic Church, separated themselves from other former Yugoslav republics. These emerging states differentiated their pasts from those of the 'Balkan states', marked by an Ottoman past and tainted by association with the 'exotic' eastern other.

More recent journalistic discourse has proposed yet another shift in the definition of Central Europe. In 2000, admitting that membership in Central Europe has largely been 'a state of mind', *The Economist* labelled Garton Ash's Central Europe 'old central Europe, 1989 (Warsaw Pact)'. 'Core central Europe, 2000' included Slovenia and excluded Germany, Rumania and Bulgaria. The quieting of the Yugoslav conflict, continuing turmoil in Russia and debates linked to security issues and the expansion of the North Atlantic Treaty Organisation had shifted Central Europe yet farther east. The magazine predicted that the 'new central Europe 2010?' might include Poland, Lithuania, Belarus and Ukraine.[22] Some now view these countries are already well ensconced in Central Europe. What these contemporary Central Europes share is an identity bound up in opposition to former allegiances based on Cold War alignments. 'Fortunate' to have fallen into the western camp during the Cold War, Trieste and other former Habsburg lands including Austria, once considered the heart of Central Europe, are ignored in the rush to identify a new Central Europe in opposition to the former communist east.

Recognition of the dynamism of the mapping of territorial affiliation complicates understanding of individuals' identities and historic affiliations. It justifies competing claims to territory and helps to explain the complicated and prolonged international dispute over territory at the head of the Adriatic Sea. Italy and Italianness became predominant in Trieste as a result of the extension of Italian statehood and the western emphasis on anti-socialism and anti-communism after 1918. Triestine Central Europeanness was (and continues to be) bound up in integration with the lands of Slavic Central Europe as well as with Austria.

Fundamentally, this study addresses larger questions facing Europe after the First World War: the local effects of the transformation of European empires to nation states and the shaping of inhabitants of European societies into national citizens. Italian involvement in the north-eastern borderland from the viewpoint of the provincial capital of Trieste offers a window on Italy's experience as a successor state bent on constructing a national community after the First World War.

On one level, this book attempts, as Alon Confino did for Württemberg

---

[21] T. Garton Ash, 'Does Central Europe exist?', *New York Review of Books*, 9 Oct. 1986, 45–52.
[22] 'Where is Central Europe?', *The Economist*, 8 July 2000, 49–50.

Germany, to 'explore the ways people turn national: how they devised a common denominator between their intimate local place and the abstract national world'.[23] Some 'common denominators', including cultural and linguistic links, already tied Triestines to this 'abstract national world' when the city was joined to Italy, but the process of assimilating Triestines as full members of the Italian community was complicated by the persistence of local allegiances and particularist expectations shaped by everyday experiences in the borderland. This account sees borders as more than metaphoric constructions.[24] It examines the political, economic and cultural impact of Trieste's proximity to 'the edge of the state'.

This portrait focuses on the voices of Triestines, overlooked in accounts of international diplomatic and political squabbles in which the city generally forms a short scene enacted on the Cold War stage. The analysis of local sources demonstrates that the binary view of Italian and Slavic culture does not fit the reality of Triestine experience. International political expectations after the First World War placed ethnic tensions between Italians and Slavs in the foreground. However, Triestine identity was predicated on ties to both Habsburg Central Europe and to Italy. It reflected local understandings of political and economic allegiances. Memoirs, government documents, literature, local periodicals and other published sources illuminate the complexities of the situation.

In general, those involved in quotidian commerce neither sought nor gained sustained public attention on the national or international stage. Commercial players in Trieste were reluctant to enter public, ethnically charged political debates. They left behind few narrative sources making their involvement and influence on community life in Trieste somewhat difficult to trace. None the less records of their interactions with governmental agencies and with other segments of the population offer evidence of their co-operation with the Italian state and their willingness to assume an Italian identity. For them, Italy emerged as the only territorial contender with the potential to protect their interests developed under the patronage of Vienna. Only Rome appeared able to supply government aid in an ostensibly liberal economic atmosphere.

Chamber of commerce correspondence and the papers of Igino Brocchi, a Triestine linked to various ministries in Rome in the 1920s and 1930s, offer insight into the economic life of the city and the position of commercial interests under Fascism. Various collections, including documents on repatriation after the First World War and name changes instituted by Liberal and Fascist authorities, describe the interactions of individuals from all walks of life with local and national government officials struggling with the complexities of nationalisation of the population.

---

[23] A. Confino, *The nation as a local metaphor: Württemberg, imperial Germany, and national memory, 1871–1918*, Chapel Hill 1997, p. xii.

[24] H. Donnan and T. Wilson, *Borders: frontiers of identity, nation and state*, Oxford 1999, 10.

The melding of commercial elites with Italian nationalist professional classes and intellectuals in the period following the First World War is evident in the letters and correspondence of two Triestine natives, Attilio Tamaro and Silvio Benco.[25] Tamaro, active in irredentist circles prior to the First World War, served as a career Italian diplomat and a leading nationalist historian. Benco, a noted writer, critic and local political figure, was a lifelong proponent of the Italian national cause. Interned at Linz by the Austrians for his political views during the First World War, he proved a loyal and devoted servant of Fascism in the interwar years. During the German occupation of Trieste he served as editor of *Il Piccolo*, the Triestine daily.

This study explores the development of Trieste's relationship with Rome and Trieste's assimilation into the Italian state from a variety of perspectives. Chapter 1 studies how Trieste fitted into the Italian political framework. The city's prominence in nationalist and irredentist debates and its symbolic importance as the guardian of the eastern border served as the bases for engagement between centre and periphery. The extension of Italian sovereignty included the promotion of political institutional ties, but these links were formed with an eye to preserving vestiges of the territory's political past. Maintenance of relations with former imperial lands in foreign states served as a basis for the promotion and spread of Italian influence abroad.

Chapter 2 explores the Triestine struggle to reconcile political assimilation and economic integration. Triestines eyed formerly profitable markets in Danubian Central Europe as a natural commercial outlet; Italy focused on Triestine involvement in Central Europe and the Balkans as part of a broader programme to infiltrate markets to the east and northeast. Local hopes for the revival of free port privileges clashed with Italian ambitions to control trade through Trieste to feed irredentist and imperial Italian appetites.

Chapter 3 looks at how states and nationalist interests competing for control in the area cast the landscape to fit their political agendas. Many Triestines envisaged an organic order imposed by the landscape. Territorial claims, political aims and economic demands relied on this view of the natural world.[26] Italians on the peninsula looked at Trieste as a city on the geographic periphery. The border delineated the extent of the state, but at same time formed a frontier, 'a front or vanguard' for the Italian nation seeking to exert its power in Europe.[27]

Chapter 4 explores Triestine conceptions of nationalism and ethnicity with an emphasis on individual relationships to the Italian state and nation. For the purposes of the study, 'ethnic associations' and 'ethnicity' refer to the

[25] A. Millo, *L'élite del potere a Trieste: una biografia collettiva, 1891–1938*, Milan 1989, and G. Sapelli, *Trieste italiana: mito e destino economico*, Milan 1990, explore the formation of a new elite after the First World War.
[26] Several scholars have noted the political cast of geographical accounts of Trieste. On the debate see Sapelli, *Trieste italiana*, 152.
[27] Donnan and Wilson, *Borders*, 49.

complex and variable sets of characteristics perceived as defining a 'people' or social or cultural group. In contrast, 'national associations' or 'nationalism' implies ties or the desire for ties to the state. This chapter suggests that the traditional focus on ethnic difference obscures the importance of social status, cultural associations, political practice and even individual judgements in the articulation of loyalty to the state and the nation. It emphasises the malleability of personal identity and suggests that enmities did not spring from primordial ethnic difference but from politically and socially constructed interpretations of identity.

While chapters 1–4 take a chronological approach, examining developments from 1918 to 1954, chapter 5 takes a different tack. It eschews emphasis on changes over time for emphasis on continuities in an examination of overlapping and competing associations and loyalties at the community level. It explores the ambiguities of nationalist and ethnic associations in Triestine culture.[28] Associations with Slavism were cast in opposition to Italianness and ties to the city's Germanic Habsburg past were overlooked, remained unrecognised or were dismissed unless they served an immediate political purpose. These 'foreign' associations continued to form a part of Trieste's cultural landscape. They were instrumental in shaping the city's relations with the Italian state but also provided the bases for challenges to Italian claims to Trieste.

Taken together, the examinations of the various ways in which Trieste 'became Italian', illustrate the intersections and interstices of political life with economic, institutional and cultural associations. They suggest that making Trieste Italian did not simply require de-legitimising Slavic claims and disenfranchising members of minority populations. It entailed recasting Trieste in light of changing interpretations of the city's relationship to Rome and Italy's relationship to neighbouring states in Danubian Central Europe and the Balkans.

---

[28] 'Culture' is intended in broad and popular terms to mean 'the totality of socially transmitted behavior patterns, arts, beliefs, institutions, and all other products of human work and thought characteristic of a community or population': William Morris (ed.), *The American heritage dictionary of the English language*, Boston 1981, 321.

1

The Politics of a Borderland

On 3 November 1918 the Italian destroyer the *Audace* entered the harbour of Trieste and tied up alongside the San Carlo jetty. Italian troops disembarked into the heart of the city and amassed in the Piazza Grande, the city's central square and its stage for national political celebrations and urban politics.[1] In March 1921 that same square, renamed the Piazza dell'Unità in honour of the joining of Trieste and Trent to Italy, saw Triestines commemorate official annexation.[2] In September 1938 Mussolini stood in the grand piazza addressing the crowd on the eve of the initiation of his racial campaign. On 12 June 1945 Yugoslav troops quit the square as the pro-Italian western Allied military authorities arrived to take control of Zone A of the Free Territory of Trieste. On 26 October 1954 the square formed the stage for the transfer from Allied authority to Italian control, and on 4 November it served as the locus for public celebration of the return to Italian sovereignty.[3] The scenes played out on the square at the heart of the city marked the transformation of Trieste from an internationally oriented commercial port serving Germanic and Slavic interests to an Italian border city symbolising Italian and western European political aims.

The arrival of the *Audace* in November 1918 marked the shift to Italian sovereignty on the heels of the Austrian defeat, and, at the same time, it underscored a symbolic tie between the port of Trieste and the seafaring culture of Italy. Italian control extended across the Adriatic and radiated out from the city to reinforce Italian hegemony on the eastern Adriatic shore. Military authorities took control of the new eastern territory dubbed Venezia Giulia. Commander Carlo Petitti di Roreto, reporting directly to the Italian prime minister, administered the city of Trieste and twenty-nine other localities of the former Habsburg Adriatic Littoral. By March 1922 the San Carlo jetty, the site of the Italian landing, had been renamed Molo Audace, in honour of the destroyer *Audace*. This change erased the reference to the sunken Austrian warship over which the jetty had been constructed. It effec-

---

[1] On the role of the central square in Italian political life see M. Berezin, *Making the Fascist self: political culture of interwar Italy*, Ithaca 1997, and M. Isnenghi, *L'Italia in piazza: i luoghi della vita pubblica dal 1848 ai giorni nostri*, Milan 1994.
[2] Known as the Piazza Grande prior to the First World War, the square was renamed in 1916 for Franz Joseph and then called the Piazza dell'Independenza prior to Italian takeover.
[3] V. Scrinari, G. Furlan and B. Favetta, *Piazza Unità d'Italia a Trieste*, Trieste 1990, 127.

11

tively entombed the power of the imperial monarchy below that of the Italian state.[4]

Trieste's municipal council willingly collaborated in assimilation into the Italian national framework and actively transformed the city's administrative toponomy to reflect Italian sovereignty.[5] Several factors encouraged Triestine acquiescence in Italy's control. The collapse of Habsburg Austria left the city with few alternatives. Since the turn of the century, the city administration had been in the hands of Italian nationalists. Their influence was decisive in the administrative transfer of power. Local leaders presumed that Rome viewed Trieste as an important commercial centre and an asset for foreign policy. This confidence in Trieste's importance within the Italian framework was misplaced. Triestines failed to see that their city's role would be largely symbolic. Its fate would be tied to its usefulness in promoting Italian irredentism and expansion.

The Austrian Adriatic Littoral

Italian sovereignty in 1918 brought an end to more than five centuries of Austrian guardianship of Trieste that had begun in 1382, when the municipal council requested Habsburg protection against Venice. By the beginning of the sixteenth century, the Monarchy had held the upper Adriatic area with the exception of western Istria. Austrian flirtation with legislative experimentation, linked to the political and economic ideas of the Enlightenment, promoted the growth of the port in the eighteenth century. By the turn of the nineteenth century, Napoleonic occupation, the fall of the Venetian empire and brief French administration had encouraged western European political associations and created links between the upper Adriatic region and areas of the Italian peninsula as far south as Rome.

In other Italian-speaking cities within the Habsburg realm, particularly in the Veneto and Lombardy, the taste for western political ideologies spurred political revolution by 1848 and Italian nationalists threatened Habsburg control. In Trieste, by comparison, revolutionary activism held limited appeal. The city had its share of civic unrest in March 1848, but civilian and military leaders, guided by pragmatic concerns based on the port's commercial reliance on Vienna, took firm control and maintained calm. Vienna recognised Trieste's loyalty in the wake of 1848 by making it home to the Austrian navy, transferred from revolutionary Venice.[6]

[4] L. V. Bertarelli (ed.), Le Tre Venézie (Guida D'Italia), Milan 1925, iii. 238, and A. Trampus, Vie e piazze di Trieste moderna: toponomastica stradale e topografia storica, Trieste 1989, 47, 381, 610.
[5] M. Benvenisti, Sacred landscape: the buried history of the holy land since 1948, Berkeley 2000, 11–54, discusses how the modern state of Israel created an administrative toponomy.
[6] L. Sondhaus, The Habsburg empire and the sea: Austrian naval policy, 1797–1866, West Lafayette 1989, 163.

In the 1860s Italian unification, particularly the inclusion of Habsburg Venetia and Lombardy in Italy, exacerbated tensions over the fate of the Italian-speaking populations of the Adriatic Littoral. The Austro–Hungarian Compromise of 1867 brought questions of autonomy and minority rights to the fore and Trieste, along with Trento, Isontine Fruili, Istria and Dalmatia caught the attention of irredentists. 'For Trento and Trieste' became the war cry of Italian nationalists. Still, Trieste remained relatively content within the Habsburg realm. Triestine historian and archaeologist Pietro Kandler described the city as 'with Austria but not in Austria'.[7] His attitude mirrored that of many others in the city who trusted in the survival of a federated Habsburg Empire in which Trieste would continue to serve as a pillar of Habsburg maritime commerce. In 1882 Triestines commemorated the 500th anniversary of the city's union with Austria in a lavish celebration and exhibition on the new San Andrea exposition grounds and promenade overlooking the sea.[8]

Trieste's seeming loyalty did not prevent the spread of violence spurred by revolutionary nationalists and anarchists active throughout the Habsburg empire and Europe to the upper Adriatic area. The most famous local incident involved Guglielmo Oberdan (or Oberdank) who plotted to assassinate the monarch Franz Joseph on a visit to Trieste. Although Austrian officials arrested the would-be assassin even before he reached Trieste and the monarch was never directly threatened, officials' discovery of the plot shook Habsburg confidence in the loyalty of the Adriatic provinces. Oberdan's execution on the charge of treason furnished the irredentist movement with a local martyr.

By the turn of the twentieth century, nationalist pressures had mounted throughout the empire. The Habsburgs enacted policies designed to draw border provinces, including those in the Adriatic, into closer alignment with the centre. Foreigners resident in Trieste during the final decades of Habsburg rule observed the unfolding struggle between Austrian imperial affiliations and Italian irredentist aspirations. James Joyce's depiction of 'tarry easty' or the land of the east related the tensions and complexities of political and ethnic life in the city. At first, Joyce had sympathised with the internationalism espoused by the unlikely duo of the committed socialists and pro-Austrian commercial elite. Later, he turned to support the cause of professional pro-Italian factions and pointed to parallels between the Triestine situation in Austria and the Irish dilemma in Great Britain.[9]

Until the outbreak of the First World War, imperial political institutions continued to function well in the Adriatic Littoral. Pro-Italian elements

---

[7] P. Kandler, 'Federalismo, dualismo', in G. Cervani (ed.), *Nazionalità e stato di diritto per Trieste nel pensiero di Pietro Kandler*, Udine 1975, 190.
[8] 'L'esposizione di Trieste', *L'Illustrazione Italiana: rivista settimanale degli avvenimenti e personaggi contemporanei* ix/33 (13 Aug. 1882), 107
[9] J. McCourt, *The years of Bloom: James Joyce in Trieste*, Madison 2000, 3, 65–70, 98–101.

dominated the diets that served Trieste and Istria, but elected representatives were by no means revolutionary. Ensconced political interests felt pressures from the left, particularly from the reformist socialists and the power of the socialists increased. However, provincial diets ministered to local needs, and these bodies continued to serve as stepping stones for representatives to move on to careers in imperial service throughout the Habsburg lands. The local bodies served as release valves, providing outlets for political participation and limited local control in the polyglot empire.

The First World War

Wartime propaganda aroused the political and territorial ambitions of both Italians and Slavs in the Austrian Adriatic provinces. Triestine loyalties were complex and ambiguous. Slavic propagandists championed the rights of the Slovene and Croat populations and charged that the appeal of the Italian programme was limited to the 'small group of intellectuals, four or five journalists, and several members of the professions' encouraged by intellectuals and politicians on the peninsula.[10] Italian nationalists clamoured for the redemption of 'Trento and Trieste', seeking to unite all Italian populations under the flag of Italy. The ruling political faction in the city had a decidedly pro-Italian cast, but support for annexation was far from unanimous.

At the outbreak of war in 1914, the public squares in Trieste rang with cries of both 'Viva L'Austria' and 'Viva L'Italia', a testament to Triestine hopes for a continuing relationship between Italy and Austria and the maintenance of official ties through the Triple Alliance.[11] Rome declared its neutrality on 3 August 1914, but pressure mounted for Italy to enter the war. Many Triestines were caught between Italian cultural ties and Austrian political affiliations. The enactment of wartime restrictions increased surveillance along Italy's border with Austria. Italian nationalists, including Attilio Tamaro and the lawyer Camillo Ara, fled the Adriatic city. The general population suffered under the weight of increasing Austrian suspicion.[12] An engineer who regularly travelled from Austrian Trieste to visit his two sons in school in Italy was interrogated and harassed by officials on both sides of the border.[13]

At the official level, National Liberals in Trieste initiated contacts with Rome with two intents. The more public justification for their approach was to secure access to disrupted grain and food shipments to the eastern Adriatic

[10] For M. Alberti's assessment that only 2 % of Trieste's population was irredentist in 1914 see I. Mihovilovic, *Trieste et son port*, Susak 1945, 43.
[11] L. Fabi, *Trieste, 1914–1918: una città in guerra*, Trieste 1996, 16–18.
[12] H. Astori and B. Astori, *La passione di Trieste: diario di vita triestina (luglio 1914–novembre 1918)*, Florence [1920], 46.
[13] Ibid. 90.

lands. The contacts also no doubt aimed to establish channels of communication and ties to the administration in Rome.[14] In histories of Trieste recounted after the war, these men stand as Italian patriots, intent on saving the city from starvation and ensuring its 'salvation' by Italy. From the ground level at the time their patriotism and loyalty were less clear.

In Italian nationalist lore, riots that erupted in Trieste in the spring of 1915 have been cast as local reaction against Austrian authoritarianism. In fact, the disturbances were bread riots related to the disruption of trade in foodstuffs that local negotiators sought to address in Rome. In the city, the shortage of flour became acute in March 1915.[15] For political reasons associated with the British blockade of the Central Powers, Italy had refused to supply foodstuffs to the city, thus heightening the resentment of the local population. After Italian entry into the war in May, the disturbances took on a nationalist tint that was anti-Italian, not anti-Austrian. Offices of the pro-Italian Liberal daily Il Piccolo were destroyed. The statue of Giuseppe Verdi was shattered. The pro-Italian Triestine Sports Club and the Chiozza and San Marco cafés, meeting places for Italian nationalists, were attacked.[16] Many Triestines remained loyal to the monarchy. Between 1914 and 1918 more than 50,000 men from the Adriatic Littoral served under the Habsburgs. Only an estimated 1,000 irredentists fled Austrian service to volunteer in the ranks of the Italian military.[17]

The annexation and Liberal Italy

At the end of the First World War, irredentists heralded the joining of Trieste to Italy as a nationalist victory. However, Italian control of Trieste resulted more from the circumstances of the First World War and the void created by the dissolution of the Habsburg empire than from international recognition of irredentist claims. Negotiators favoured open covenants and ethnic self-determination. Under their criteria, populations on the eastern coast of the Adriatic, particularly in Istria and Dalmatia, were not clearly Italian. Italy traced claims to the secret pact of the 1915 Treaty of London, by which the country had entered the war. Irredentists and even moderate elements viewed negotiators' refusal to grant Italy's territorial wishes as a proverbial 'stab in the back', an abandonment by wartime allies and a failure to acknowledge Italy's 'sacrifices' in the fight against Austria.

---

[14] L. Riccardi, Francesco Salata tra storia, politica e diplomazia, Udine 2001, 122–4.
[15] For S. Benco's account see Fabi, Trieste, 1914–1918, 26–30. Astori and Astori, La passione, 74–87, attribute the disturbances to the shortage of bread. Save for a brief mention in McCourt, Years of Bloom, 246, the riots are ignored in English-language literature.
[16] Fabi, Trieste, 1914–1918, 43, 50–4.
[17] L. Sondhaus, In the service of the emperor: Italians in the Austrian armed forces, 1814–1918, Boulder, Col. 1990, 105.

Wrangling over eastern border issues after the First World War shook the Liberal Italian government to its foundations. Government leaders had counted on a favourable settlement of territorial claims to salvage tarnished reputations and bolster national spirits in the wake of a war that had been costly and politically divisive. Prime Minister Vittorio Orlando's support for radical nationalism rather than compromise with the Slavs and Wilson exacerbated political tensions. In December 1918 Leonida Bissolati, a leading supporter of compromise, departed Orlando's cabinet. Effective opposition to the irredentists, led by Sidney Sonnino at the foreign ministry, was eliminated.

In Paris, Italy negotiated from a position of relative weakness. Italy had entered the war late, and, arguably, as the 'least of the Great Powers'.[18] Of the Big Four, Italy alone was more concerned with Austria-Hungary than Germany. For the Americans, British and French, the fate of Trieste and areas of the Upper Adriatic aroused interest in theory, but the particulars of local territorial settlements were not a high priority. Their attention focused on the western front. Pre-conference guidelines for the peace included an American recommendation that both Trieste and Fiume be granted the status of international ports.[19] Orlando proved intransigent and vociferous demands by Italian nationalists irritated other parties at the peace table. In late April, Orlando quit the negotiations in protest at the negotiators' perceived slights to Italy. Italy's absence from the table had little effect. The conference continued, and negotiators drafted the key clauses of the German treaty that were to serve as a model for other agreements. Orlando made an unceremonious return to Paris in early May, but by then settlements had been outlined.

Rome's wrangling over the eastern border regions had negative repercussions on the city of Trieste. A squabble in early 1919 between the Central Warehouse Authority (the local port authority) and the military government illustrates the difficulties of Italian military administration in the city. Claiming coastal facilities should remain at the military's disposal given the 'actual state of war', Petitti di Roreto refused to release office space for commercial use. Authorities at the ministry of the treasury in Rome admitted to being baffled by the existing protocol for authority and regulation in the port. They turned to local officials for an explanation of the functioning of the port administration and the duties of the Central Warehouse Authority. Commercial interests gained the upper hand, and the military government relocated its headquarters at the end of March 1919.[20] But at least until 1921

---

[18] R. J. B. Bosworth, *Italy, the least of the great powers: Italian foreign policy before the First World War*, Cambridge 1979.

[19] R. Albrecht-Carrié, *Italy at the Paris Peace Conference*, New York 1938, repr. Hamden, Conn. 1966, 64. Fiume is the Italian name for the port city of Rijeka, located at the head of the Istrian peninsula and now in Croatia.

[20] Ufficio VI and affari militari, AdS, CGCVG (ag), div. VII –1919, busta 15.

confusion lingered regarding the scope of responsibility of various officials and the channels of administration in the port.[21]

Population dislocation and the lack of adequate housing posed further challenges. In January 1919 the 12,000 refugees who had either newly arrived or were returning to the city, found that private charities were overwhelmed, and aid programmes were poorly co-ordinated. Barracks and compounds were set up to assist those awaiting repatriation. By February the influx prompted officials to adopt 'severe and prudent' economic and political criteria when screening those wishing to return. By June local officials requested the assistance of additional national police officers or *carabinieri* to deal with the 400 to 700 refugees making their way through the city each day.[22]

In July 1919 a civilian governor replaced the military commander in Trieste. This administrative change did little to rectify the bureaucratic tangle or to improve conditions in Trieste. The Triestine writer Giani Stuparich captured Triestine disappointment:

> Enamoured of the 'great Italy', Triestines have felt day by day since its arrival more and more uncomfortable in contacts with the real Italy that is still small, that is officially anything but genial with its cumbersome apparatus and the inertia of its bureaucracy, with the superficiality and bombast of its character and with the thousand defects that accompany its values.[23]

Rome's approach to the assimilation of the new provinces exacerbated the political muddle. Despite the national obsession with eastern border issues, little attention was paid to the specifics of integrating the newly annexed lands. Poor communication and misunderstanding frustrated efforts to normalise relations between Trieste and Rome. The responsibilities and powers of the Triestine chamber of commerce, the council of the stock exchange and an advisory board, set up after the First World War with the vague charge to oversee local economic affairs, were not clearly delineated. Local officials, including Antonio Mosconi, municipal commissioner and then civilian commissioner for Venezia Giulia after December 1919, received uncoordinated and contrary signals from a weak and divided national leadership.

Orlando and his successor Nitti favoured the extension of limited provincial power to the newly annexed eastern borderlands. Nitti, in particular, viewed the situation in border areas with optimism. He advocated limited federalism in the new north-eastern territory. He hoped to prove that federalisation could simplify the management of diverse regions and strengthen the Italian nation. Francesco Salata, appointed to head the Central Office for the New Provinces, was attractive both to national officials who sought stability

---

[21] Ibid. busta 24.
[22] Ibid. busta 41.
[23] S. Arosio, *Scrittori di frontiera: Scipio Slataper, Giani e Carlo Stuparich*, Milan 1996, 136–7, quotes this sentiment expressed in November 1919.

and to locals in Venezia Giulia who hoped to benefit from his experience in the Istrian diet and ties to the region. An active irredentist prior to the First World War, Salata had spent the war in Italy.[24] He then served as Italy's technical expert on border matters at the peace negotiations. His arguments for Italy's claims under the Treaty of London earned him the respect of Rome and the trust of irredentists. His loyalty to Italy was beyond question, but he was not a vociferous assimilationist. He had Istrian roots, was educated in law in Vienna and had been a member of the Austro-Hungarian administration in the Istrian diet. He recognised the necessity for compromise and collaboration between Rome and the pro-Italian political leaders and economic elite of the Adriatic provinces.[25] Triestines who relied on Salata and other officials to push their interests in Rome were to be sorely disappointed. Salata's hopes for the new territory's autonomy came to naught. Despite their grand hopes for a voice in Italian affairs, Triestines found that they had traded rule by Vienna for rule by Rome.

Possession of the new territories eased Italian relations with the independent successor states, but did not necessitate the actual involvement or co-operation of Trieste in Italian foreign affairs. The headquartering of a conference of the successor states in Rome rather than in Trieste in 1921 and 1922 sent a clear signal that Trieste lacked importance. The Adriatic port was merely a provincial capital; Rome took complete charge of Italian involvement in post-First World War Central Europe.

On the heels of Italian failures at the peace conference, Orlando's government collapsed in June 1919. The stand-off over the eastern border issue had contributed to broader domestic problems and accentuated the instability of the central government. In September 1919 Prime Minister Nitti ordered the withdrawal of Italian troops from Fiume, the former Hungarian port, occupied by Italy but established as an international city by the terms of the peace. The Italian poet-patriot Gabriele D'Annunzio, pledging to protect Fiume's Italian integrity, gathered volunteer corps at Ronchi near Trieste and proceeded to march on Fiume. He occupied the city and established the Regency of Carnaro. Nitti proved incapable of dealing effectively with the situation. Raging debate over the fate of regions along the eastern border fuelled 'Nittian chaos'.[26] Conciliatory policies failed to affect a compromise, and by June 1920 a new government under Giovanni Giolitti, the master statesman and dominant politician of the pre-war period, took power.

Rather than simply subverting Habsburg institutions and legislation in the new territories, the Giolitti government (like its immediate predecessors)

---

[24] His family was interned in Austria as a result of his political activities.
[25] P. Ziller, 'Le nuove provincie nell'immediato dopoguerra: tra ricostruzione e autonomie amministrative (1918–1922)', in F. Salimbeni (ed.), *Dal litorale austriaco alla Venezia Giulia: miscellanea di studi giuliani*, Udine 1991, 244–51, and Riccardi, *Francesco Salata*, 210–12.
[26] G. Roncagli to A. Tamaro, 29 Nov. 1919, BC, RP, MS Misc. 152, Tamaro papers.

favoured maintaining regional liberties to smooth the transition to Italian sovereignty. Co-ordination of Italian and Austrian administrative practices was proposed in July 1920. Provincial diets in Venezia Giulia and the Trentino were preserved, but with limited powers. Austrian legislation remained in force despite an agreement that accompanied Italy's signature on the Treaty of St Germain allowing Italians to co-ordinate the laws of Venezia Giulia with Italian statutes.[27] Italian measures superseded Austrian laws only as dictated by immediate needs. Revived local institutions were remodelled haphazardly along Italian national lines. For example, the local tourist association came under the oversight of the Italian National Tourist Office in 1922. Prior to that, the chamber of commerce, the city of Trieste, the provincial administration for Venezia Giulia, the administration of the national railroads, the Federation of Ship Owners in Venezia Giulia, principals of the Triestine Association of Navigation and other municipal and regional public corporations had collaborated in efforts to promote tourism.

Local administrative confusion reflected the uncertain status of Trieste and the border territory. Carlo Sforza, Giolitti's foreign minister, worked diligently toward a settlement of the eastern border question and the Fiume crisis. The Italian parliament's ratification of the Treaty of Rapallo in 1920 cleared the way for the definitive annexation of Venezia Giulia including the city of Trieste. On 20 March 1921, nearly two and a half years after the cessation of the hostilities of the First World War, Triestines celebrated official unification with Italy. However, Sforza had been forced to compromise. Italy relinquished claims to Croatian Dalmatia and agreed to the creation of an independent Fiume under international supervision.

Rapallo, and juridical settlement of Italy's eastern border claims, proved to be a pyrrhic victory for Giolitti's government. The perceived 'surrender' of Italian territory and the expulsion of D'Annunzio and his forces from Fiume by the end of January 1921 excited public indignation. Right-leaning politicians enjoyed increased support for irredentist and anti-socialist policies. For Italian irredentists, whom writer Giani Stuparich noted 'lacked any sense of criticism' with regard to the eastern borderland, defence of Italy included using Trieste as a launching point for national expansion.[28]

Posters and publicity materials prepared for the 1922 International Trade Samples Fair in Trieste depicted the city as a beacon guiding Italians to the country's borders. Triestine painter Vito Timmel used a spinning roulette wheel with a swirling vortex composed of three colourful rings to join the coats of arms of Trieste, Istria, Friuli and Dalmatia with the coat of arms of the House of Savoy. In his advertisement for the state-sponsored lottery to finance the fair, figures representing Trieste, Istria and Friuli, arranged carefully in the centre of the vortex, demonstrated the equilibrium these prov-

---

[27] *Gazzetta Ufficiale del Regno d'Italia: parte prima: leggi e decreti: anno 1920*, Rome, 1 Oct., no. 232, 1322.
[28] This is quoted in Arosio, *Scrittori di frontiera*, 136.

inces had attained in the 'new Italy'. A castle not yet anchored to the centre and a detached head of a three-headed House of Savoy lion represented an unredeemed Dalmatia. The edge of the lion's collar 'reached out toward the head in an act of comfort and goodwill', signalling high hopes for the 'recovery' of the area.[29]

Fears of communist and socialist infiltration and Slavic expansionism from the east combined with the threat of the rising strength of the political left to mobilise forces on the right. From 1919 to 1921, during the so-called 'red biennium', the attention of the Liberal government focused on the increasing militancy of socialists and continuing economic difficulties. The government's reluctance to intervene forcefully in labour's 'occupation of the factories' which spread from Milan across the country in September 1920 clearly demonstrated the weakness of central leadership.

The particularities of local alignments linked to the city's former position within the Austrian empire exacerbated political instabilities. Immediately after the war, the National Liberal party was in disarray. The primary goal – annexation to Italy – had been achieved. Two major factions emerged trying to capture National Liberal support. *Rinnovamento*, or Renewal, welcomed the Italian takeover of the city but insisted on local exceptionalism. Its mouthpiece *La Nazione*, first published on 30 October 1918, emphasised the importance of retaining special protection for Triestine shipping, Istrian agriculture and local industry.[30] A more conservative offshoot of the National Liberal party took a more nationalistic stance. *Il Piccolo* announced this faction's dedication to the 'strenuous defence of the general interests of the city and surrounding regions in the interests of the [Italian] Nation and the State'.[31]

As in many other central European cities, renascent socialist parties emerged after the First World War with strong popular support. Ethnic Italian socialist leaders, adhering to reformist Austrian models of socialism, cooperated with other political groups in Trieste. The reborn socialist newspaper *Il Lavoratore* advocated moderate reforms. Despite an initial surge in power, the political left failed to capitalise on broad post-war support. The intransigence of the Italian Socialist party and its alignment with the Bolsheviks alienated moderate socialist factions throughout Italy. Trieste was no exception. The local socialists split between maximalist and reformist branches. Members of the traditional governing classes and members of the middle class turned to conservative and nationalist elements for leadership. Migration of irredentists and former exiles, reassigned to the city from duties on the peninsula, contributed to the rising nationalist tide.

Rightist groups came together to deal with particular problems related to

---

[29] F. Babudri, 'L'arte e la fiera triestina', *Fiera Campionaria Internazionale di Trieste* (May 1922), 21, illustration.
[30] D. Rusinow, *Italy's Austrian heritage, 1919–1946*, Oxford 1969, 86–7.
[31] 'Vita nuova', *Il Piccolo*, 20 Nov. 1919, 1.

life in the border region. Patterns of migration and industrialisation had attracted Slovene and Croatian workers to Trieste in the late nineteenth and early twentieth centuries. Regardless of individual political bent, members of these groups, minorities in the city, were associated with the working class and working-class politics and were vulnerable to rightist accusations of association with socialism. The political shift to the right encouraged anti-Slav prejudice and tolerance of extremist tactics of persecution and violence.

The most famous attack on Slavs in Trieste came in July 1920 when a crowd guided by Francesco Giunta, a young lawyer appointed by the central committee of the *fascio* in Milan to lead the nascent movement in Trieste, torched the Slovene Cultural Centre, the Narodni Dom. The centre had housed one of the oldest Slovene banks in the city, the Slovene theatre and library and other Slavic cultural institutions. The Triestine press and public opinion condemned the violence, but government reaction was equivocal. Civil Commissioner Mosconi found himself caught between sympathy for conservative nationalist causes and the duty to maintain public order. He ordered soldiers to defend minority interests but hesitated to act forcefully against those who participated in the attack that had taken place under the noses, and perhaps with the collaboration, of soldiers stationed in the nearby barracks.[32] Socialist, communist and Fascist groups agitating for political power contributed to the escalating confusion and violence. By January 1921 concerns for public safety prompted officials to ban the wearing of masks during the carnival season.[33]

In national elections in 1921 the Nationalist Bloc, including Fascists, rightist parties and groups of traditional elites won 22 per cent of the vote. In Trieste, the coalition captured an impressive 47 per cent. The Fascist representatives Francesco Giunta and Fulvio Suvich (a young lawyer), gained seats in the Italian parliament. Shipping lines, insurance companies, banks and large firms collaborated with the forces of the right. Their contributions directly assisted in the nationalist victory. The Assicurazioni Generali insurance firm even provided the Triestine *fascio* with office space.[34] Alarmed by the equivocation of government officials and spurred by political suspicions and pecuniary motives, commercial and political leaders had ignored the *fascio*'s violent tendencies, seeing support for the group as necessary in the fight to crush workers' organisations and political opposition. Small businessmen were also won over. The *fascio* strenuously supported Italian over 'foreign' firms operating in the city. For example, in 1920 the *fascio* demanded that a licence granted to a foreign beer firm be revoked and reissued to a local Italian producer to run the beer concession at the Triestine Fair.[35]

The *fascio*'s willingness to act in itself inspired the admiration of some

---

[32] Unione antifascista italo-slovena, *Trieste nella lotta per la democrazia*, Trieste 1945, 9.
[33] CGCVG (adg), busta 111.
[34] E. Apih, *Italia fascismo e antifascismo nella Venezia Giulia (1918–1943)*, Bari 1966, 138–9.
[35] 26 Aug. 1920, CCIA, busta 4065.19.

Triestines. Giani Stuparich claimed to deplore the blind nationalism and scorn for the rights of the people of Fascist followers, but he offered grudging praise for their willingness to upset 'the supine inertia and [expose the] cowardice of the bourgeoisie'.[36] Nationalist writer Silvio Benco felt a certain sympathy for the '*fascio* and the small group of [activist] nationalists'. He claimed that the general public shared his appreciation of the *fascio*'s efforts to 'hasten the annexation', although most did not condone the violent tactics.[37]

By September 1922, assured of public sympathy if not direct assistance, the *fascio* in Trieste aggressively promoted the nationalist, conservative agenda. A brief thaw in official relations between the new Russian government and Italy had encouraged Russian participation in the Triestine International Trade Samples Fair. Fascist thugs attacked the Russia stands.[38] Fair security stepped in to avert damage that might 'harm the delicate relationship' between Italy and Russia, but the political point had been made.[39]

Triestine acceptance of political violence in the name of nationalist and anti-socialist causes mirrored the nationalist and conservative response to political extremism throughout Italy. The 1920 attack on the Slavs and the Narodni Dom, later labelled 'a memorable night . . . a signal of Fascist conquest', served as a portent of events to come.[40] The Roman periodical *Idea Nazionale* suggested that Trieste provided a model of action in the rest of the country. It directed loyal veterans to follow the example of the Triestines that 'on their own initiative' had dealt 'with the new enemy which stabs the nation in the back'.[41] By 1921 the *fascio*'s use of violent tactics was simply part of the Italian political landscape. Giolitti failed to curb the violence; nor did his government respond effectively to the conservative challenge. In July 1921 his government collapsed, paving the way for the March on Rome and Fascist takeover in 1922.

---

[36] This is quoted in Arosio, *Scrittori di frontiera*, 196.

[37] S. Benco to Tamaro, 12 Nov. 1920, Tamaro papers.

[38] Meetings linked to the April 1922 Genoa Conference generated high hopes. Triestine commercial leader Oscar Cosulich served on an Italian committee that met with Soviet representatives: Giorgio Petracchi, 'Italy at the Genoa Conference: Italian-Soviet commercial relations', in C. Fink, A. Frohn and J. Heideking (eds), *Genoa, Rapallo, and European reconstruction in 1922*, Cambridge 1991, 159, 164–7.

[39] For an account of the clash see 'Mancata azione fascista contro la mostra russa', *Il Lavoratore: organo del partito comunista d'Italia*, 26 Sept. 1922, 3.

[40] *Guida di Trieste e della Venezia Giulia*, Trieste 1937, 54.

[41] *Idea Nazionale* (Rome), 16 Oct. 1920, quoted in A. De Grand, *The Italian Nationalist Association*, Lincoln, Neb. 1978, 120.

Fascist Italy

The violent outbursts of the early 1920s gave way to governmental coercion and institutionalised oppression as the Fascists gained power. Leaders in Rome rewarded local Fascist leaders, including Francesco Giunta, for their loyalty but remained uncertain of the allegiances of the borderland population living on the eastern fringes of the state. Igino Brocchi, a native of Trieste working at the ministry of foreign affairs, compared the role of Trieste in the Danubian world to that of Naples in the Mediterranean. In 1923 he urged Mussolini to invest in the Adriatic city for its political potential to support Italian foreign policy and to satisfy Italian ambitions as the 'base for action' in Central Europe and the Balkans.[42]

Brocchi and other Triestines failed to realise that direct aid and special privileges for Trieste would not serve the interests of Rome. Italy was already well served by international ports. Rome's support for the city hinged on Italian ambitions to clearly establish Italian power, to assimilate Trieste into Italian Fascist society and to promote cultural Italianness. In 1923 a participant at the National Congress for Commercial and Economic Expansion Abroad argued that Rome justified expenditure on Trieste as investment but suggested that aid to the city really had 'other political and sentimental purposes'.[43] Investment was tied to Rome's attempt to secure visions of Trieste as a custodian of Italian power.

Triestine international expertise and personal contacts might be helpful in obtaining intelligence useful in diplomacy, but Trieste and Triestines would play little actual role in Italian foreign relations with successor states to the interior. A request for Attilio Tamaro's assistance prior to diplomatic meetings being held in Austria in 1923 was typical of the kind of help Italian officials sought. They contacted Tamaro in the hope that he might provide the name of a 'very rich Triestine Italian' living in Vienna, someone who might exercise influence on behalf of the Italian representatives. They asked him to 'put himself immediately in contact' with Yugoslav representative Radic to discover Yugoslavia's intentions with regard to proposed Austrian co-operation with the Little Entente. An intricate web of alliances aimed against the Little Entente formed the core of Mussolini's strategy in Danubian lands. The country would act 'against the Little Entente, that is against the French, in the Balkans',[44] regardless of the interests of Trieste.

Trieste's primary foreign policy importance lay in its relationship with Italy's new eastern neighbour the South Slav State, a successor state of

---

[42] Igino Brocchi to Mussolini, 22 Mar. 1923, AdS, Archivio Igino Brocchi, 1914–31, busta 12, fasc. 114.

[43] C. Moschitti, 'Per il disciplinamento delle fiere campionarie in Italia', *Congresso nazionale per l'espansione economica e commerciale all'estero* [Trieste, 4–8 Nov. 1923], Naples 1923, 17.

[44] Roncagli to Tamaro, 11 Nov. 1923, Tamaro papers.

limited power and little importance to continental relations. The position of Italy's eastern border continued to be at issue, and Trieste served as a launch point for irredentist ventures. In March 1922 Francesco Giunta had marched on Fiume with 1,000 Fascist *squadristi*. He aimed to control Fiume and Dalmatia for Italy and to force revision of the Treaty of Rapallo. His force succeeded in occupying the former Hungarian port, and the elected autonomist mayor fled to Croatia. Throughout 1923 Mussolini's government used the *de facto* occupation and diplomatic pressure to strengthen Italy's hold, and, in January 1924, in return for Italian concessions on Port Baros, the Yugoslavs relinquished their claim to Fiume. By the Treaty of Rome of 27 January, Italy annexed the city.

The 'redemption' of Fiume did little to ameliorate the borderlands' uneasy relationship with Rome. Local nationalists were disappointed at Rome's seeming inattention to the needs of the city. Rino Alessi, a boyhood companion of Mussolini and the director of *Il Piccolo*, found fault in local parochialism: '[V]ery few know the rest of the country. So the misunderstanding [between Rome and Trieste] perpetuates itself.' He saw the lack of local leadership as the crux of the problem. 'Lacking is a man of great authority who could dispel the thick fog that obfuscates even the most agile minds', he opined.[45] Camillo Ara, who worked for Assicurazioni Generali prior to serving in a number of public administrative posts, called Rome's care for the city 'absolutely insufficient, inadequate, and not [conducive to] amicable [relations]'.[46] Attilio Tamaro blamed Rome's inattention on ignorance and the failure of the post-war Liberal government to develop the city's potential.[47]

These Triestine commentators failed to recognise that local needs were not a top priority for Rome. The official 1925 Italian Touring Club guide to the Three Venices summed up the national perspective on both the city's architecture and its affairs. Trieste was 'of little monumental importance . . . but interesting in light of ties to Istria and Dalmatia and its appeal to tourists'.[48] By 1925 even Igino Brocchi proved reluctant to champion Trieste from his post in Rome. He sympathised with old friends, but he offered little encouragement or assistance. In response to an inquiry about policies for the conversion of pre-war capital gains to lira, an issue of grave importance to members of the Triestine chamber of commerce, Brocchi suggested that the matter be brought again to the attention of Rome. He confided that earlier inquiries had probably been ignored and never passed on to the ministry of foreign affairs.[49] Brocchi refused to intervene on behalf of a Triestine who sought help regarding his application for Italian citizenship. He cautioned

45 R. Alessi to Tamaro, 21 June 1927, ibid.
46 C. Ara to Tamaro, 27 Nov. 1925, ibid.
47 Tamaro to G. Volpe, 15 Sept. 1928, ibid.
48 Bertarelli, *Le Tre Venézie*, iii. 236.
49 Brocchi to chamber of commerce, 10 Nov. 1925, Brocchi papers, busta 15, fasc. 123.

that officials in Rome were 'adverse to considerations and opinions of local elements' and would therefore be disinclined to help.[50]

Understandings of nationalism and loyalty diverged between centre and periphery. Borderland politics magnified nationalist concerns, and nationalist patriotism took on an extremist cast. Rome readily accepted individual Triestines into the national fold. Economic leaders, who co-operated in assimilation and integration but were pragmatic in voicing their political support, were welcomed and even honoured. Such individuals were attacked as insufficiently nationalist in Trieste. Arminio Brunner, a member of one of the city's leading commercial families with controlling interests in the Triestine Commercial Bank and ties to Assicurazione Generali, maintained his economic relationships with Vienna after the First World War. The Fascist government decorated him for his business acumen and contributions to national economic development.[51] In Trieste, Brunner fell prey to attacks by local nationalists exercising 'uncontrollable patriotism'. Local elements also targetted Arturo Castiglioni, a respected professional. A loyal servant and supporter of Austria before and during the First World War, Castiglioni wrote that his distress at the personal assault extended to a general disappointment with local intolerance for those who did not openly support the Fascist cause.[52]

Trieste's distance from the capital and Rome's general disinterest in local affairs caused misunderstandings. At the same time, it promoted an inflated local sense of autonomy and self-reliance. Until the enactment of Fascist legislative reforms in 1926, haphazard and piecemeal changes to the Habsburg and Liberal Italian codes governed Triestine life. The Fascist government appointed a non-Triestine mayor to help oversee the legislative reforms, but this attempt to smooth the transition and speed assimilation resulted in 'an insurrection . . . The city declared its humiliation by the choice' and expressed a preference for Camillo Ara, 'a man prepared to represent the major interests of the citizens and to make himself valuable to the centre'.[53] Rome withdrew its candidate. Central authorities looked on the incident as a minor irritation. They did not see the Triestine protest as interfering in broader Fascist policies or priorities. Triestines misinterpreted their minor triumph, seeing it as a sign that Rome was willing to negotiate due to Trieste's power and importance rather than as an inconsequential concession that reflected Rome's relative lack of interest.

In 1931 Attilio Tamaro asserted that Trieste 'never bent to the will of rulers if not constrained to by force or if it was not to its advantage'.[54] Influential Triestines banked on ties to Rome after the Habsburg collapse. After

---

[50] Brocchi to chamber of commerce, 11 Apr. 1926, ibid. fasc. 124.
[51] A. Millo, *L'élite del potere*, 250.
[52] A. Castiglioni to Tamaro, 20 Nov. 1925, Tamaro papers.
[53] Alessi to Tamaro, 21 June 1927, ibid.
[54] Tamaro to P. Sticotti, 13 Oct. 1931, ibid.

1922 the Fascist government drew Trieste into the national fold by increasing the Italian public's familiarity with the city and affirming its role as the guardian of the eastern border and protector of Italian-speaking populations 'stranded' outside Italian borders by an unfair peace. Further, the Fascists enticed influential Triestines to support the regime, offering patronage and fostering an illusion of respect for Trieste's past autonomy and prestige.

In 1931, with the blessing of Rome, local leaders initiated a 'June Tourism Week', the Giugno triestino, to 'attract an influx of visitors . . . for moral reasons', and to make Trieste 'known to its brothers at home and abroad'. The ministry of corporations recognised the Triestine June as a national fair to lend the initiative national legitimacy and prestige. However, the official calendar's description of the event as 'provincial in character, organised by the Committee for the Triestine June in Trieste' revealed local appeal rather than national importance.[55] Municipal officials bore the lion's share of responsibility for planning and execution. National officials played a largely ceremonial role. Financing came from the government, state-sponsored organisations including the Central Warehouse Authority and the chamber of commerce, and, in the closely regulated Fascist economy, from private firms invited or coerced to invest.

Government-sponsored radio programmes advertised the attractions of the Triestine June throughout Italy,[56] and government-financed rail and cruise discounts enticed visitors. Special coupons promoting trips to nearby resorts, historic sites, battlefields and even cemeteries underlined the area's sacrifices for Italy. The festival succeeded in bringing tourists to the region. In June 1931 nearly 30,000 visited. By 1934 between 15 May and 30 June, 45,710 visitors came. In 1935 an estimated 30,000 took advantage of rail reductions.[57]

The Giugno triestino mirrored other local events taking place throughout Italy. Exhibitions honouring the port police and celebrations recognising the presence of the Italian Fifth Naval Division underlined the authority of the state. Hunting competitions, automobile and motorcycle rallies and boat races emphasised physical fitness and highlighted virility and youthful aggression. Events showcasing Italy's military prowess and capabilities demonstrated local contributions to national efforts. Emphasis on First World War battles convinced Italians from the peninsula that Trieste merited the 'sacrifices made by the nation for liberation from Austrian dominance and the Slavic menace'.[58] A rally planned during the 1933 Giugno by the RACI

---

[55] Consiglio provinciale dell'economia corporativa, 21 Nov. 1934, CCIA, gruppo 16 (1934).
[56] 'L'importanza e le finalità della Mostra del Mare', Il Piccolo, 30 Mar. 1934, 4.
[57] 'Giugno triestino', Il Piccolo, 28 June 1934, 4; 'Giugno triestino', ibid. 1 Aug. 1934, 3; 'La Mostra del Mare chiusa', Il Popolo di Trieste, 21 Aug. 1934, 2; 'Il Giugno triestino dell'anno XIII', Il Piccolo, 31 Oct. 1935, 4.
[58] 'Il Giugno triestino', RMCT v/6 (1932), 245.

(Reale Automobile Club d'Italia) brought together automobile enthusiasts from all over Italy. Guided visits to battlefields and memorial services for drivers killed in the First World War emphasised the political purpose.[59] Two new flagpoles were placed at the head of the Piazza dell'Unità, on the site of an Austrian garden, in memory of drivers killed in the line of duty during the war.[60]

The Giugno triestino was part of a trend epitomised in Rome by the *Mostra della rivoluzione fascista* (Exhibition of the Fascist revolution) held to mark the tenth anniversary of the March on Rome. Exhibitions in Rome were designed to engage the public in the Fascist project and to set a standard for national desires, comportment and policies. Fascism's early political triumph in Trieste and the leading role the city had played in the 'redemption' of Fiume took centre stage in local contributions to the national event. Triestine Fascist organisations provided documents and local memorabilia for a room dedicated to the conquest of Fiume.[61] The dominating mural of the Triestine artist Giannino Marchig emphasised Italian cultural hegemony in the Adriatic. Superimposed upon a map of Italy was the Lion of St Mark, casting a shadow over lands in Dalmatia still waiting to be redeemed.[62] Trieste's position under the Lion of St Mark emphasised the city's integration into the Three Venices and at the same time affirmed the leonine link to the House of Savoy. It suggested Trieste's potential role in the further extension of Italian power.

As part of the attempt to win over the public and create a 'standardised' image of Italy, the Fascists attempted to bottle local cultures. Exhibitions in Trieste presented the provincial particularities of the Adriatic city and Venezia Giulia as typical of the diversity of Italy. The borderland's past was enveloped in Italianness. For example, equestrian competitions revived popular Austrian events that historically had highlighted the city's proximity to the village of Lipizza, the home of the famed Lippanzaner stallions. Recast by the Fascists, these shows highlighted Italian prestige, military preparedness, fitness and athleticism.

The road to empire and the German question

After 1935 irredentist ambitions offered some prospect of Trieste being able to participate in Italy's foreign policy. However, Italian imperialism in the Mediterranean marginalised Trieste at the head of the Adriatic Sea.

---

[59] E. Bartolini, L. Menegazzi and R. Curci, *150 manifesti del Friuli-Venezia Giulia: vita e costume di una regione, 1895–1940*, Padua 1982, 59–60.
[60] Scrinari, *Piazza Unità d'Italia*, 125.
[61] 'Mostra del fascismo', *Il Piccolo*, 17 Apr. 1932, 2; 'Trieste e la Mostra del fascismo', ibid. 28 Apr. 1932; 'La rivoluzione fascista', ibid. 19 Oct. 1932, 4.
[62] L. Andreotti, 'Art and politics in Fascist Italy: the exhibition of the Fascist revolution (1932)', unpubl. PhD diss. MIT 1989, 120–2, 258.

Condemnation by the League of Nations after the foray into Africa and adventures in Spain led Italy into increasing alignment with Nazi Germany. Italian attention turned from expanding influence in the Danubian sphere to the pursuit of overseas empire.

Prior to 1935 the Fascist government had encouraged and capitalised on anti-German sentiment, particularly in Trieste. While most Italians tended to conflate Germany with Austria, the two were separate in Triestine minds.[63] For Triestines, Austria was a former patron while Germany was a rival. Triestines resented Germany's historical support for Hamburg, seen as a competitor in maritime networks. They also blamed the Germans, rather than the Austro-Germans, for provoking the First World War. The Fascists manipulated Triestine anger to enhance Italy's position in Austria. Prior to 1935 Trieste played a symbolic, if minor, role in Mussolini's policies championing the independence of Austria. Italian interest, expressed in particularly warm relations between Trieste and Vienna in the early 1930s, bolstered Mussolini's position when he chose to dispatch troops to Italy's northern border to counter German aggression in the wake of the assassination of the Austrian prime minister, Dollfuss. Mussolini's *rapprochement* with Germany after 1935 meant a shift in attitudes throughout Italy. In Trieste, it called for a complete turnaround and tested the loyalty of Triestine Fascists.

Fulvio Suvich, who through his long and loyal service to Fascism had reached the rank of under-secretary of foreign affairs by 1936, proved unable to overcome his anti-German stance and sentiments. In the foreign ministry from 1932 to 1936, he played an important role in formulating Italian policies designed to check the expansion of German influence. The turn toward Germany and the ascendancy of Galeazzo Ciano to head the foreign ministry effectively derailed Suvich's career. In 1936 he was banished from Rome to Washington, DC, to serve as Italian ambassador to the United States. In 1938 he retired from public life and returned to Trieste to assume the management of the major insurance company, Riunione Adriatica di Securtà, replacing Arnoldo Frigessi, a victim of the racial laws. He, like other native Triestines including Franceso Salata could not renounce opposition to Germany. Salata had never been in the Fascist vanguard, but he had played an important role in Italian relations with Austria from 1933 until the *Anschluss* rendered his attachment to an independent Austria a political liability.[64]

The experience of Suvich and Salata contrasted with that of Tamaro who showed himself willing and able to adapt to the new political climate. The shift in policy actually furthered his career. In 1936 he was transferred from Helsinki, where he was the Italian ambassador (an assignment he considered akin to exile) to Berne, as ambassador to Switzerland. In a report to Rome in

---

[63] J. Berghold, *Italien-Austria: von der Erbfeindschaft zur Europäischen offnung*, Vienna 1997, 128.

[64] Riccardi, *Francesco Salata*, 337–64.

early 1937 he explained his support for the Fascist policy based on his perspective from Berne. At first he had opposed Italian *rapprochement* with Germany for fear that it would place Switzerland between 'two anti-democratic and irredentist powers' (France and Germany). His experience in Switzerland (and no doubt the desire for self-preservation) convinced him that warmer relations between Rome and Berlin were 'a guarantee of security and of peace for the future of the [Swiss] Confederation'.[65]

In Trieste, the shift to support for Germany manifested itself in an increasing 'Fascistisation' and overt commitment to national, rather than nationalist, agendas. Italian imperialism was the focus of the centennial celebration of Lloyd Triestino in 1936, which lauded the firm's participation in the 'founding of the empire' and its role in supporting Italian networks overseas.[66] The local tourist agency, exercising influence through the Italian National Tourist Bureau and affiliated organisations, intensified efforts to attract visitors to Trieste from German-speaking regions. In 1938 the official guide to the city produced by the local tourist agency even appeared in German.[67] In September 1938 Mussolini visited the city for the first time since taking power. This did not reflect any increased attention to the city itself, but rather to its ties to Austria and the Germanic world.

Changes to Trieste's administrative toponomy reflected the increased attention to Fascist priorities. The Piazza della Borsa (marketplace), dedicated to the city's history of commerce, became Piazza Costanzo Ciano in 1939, in memory of the recently departed Fascist official. Via dell'Istituto, named for the location of the poor house, was transformed to Via Giovanni Pascoli to honour the Italian poet and lyricist. Other streets were renamed for local heroes of Italy's Africa campaign including Arrigo Protti, Odorico Panfili and Arturo Zanolla. In 1940 Via Sara Davis, commemorating a local benefactress, became Via Casala in honour of the conquest of that city in Eritrea. Via Raffaele Abro, named in memory of a nineteenth-century diplomat, became Via Guido Presel in honour of a soldier killed in action in Spain. Both emphasised recent Fascist exploits and activities. Raffaele Abro's name was erased at the same time as that of others including Guido Brunner, a volunteer killed fighting for Italy in the First World War, to eliminate traces of Jewish participation and influence in Italian nationalist circles.[68]

Many Triestines found the initiation of the racial campaign, mimicking Nazi policies, disconcerting. Antisemitism gained ground in Italy as Rome drew closer to Berlin, but the extension of discriminatory legislation caught many in Trieste by surprise. Members of the Jewish population of approximately 5,000 (generally acknowledged as the third largest in Fascist Italy)

---

65 'La Svizzera e l'Italia' [report], 8 Jan.1937, Tamaro papers.
66 'La missione imperiale di Trieste illustrata da Alberto Pirelli', *Il Piccolo*, 7 Nov. 1936, 4.
67 Azienda autonoma di soggiorno e turismo von Trieste, *Das Trieste der Touristen*, Trieste 1938.
68 Trampus, *Vie e piazze*, 29ff.

exerted considerable political and economic influence, had unabashedly supported Italian nationalism and saw themselves as full Italian citizens.[69] Prior to 1938 Mussolini had generally distinguished between Italian Jews loyal to the state and those linked to financially motivated 'world Jewry'.[70] After the Manifesto of Race was issued, many influential Jews hoped to gain special dispensations, relying on service to the regime or past loyalty to Italy, to exempt them from the effects of the racial laws. Most were to be disappointed.[71]

Triestines had mixed reactions to the increasingly militant stance of Fascism. The March 1938 *Anschluss* raised fears of German domination, and the 1939 Pact of Steel exacerbated local trepidations regarding German designs on the region. Fear of alliance with Germany tempered the enthusiasm of some Italian Triestines and former irredentists for the regime after 1938. Small anti-Fascist groups spanned the political spectrum and included members of Justice and Liberty, a movement organised in the early 1930s. However, the republican opposition remained weak and isolated. Most people in the city either failed to grasp the gravity of the change in Italian policy or chose to ignore it.

Resistance did emerge, but under the leadership of those who had opposed Italian Fascism in the 1920s and early 1930s. The communist and revolutionary opposition, fed by links to nearby Yugoslavia, had periodically surfaced throughout the Fascist *ventennio*. Slavs had been under particular suspicion. Between February 1927 and July 1932, the Special State Tribunal condemned 106 Slavs to 1,124 years of prison for anti-Fascist activities.[72] In 1936 Italian communists and Slovene and Croatian revolutionaries in Venezia Giulia had entered into a pact for unified anti-Fascist action.[73] In February 1939 the communist Pino Tomasich led a clandestine meeting in the village of Opicina in the hills above Trieste at which a concrete plan was laid out for action against German and Italian Fascism. After the Soviet-German pact of 1939, the group turned to anti-military and anti-war propaganda and activities. However, by 1941, key members of Tomasich's

[69] For various estimates of the Jewish population see S. Della Pergola, *Anatomia dell'ebraismo italiano: caratteristiche demografiche, economiche, sociali, religiose e politiche di una minoranza*, Assisi 1976, 60 (table 6); G. Reitlinger, *The final solution: the attempt to exterminate the Jews of Europe, 1939–1945*, London 1968, repr. Northvale, NJ 1987, 356–7; R. De Felice, *Storia degli ebrei sotto il fascismo*, Turin 1993, 10; C. Ipsen, *Dictating demography: the problem of population in Fascist Italy*, Cambridge 1996, 191.

[70] B. Mussolini, *Opera omnia*, XXIX : *1 ottobre 1937–10 giugno 1940*, ed. E. Susmel and D. Susmel, Florence 1959, 146.

[71] For more on the impact of Fascist racism in Trieste see M. Hametz, 'The ambivalence of Italian antisemitism: Fascism, nationalism, and racism in Trieste', *Holocaust and Genocide Studies* xvi (2002), 376–401.

[72] E. Apih, *Dal regime alla resistenza: Venezia Giulia, 1922–1943*, Udine 1960, 28.

[73] R. Pupo, *Guerra e dopoguerra al confine orientale d'Italia, 1938–1956*, Udine 1999, 30.

conspiratorial network had been caught and were being tried by the Fascist special tribunal in Trieste. Others would soon take their places.

Graffiti scribbled on a wall in Trieste in 1940 warned, 'Mussolini, be careful of the steps you take! The dream of Bismarck was and will be fatal for us!' The warning reflected a preoccupation with Trieste's past experience at the hands of Germans. The slogans 'Viva Stalin' and 'Down with Italy' testified to the seething rivalry which would break out during the war and result in the division of the territory at the end of the hostilities.[74]

In response to Yugoslavia's entry into the war in 1941, Triestines rallied around anti-Slavism. Pro-Italian forces came together in a consensus built against 'enemy Slavs'. Italian nationalists celebrated the annexation of Slovenia including the capital, Ljubljana, and parts of Croatia.[75] Communist groups, on the other hand, taking their cue from Yugoslav cells, coalesced in opposition to Fascist authority throughout Italian lands. Italian nationalists who opposed the Fascist alliance and the democratically minded found it difficult to organise. Resistance supporters remained scattered, lacking in consistent social aims and a unified political platform.

The Nazi Adriatic Littoral

In the autumn of 1943 German forces occupied Trieste. In recognition of the area's association with the Habsburgs, the Nazis absorbed the city and surrounding regions into Greater Germany rather than including it in northern Italy under the emerging puppet regime of Salò. From the German perspective, the creation of the German Adriatic Coastland simplified the structure of Nazi administration and restored territory to the German 'national' fold. From the perspective of inhabitants, the fusion of Trieste, Slovenia and Istria raised the spectre of Germanisation in lands contested for twenty years between Yugoslavs and Italians.

The German occupation pushed some that had been complacent under Italian Fascism into resistance. The persecution of influential Jewish Triestines raised concerns prior to 1943, but the enactment of German racial policies scared local elements that saw the Nazi policies as unwelcome and dangerous German interference. The deportation of members of the influential Morpurgo family rocked commercial circles. German attempts to coerce or entice commercial leaders into supporting Nazi leadership were not particularly effective. Among the local notables detained by the Nazis on suspicion of resistance were the Cosulich brothers, including Antonio Cosulich, head of the provincial economic advisory board and president of Assicurazioni

---

74 Apih, *Italia fascismo*, 387.
75 Pupo, *Guerra e dopoguerra*, 33.

Generali. Members of the Cosulich family were well known for their Italian nationalist leanings.

However, resistance forces remained fragmented. Pro-Italian forces on the right sympathised with the anti-Nazi stance of the socialist and communist resisters, but could not reach ideological agreement. In addition, the various groups had different visions of the post-war order. By December 1944, Giulian representatives of the Action, Italian Socialist, Christian Democrat and Liberal parties came together to defeat the Nazi occupiers. Ideological and ethnic fissures among the various factions made the pact shaky. Italian nationalists walked a political tightrope. Their support for resistance was based on opposition to Germany.

Further confusing the situation, Italian nationalist collaborators maintained ties with nationalist resisters throughout the war. In addition to Italian nationalist aspirations, they shared opposition to Slav and communist influence. Prefect Bruno Coceani and Mayor Cesare Pagnini claimed that collaboration offered the only viable plan for maintaining Italian interests and the only alternative to co-operation with the communists and Slavs.[76] Leftist elements were naturally suspicious of links between collaborating and resisting Italian nationalists and were therefore reluctant to trust members of the right-leaning resistance.

By 1944 Allied forces were fighting their way north on the Italian peninsula. Attention focused on the upper Adriatic region as an arena for a potential showdown between Allied and Fascist forces. Equally important was the likely meeting of eastern and western Allied forces in the upper Adriatic. At the end of April 1945 Yugoslav partisan groups neared Trieste. Yugoslav troops, who had defeated the German forces in Istria single-handedly, beat the German forces occupying Trieste into submission in all but a few scattered areas including the castle of San Giusto on the Capitoline Hill, Miramare castle, the law courts and Villa Opicina in the hills above the city. The German troops held out in these enclaves until their surrender to the western Allied forces at the beginning of May. The Second New Zealand Division negotiated with them and then consented to Yugoslav civil administration of the city.

On the local level the effects of the emerging politics of the Cold War were already being felt. Geoffrey Cox, one of the first western Allied soldiers to enter Trieste in May 1945, called the situation highly flammable in 'diplomatic and not military' terms. The real problem lay in the 'tension and strain between Russia and her Allies on one side and Britain and America on the other', he observed.[77]

---

[76] B. Marin to Tamaro, 17 June 1947, Tamaro papers, discusses Bruno Coceani and his role during and after the war.

[77] G. Cox, *The road to Trieste*, London 1947, 200–1, 248–9.

The Forty-Two Days

From 1 May until 12 June 1945 Yugoslav forces ruled the city. Official aims for former Italian territory and the treatment of ethnic Italians were unclear, but absorption into a federated Yugoslavia seemed the ultimate aim of Yugoslav policy. Clocks in the city were immediately moved ahead an hour to conform to Yugoslav rather than Italian time.[78] Yugoslav authorities concentrated on de-Fascistisation, but efforts to dismantle Italian Fascist administrative frameworks in favour of communist models inevitably degenerated into violence. Arrests and deportations were motivated, at least in some cases, by nationalist and ideological enmities.

Observers on the ground, including the American officer R. C. Dunlop, reported that the reception of the Yugoslav administration by the general public was guarded. 'The streets of Trieste give an impression very different from that of any other "liberated" city I have seen lately', he observed. 'The people are going about quietly and there is no manifestation of enthusiasm of any sort.'[79] For most members of the population, steeped in Italian nationalism and accustomed to Fascist rule, the extension of Yugoslav power over the city confirmed fears that the communists had aggressive and expansionist intentions. Preliminary agreements between Tito and the Allied commander, Harold Alexander, after May 8, regularised Yugoslav control and violence decreased.[80] None the less, the urban climate remained tense.

Yugoslav control was short-lived. A hastily drawn-up compromise signed in Belgrade on 9 June 1945 divided the contested upper Adriatic region into two zones in the Free Territory of Trieste. Allied military officials supervised Zone A, which included the city of Trieste. The Yugoslavs retained control of Zone B. On 12 June the population of Trieste once again assembled on the Piazza Unità. 'There was an air of expectation of great events to come', Sergeant R. J. Corrie, a New Zealander, reminisced. He mentioned a lone dissenter in the day's celebration, but his overall depiction was of the jubilation in the city as the Yugoslav troops withdrew from the city in compliance with the agreement.[81]

Several factors probably contributed to the orderly transfer of power. In the city itself, Italians were in the clear majority. The Yugoslavs may have hoped that early compromise would appease anti-Yugoslav elements and affirm the legitimacy and rationality of Tito's rule, strengthening Yugoslavia's hand later in the peace process. In addition, although the upper Adriatic area had been an arena for showdown between eastern and western Allied forces, the wartime alliance between the Soviets, British and Americans still held. Tito and Stalin were still on good terms. Stalin, probably at the prompting of

---

78 De Castro, *Il problema di Trieste*, 123–4.
79 This is quoted in Sluga, 'Liberating Trieste', 36.
80 De Castro, *Il problema di Trieste*, 124–5.
81 Dinardo, 'Glimpse', 378.

the British and Americans, may have convinced Tito to relinquish control of Trieste.

As Sergeant Corrie described, western forces and Italian elements in the city hailed 12 June as a day of liberation. The withdrawal brought an end to communist rule and what Italian nationalists and western Allies referred to as the 'forty days', a clear biblical reference to the end of the deluge. Slavs, on the other hand, remembered the years of Fascist and Nazi persecution. For them the end of Yugoslav administration was 'a "liberation" denied'.[82]

Allied military government

While the withdrawal of Yugoslav authorities removed the communists from power, it did not settle the outstanding political and territorial conflict. The Council of Foreign Ministers debated the future of the former Italian provinces of Venezia Giulia in their preparation of the Italian peace treaty. Despite obvious parallels between the post-First World War and post- Second World War international situation, the circumstances in the upper Adriatic region after the Second World War caused considerably more international concern. The emerging politics of the Cold War placed territorial politics and Trieste in the spotlight. To the British foreign secretary, Anthony Eden, the Trieste problem appeared 'always vexing, sometimes volcanic'.[83] American state department officials referred to Trieste as a 'powder-keg'.[84] Bearing in mind the American demonstration of nuclear capabilities in August 1945, international leaders saw the potential for conflagration.

In a particularly lucid description of the city's position, local historian Fabio Cusin called Trieste a 'small and perhaps negligible pawn in a European, perhaps worldwide game'.[85] Unlike most local historians, who focused narrowly on Trieste and inflated the importance of parochial interests, Cusin identified Trieste's reputation, rather than its innate strategic, material or political importance as the central factor that captured Allied attention. Trieste's location on the frontier between east and west encouraged western 'idealist fantasies' that emphasised the superiority of western democracy and glorified western humanitarianism and godliness in the face of the communist threat. It fed British and American beliefs that their exceptional capacity to maintain disinterested neutrality and to take the moral high ground gave them the upper hand in settling territorial conflicts.[86]

---

[82] Sluga, 'Liberating Trieste', 47, 87–8.

[83] A. Eden, *Full circle: the memoirs of Anthony Eden*, Boston 1960, 195.

[84] 'The Trieste powder-keg', 29 Sept. 1947, National Archives, Washington, DC, George C. Marshall Foundation, drawer 1600 [hereinafter cited as GMF], xerox 2055.

[85] F. Cusin, *La liberazione di Trieste*, Trieste 1946, 11.

[86] On the influence of 'idealist fantasies' in American foreign policy see G. Tuathail, 'Foreign policy and the hyperreal: the Reagan administration and the scripting of "South

In the upper Adriatic, the western Allies faced the choice of rewarding their former enemy, Italy, with the return of territory, some of which was gained under the Fascists, or siding with their ally, Yugoslavia, and increasing the amount of territory under communist control. Return of the Brenner provinces of the Trentino and Alto Adige to Italy, while contentious on the ground level due to the strong German ethnic presence, aroused little opposition in international circles. None of the Allied powers supported annexation to Austria, the other possible claimant, and the provinces did not lie on the fault line between east and west. In the Adriatic provinces, Yugoslav contributions to liberation and the anti-Fascist campaign could not be denied or dismissed.

On 10 February 1947 the Council of Foreign Ministers announced the peace treaty with Italy. The treaty internationalised the two zones of the Free Territory of Trieste, but they remained under separate jurisdictions, exercised by the western Allied military and the Yugoslavs. The nascent United Nations, charged with appointing a governor to oversee the Free Territory, gained supervisory power. However it did not possess the means to protect the Free Territory or its interests, nor was the extent of its powers clear. In January 1947 the Security Council approved the statute outlining the responsibilities of governorship. The United States expressed confidence that a civilian governor would be named in only a few weeks.[87] Instead, east and west locked in a stalemate over the appointment. Through five phases of negotiation France, Great Britain, Italy, the Soviet Union, the United States and Yugoslavia alternately proposed and rejected candidates for the governorship. In the first five months of 1947 alone, more than twenty candidates were rejected by the Security Council or refused the nomination.[88] A proposal by the French to allow the Yugoslavs and Italians to agree on a candidate among themselves came to naught. Control over Trieste and the entire Free Territory had drawn international attention as a matter of international prestige. The United States, Great Britain and the Soviet Union would not allow the countries directly involved to resolve the dispute.

For Italy, internationalisation seemed uncomfortably familiar. It mimicked the international approach to the creation of an autonomous Fiume after the First World War. Again the perception that Italians had been robbed of their patrimony breathed new life into rightist political factions with nationalistic and irredentist aims.[89] Irredentism presented a particular problem for the

---

Africa" ', in T. Barnes and J. Duncan (eds), *Writing worlds: discourse, text and metaphor in the representation of landscape*, London 1992, 156–8.

[87] 'Withdrawal from Italy and establishment of U.S. contingent for interim period in free territory of Trieste', n.d. [prior to Feb. 1947], GMF, xerox 3535.

[88] De Castro, *Il problema di Trieste*, 353–408, details the conflict over the appointment of the governor.

[89] Novak, *Trieste, 1941–1954*, 160.

Italian Foreign Office as it attempted to escape the imperial legacy of Fascism and establish the legitimacy of the post-war Italian government.

Internationalisation profoundly disappointed many professionals in Trieste who remained strongly nationalist. Camillo de Franceschi, an Istrian by birth and director of the civic library in Trieste, saw the creation of the Free Territory as 'a misadventure and abomination', unimaginable after the *redenzione* of 1918. He saw that Trieste's best chance lay in 'winning a part of the foreign press' to the pro-Italian cause as 'the Italian newspapers who come for the major part show little excitement in Trieste's favour, are often unknowing and of uncertain insight regarding the vital problems of our miserable province'. De Franceschi feared that 'Autonomy or independence with the absolute renunciation of the greater part of Slovene territory in the Carso and Gorizia would be the last rat'. This would be preferable at least to 'falling into the paws of the cat'.[90]

Attilio Tamaro blamed Rome and regional representatives for the city's predicament. 'The errors of the men in charge are grave', he wrote. 'However the Giulian representatives have also committed some which are neither few nor minor.'

> [They] came to Rome and went to Paris divided among themselves, factious, unprepared regarding the problems, too preoccupied by their personal positions, ignorant of the facts. . . . [T]heir fear of seeming to be nationalists was comic in itself, but had tragic consequences. . . . They played with the statistics and with the historical references, but were incapable of raising themselves by force of faith and will.
>
> Equivocation led them to concede on several points and 'by accepting several Slav ideas, they favoured the tactics of the adversaries. – Who, given a hand, took an arm'.[91]

Commercial and business leaders tended to side with professionals who favoured reunification with Italy. Fascism had tied commerce and business firmly to the Italian structure. Ties with business-minded members of the Committee for Northern Italy, headquartered in Milan, remained strong. Yugoslav communism threatened the capitalist foundations of the port society.

Members of ethnic minority populations saw annexation to Italy as an invitation to renewed persecution. These groups included only a minority of the urban population, but surrounding areas were more heavily Slavic. Many feared that they would be 'stranded' in a foreign state. They were uneasy about living near the border. Independence offered an alternative to being cut off entirely from either east or west.

No matter how logical independence might seem to segments of the Free Territory population, the western Allies proved unwilling to allow Trieste to

---

[90] C. de Franceschi to Tamaro, 16 June 1946, Tamaro papers.
[91] Tamaro to Benco, 18 Aug. 1946, BC, RP, MS Misc. 58, Benco papers.

'fall victim' to the 'Yugoslav cat'. Both the British and the Americans were convinced, prior to 1948 at least, that Trieste lay on a fault line and that the city was worth protecting for the west. The British saw the problem as strategic. Trieste formed part of its sphere of influence in the Mediterranean and Europe. The Americans focused on the city's role in the construction of a democratic world order.[92] Provocative American State Department rhetoric compared Yugoslav propaganda campaigns and military presence along Italy's border to 'Nazi build-ups before moving against Czechoslovakia and Poland'.[93]

Anti-communist and anti-socialist bias infected politics and administration on the Italian peninsula. In 1946 Italy's precarious coalition government included Christian Democrats led by the prime minister, Alcide DeGasperi, socialists led by the foreign minister, Pietro Nenni, and communists led by the minister of justice, Palmiro Togliatti. Allied pressures undermined communist and leftist elements. Internecine ideological squabbles further weakened the left. By 1947 the Italian socialists had split. Nenni's radical socialists favoured a 'third force' socialist government linking western Europe to the USSR. Giuseppe Saragat's Secessionists, in alliance with British and American leftists, founded the Social Democratic party willing to co-operate in a coalition government.[94]

Traditional moderate capitalist elements found their political home with the Christian Democrats, a party which also benefited from the support of the Roman Catholic Church and the assistance of the United States.[95] DeGasperi, bolstered by external support and international confidence, initiated a ministerial reshuffling to oust representatives of the left from national posts.[96] In 1948 the defeat of the left at the polls cleared the path for the consolidation of Christian Democratic government. Italian adherence to the Atlantic Pact and to the Council of Europe placed the country firmly among western European states. Italy became a reliable partner in the coalition against Soviet-inspired communism.

Italy's rehabilitation strengthened Rome's hand with regard to claims to Trieste. Allied policies for Zone A already reflected western protectionism and paternalism. An American officer, Benedict Alpers, noted the tendency of the British to treat 'everyone – often including their American allies – as colonials'.[97] Yet the name given to American forces stationed in Trieste, TRUST (Trieste United States Troops), clearly revealed the Americans' proprietary attitude. The Allies believed that theirs had been a triumph over

---

92 Dinardo, 'Glimpse', 365.
93 'The Trieste powder-keg', 29 Sept. 1947, GMF, xerox 2055.
94 J. Harper, *America and the reconstruction of Italy, 1945–1948*, Cambridge 1986, 144–5.
95 D. Day, 'The shaping of postwar Italy', unpubl. PhD diss. Chicago 1982, 248.
96 G. Lundestad, 'Empire by invitation? The United States and western Europe, 1945–1952', in C. Maier (ed.), *The Cold War in Europe*, New York 1991, 150.
97 This is quoted in Sluga, *The problem of Trieste*, 117.

evil Fascist forces, and garnered from this a sense of moral rectitude. The Americans, in particular, saw themselves as disinterested and altruistic negotiators struggling to decide the fate of ungrateful peoples preoccupied with self-interested squabbles. They claimed political neutrality in the administration of Zone A, but they exhibited a pronounced sympathy for pro-Italian elements.

As early as June 1945 Harold Alexander, supreme Allied commander in the Mediterranean, had interpreted Tito's evacuation of Zone A as an affirmation of the region's inherent Italian character. The Allied military government labelled the two zones the 'Italian' and 'Yugoslav' sectors demonstrating their understanding of territorial politics.[98] Alexander justified the continuation of Italian administration in Zone A by suggesting 'inasmuch as the basic law of the area is and must continue to be Italian, the Italian administrative system . . . must in its essentials be continued'.[99] Alfred Connor Bowman, head of civilian affairs for the Allied military government from 1945 to 1947, contended that the western Allies acted as caretakers to maintain the *status quo*. His version of '*status quo*' included insuring a Trieste free of communist and socialist influence and oriented decisively toward Italy.

Italian was the non-English language of choice for Allied officials in Zone A. Press conferences and meetings were held in Italian or in English with an Italian interpreter. Slavic translators did not attend.[100] Rome furnished long distance telephone. The Triestine postal system used Italian stamps overprinted with 'AMG-FTT' (Allied military government-Free Territory of Trieste). The Allied military government issued identity cards that identified inhabitants by their pre-war citizenship, making all native Triestines officially Italian. Agreements made with the Committee for the Liberation of Upper Italy provided the administrative framework for both northern Italy and Trieste. Failing to recognise the differing war experiences of northern Italy, under Salò, and Trieste, joined to the Nazi *Reich*, the Allies made the same assumptions in the Free Territory regarding the 'essential neutrality' of the bureaucracy. This allowed local administrators, even those who had collaborated with the Nazis, to resume their posts.[101]

Bureaucratic entrenchment and Allied sympathies for Italian nationalists made efforts to purge local Fascist administrators and functionaries ineffective. Of a total of 40,059 whose cases were brought to the purge commission in Trieste, 37,787 (94 per cent) were dismissed without adjudication.[102] Evidence of long public service careers, begun under Liberal Italy or even

[98] See, for example, General T. S. Airey, *Report on the administration of the British-US zone of the Free Territory of Trieste*, i-xi, Trieste 1947–51, appendices.
[99] This is quoted in Novak, *Trieste, 1941–1954*, 209.
[100] A. C. Bowman, *Zones of strain*, Stanford 1982, 88.
[101] C. Duggan and C. Wagstaff (eds), *Italy in the Cold War: politics, culture and society, 1948–58*, Oxford 1995, 3.
[102] R. Spazzali, *Epurazione di frontiera: le ambigue sanzioni contro il fascismo nella Venezia Giulia, 1945–1948*, Gorizia 2000, 391. These included state workers, public service and

Habsburg Austria and continued through the Fascist period, seemed to bear out the assertions of the many who claimed to have acted simply as loyal servants of the city. Allied assertions were backed by local nationalist support. Writers Umberto Saba and Giani Stuparich dismissed allegations of Fascist collaboration levelled at Pier Antonio Quarantotto Gambini, who had accepted the position of director of the municipal library under the Nazis. As 'a man of letters', Gambini was above political reproach. His service did not indicate loyalty to Fascism or support for Nazism, but rather an attachment to Italy and a commitment to perpetuating Italian culture in the face of foreign occupation.[103] Allied and local authorities concurred.

On 20 March 1948 the western powers issued the Tri-Partite Proposal that announced their support for Italian claims to the city of Trieste and the Free Territory. Ostensibly prompted by the inability of the United Nations to agree on a governor for the territory, the announcement was timed to support the Christian Democrats in the Italian elections. The proposal proved a useful political instrument. It helped the Christian Democratic cause and established a concrete basis for Italian leaders' later claims to western support for Trieste's return to Italy. After Italian elections in 1948, the international importance of the fate of the territories on Italy's eastern border began to diminish. The victory of republican and democratic forces seemed to secure Italy for the west.

On 29 September the Soviets renounced the Treaty of Friendship and Mutual Assistance with Yugoslavia. The expulsion of Yugoslavia from Cominform contributed to the sense that the west no longer faced monolithic Soviet communism on Italy's eastern border. Yugoslavia's willingness to accept American aid and Tito's record of co-operation during the Second World War smoothed the path for the western Allies to accept an independent, communist Yugoslavia. In 1949 and 1950 the Americans and British complained of the Soviet attempt to link the settlement for Trieste to the treaty with Austria. The Allies interpreted Soviet intervention as an aggressive step to strengthen the communist position by blocking the appointment of a governor for the Free Territory. In fact, the Soviets probably objected to the American use of Trieste to supply large numbers of troops stationed in Austria. The Soviet Union lost the bid to influence the Austrian treaty. In adherence to the agreement reached at Paris, the Soviets withdrew their troops east of the Austrian border. Other international events contributed to the Allied resolve to quit the Free Territory. In October 1949 the Greek guerrillas were defeated, allaying general anxieties over Soviet ambitions in the Balkans. The outbreak of the Korean War in 1950 diverted western attention to conflagrations in Asia.

---

utility workers, employees of cultural, educational, research, athletic, recreational and social work institutions run by the state, and workers at scattered private firms.
[103] Sluga, 'Liberating Trieste', 143.

In 1949 the United States had agreed to hold elections in the Free Territory. The American State Department hoped that a firm show of support for modern western elements might deflate the ambitions of pro-Yugoslavs and internationalists and check the power of aggressive Italian nationalists.[104] Election results were hardly edifying for Allied authorities. In all areas except the actual city of Trieste, parties advocating autonomy under United Nations' guarantee won a majority of the vote. Political prejudice may well have caused Allied authorities to misinterpret this result. Support for independence was not a veiled vote in support of Yugoslav socialism. The results of the elections were decidedly anti-Yugoslav. Overall support for communist parties was lower than expected, and left-leaning Slovenes and Italians voted overwhelmingly for candidates aligned with Italian Cominformists rather than with Titoist factions, by a margin of 42,587 to 5,344 votes.[105] The result in Zone A indicated an affinity with socialist internationalism fed by popular dissatisfaction with Italian nationalism, Fascism and anti-Slavism.

Local voices favouring independence would not, however, be heard. Initiatives to strengthen the territory's independent position were ignored. For example, local leaders dispatched Swiss journalist Gualtiero Lieblien, a resident of Trieste, to his native country to push for a Swiss nominee to take the post of governor of the Free Territory. Neither Italy nor any of the occupying military powers supported Lieblien's visit. His efforts were doomed to failure.[106]

Small details of local life and administration affirmed the western allies disregard for the independence of Zone A. Throughout Italy, the coat of arms of Savoy was removed from mail collection boxes to mark acknowledgment of the birth of the Italian Republic in 1948. In Trieste, too, the insignia of Savoy was eradicated. No one gave a thought to the fact that in an ostensibly autonomous Free Trieste, these boxes, and indeed the postal service, bore no imprint of Allied Military or independent authority.[107] By 1949 the Allied military government had lifted all constraints on travel between Zone A and Italy. Travel from the east, even from nearby interior regions, remained restricted. Yugoslav authorities in Zone B, feeling threatened by the pro-Italian sympathies of officials in Zone A, countered with the enactment of pro-Yugoslav legislation addressing similar issues in the sector under their control.[108]

Promotional literature for the trade fairs held in Trieste emphasised the

[104] US political adviser, Trieste, to secretary of state, 14 Sept. 1948, GMF, xerox 2029.

[105] Novak, *Trieste, 1941–1954*, 306–11. In the city of Trieste, of 168,108 valid votes, the Christian Democrats won 65,627 or 39%, followed by the Cominformists with 35,548 votes or 21%. The remaining votes went to smaller parties, which took less than 7% of the vote.

[106] De Castro, *Il problema di Trieste*, 367–8.

[107] A post box with the obliterated imperial coat of arms is displayed at the 'Museo postale e telegrafico della mitteleuropa' in the central post office on Via Roma, Trieste.

[108] Novak, *Trieste, 1941–1954*, 400–1.

city's debt to and ties with Italy. One article in the fair periodical described all people in Trieste as 'crazy with love for Italy'. Another traced the steps being taken toward fulfilment of the Tri-Partite Proposal to 'permit recovery and peacefulness in the zone'.[109] In 1950 the organisers of the fair sponsored an essay competition. Both prize-winning essays, 'illustrating the purpose and characteristics of the fair', assumed the city's return to Italy. An Austrian journalist whose writing emphasised 'the importance of administrative return to Italy' won an honourable mention.[110]

Representatives from Rome waxed enthusiastic about ties between the Free Territory and Italy. In his speech on the opening of the fair in 1948, the Italian minister of foreign trade identified the 'breath of Italy in the economy of Trieste'.[111] Trieste also hosted the national meeting of the Institute for the History of the Italian Risorgimento. Situating the conference in Trieste emphasised Rome's support for the city and highlighted its importance to Italian nationalist struggles. It implied that the city belonged within the borders of 'redeemed' Italy.

By the late 1940s irredentist politics took an antagonistic tone in the city. By 1951 virulent Italian nationalism taxed the sympathies of Allied officials. Tito's increasing distance from Moscow and willingness to compromise with the west stood in stark contrast to Italian intransigence on nationalist issues. For a brief moment, Tito's government appeared conciliatory, and the western Allies' support for Italy appeared to waver. However, the spread of communism (in any form) was simply unpalatable. Allied commitment to western agendas proved decisive.

Allied administration distanced Italy from its Fascist past. Allied programmes promoted exalted notions of western humanitarianism. Refugee camps, including one established in San Sabba, the site of the former Nazi concentration camp and crematorium in Trieste, served as an example of western beneficence. Set up to provide an institutional framework for Allied officials dealing with refugee problems that plagued the city, the camps provided a home for 'foreign' refugees. They also incidentally relieved pressure on local administrators to assimilate members of 'foreign' populations, especially Slavs. An array of organisations contributed to improving the lives of the 3,000 people living in the San Sabba camp who sought a 'haven' in the west. The World Council of Churches and the National Catholic Welfare Conference attended to the spiritual as well as material needs of the 'refugees' from '18 different European nations'. The YMCA and YWCA provided recreational and educational facilities. Under the aegis of the World Council

---

[109] U. Sartori, 'Richiamo irresistible', *Fiera di Trieste* i (Sept. 1948), 59; Mario Polla, 'Per la rinascita economica', ibid, 63.
[110] Commissione giudicatrice del concorso giornalistico, 17 Oct. 1950, and Fiera di Trieste to CCIA, 24 July 1950, CCIA, cat. XXVIII–1950.
[111] C. Merzagora, 'Il respiro dell'Italia nell'economia di Trieste', *Fiera di Trieste* i (Sept. 1948), 103.

of Churches, a vocational training programme offered classes in skilled trades to help the camp's inhabitants to prepare for 'their opportunity to establish new homes in the free world'.[112]

Allied beneficence in Trieste did not prompt Italy to invest in the city. Trieste remained low on the list of national priorities. The chamber of commerce complained that the city 'had the worst ties to the centre [Rome] and was therefore the latest and least informed' of national plans.[113] Particularly irksome were suggestions made by central officials that Triestines should feel an affinity for Sicilians and others from southern Italy with whom they shared similar experiences of living 'on the peripheries'.[114]

Diego De Castro, Italian representative in Trieste, drove home Trieste's unimportance in his assessment of a squabble with Padua over the timing of trade fairs in 1953. National elections caused officials to postpone Padua's event, shifting it to Trieste's slot in the Italian national calendar. Trieste complained to Rome. DeCastro chastised the Triestines for their narrow self-interest. He urged those in the city to view the problem more broadly, reminding them that 'no one gets angry that Trieste costs a lot'. Italy had 'higher priorities that require[d] attention'.[115]

With the change in the American administration in 1953, when Eisenhower replaced Truman, the Triestine conflict figured less prominently on America's list of priorities. The Balkan Pact of Friendship between Yugoslavia, Greece and Turkey laid to rest lingering western fears of the spread of communism into the Adriatic region. Parliamentary crises in Rome and the threat of a resurgent left weakened Italy. Stalin's death brought a slight thaw in relations between Yugoslavia and the Soviet Union, strengthening Tito's hand. General Winterton, Allied commander of the Free Territory, announced the western Allies' intention to withdraw troops from the territory. A broadcast by Giorgio Borsa for the BBC's 'The Listener', that went on air on 15 October 1953 presented the western Allies' position as a vote of confidence in Italy. British and American withdrawal would 'fully restor[e] Italian confidence in her allies'. It would also counter communist and Fascist propaganda charging the western Allies with imperial intentions.[116]

In late 1953, to end the stalemate over the Free Territory, the Americans and the British abandoned their previous interventionist stance and turned to support for bilateral talks between Italy and Yugoslavia. The United Nations once again became an arena for debate. The Soviet Union charged that Britain and the United States had procrastinated intentionally over the appointment of a governor in order to 'convert [Trieste] into an illegal

---

[112] 'San Sabba's camp for DPs offers new life to homeless', *The Blue Devil*, 17 July 1954, 2.

[113] CCIA to ministero del commercio estero (Rome), 8 Aug. 1950, CCIA, cat. XXVIII–1950.

[114] Fiera di Trieste, press release, 9 June 1951, ibid. 1951.

[115] Consiglio d'amministrazione, Fiera di Trieste, 30 Apr. 1953, ibid. 1953.

[116] G. Borsa, 'What Trieste means to Italy', *The Listener* (BBC), 15 Oct. 1953, 620.

military and naval base'.[117] The Russians called on the United Nations to name a governor for the Free Territory and end the bilateral talks. However, the Security Council remained at an impasse. The western allies forged ahead. Their actions underlined the impotence of the United Nations, the impossibility of international oversight, and the weak position of the USSR in the Triestine affair.

In a series of secret talks, western diplomats approached first Yugoslavia and then Italy. The American ambassador to Vienna, Llewellyn Thompson, negotiated on behalf of the United States. Geoffrey Harrison, assistant undersecretary of state to the British Foreign Office, represented Great Britain. The French, distraught at their recent defeat at Dien Bien Phu and distracted by negotiations of the Geneva Agreements on the fate of Indochina, demonstrated little interest in Trieste. The French Assembly's rejection of the European Defence Community and French dissatisfaction with German rearmament compromise probably also made Paris disinclined to co-operate with Washington. Rebuffed by the inaction of the United Nations, preoccupied with domestic issues and distanced from local politics by Tito's non-aligned stance, Moscow avoided involvement. The British and Americans neither requested nor welcomed Triestine involvement. The eagerness of influential locals to co-operate with the western powers and Italian agendas had undermined any independent prerogative by 1953. Triestines had welcomed the United States' 'empire by invitation' and were subject to its constraints as well as privileges.[118]

The return to Italy

On the afternoon of 5 October 1954 the Italian flag was hoisted above the town hall overlooking the Piazza dell'Unità. General Winterton told Triestines that Yugoslavia and Italy had agreed to the Memorandum of Understanding, effectively ending the Allied occupation.[119] The memorandum, a provisional agreement signed by representatives of the Yugoslav, Italian, British and American governments extended Italian and Yugoslav civil administration over Zones A and B respectively.[120] The United States and Britain declared that they would no longer support 'claims of either Yugoslavia or Italy to territory under the sovereignty of the other'.[121] France and the Soviet Union expressed their approval. Resolution of the territorial

---

[117] 'Political and security questions: the question of the Free Territory of Trieste', *Yearbook of the United Nations*, Lake Success, NY 1953, 249.

[118] See Lundestad, 'Empire by invitation', 143–65.

[119] Officially, the terms of the Italian peace treaty remained in force. Juridical abrogation required the agreement of all parties. Neither the Soviets nor the French were involved in the negotiation or signing of the memorandum.

[120] A few small border modifications were made.

[121] Novak, *Trieste, 1941–1954*, 460–3.

conflict over Trieste, a spark with potential to light European and east/west conflagration, had ultimately caused 'scarcely a ripple on the international waters'.[122]

Predictably, for Italy the settlement proved bittersweet. Representatives on both political extremes protested against the compromise and the separation of the two zones. The left decried capitulation to western ambition and capitalist domination. Those on the right mourned the abandonment of Italian territory and the desertion of Italian nationals in Istria. None the less, Prime Minister Mario Scelba held firm and the agreement passed in the Italian senate and the chamber of deputies by a slim margin.[123]

In Trieste dissenting voices cried out over the perceived injustices. *Il Lavoratore*, reflecting the Italian left's Cominformist stance, objected to the extension of national sovereignty over a region that had been promised independence. It urged readers to fight for an agreement 'in support of . . . unification of the two zones, application of the Italian Peace Treaty [of 1947], and local plebiscite'.[124] It also bemoaned the absorption of populations in Zone B into Tito's state. At the opposite end of the political spectrum, irredentists decried the 'loss' of Istria and other lands once a part of Fascist Italy. By and large Trieste's population, hoping for a return to normalcy, welcomed the 1954 Memorandum. The major daily, *Il Giornale di Trieste*, rejoiced at the end of Allied administration, but hastened to remind Triestines that entry into Italy would require a difficult period of assimilation and local political disruption. The paper underlined the importance of accepting Italian assistance to allow the city to fulfil its 'economic and political duties in the interests of the nation'.[125]

On 26 October crowds gathered on the Piazza dell'Unità to watch the transfer of authority from Allied troops to Italian authorities. *Il Giornale di Trieste* ceased publication. *Il Piccolo*, the right-leaning newspaper published by pro-Italian factions from the end of the nineteenth century and maintained by the Fascists until the end of the Second World War, returned to the scene. Nine years of Allied rule had been sufficient to rid the paper of its Fascist taint. More than forty pages of the 26 October edition explored Trieste's institutions, activities, history and prospects within Italy.

On 4 November crowds thronged the Piazza dell'Unità once again.[126] Scelba welcomed Triestines into the nation promising that the Memorandum of Understanding would constitute a jumping-off point for future collabora-

---

[122] Campbell, *Successful negotiation*, 21.

[123] Novak, *Trieste, 1941–1954*, 462–3. The senate voted 122:99 to accept the memorandum; the chamber of deputies voted 295:265 with seven abstentions.

[124] 'Dichiarazione del partito comunista sulla spartizione del territorio libero', *Il Lavoratore*, 4 Oct. 1954, 1.

[125] 'I compiti che attendono l'Italia a Trieste: l'ora della revisione di tutti i nostri problemi', *Il Giornale di Trieste*, 6 Oct. 1954, 1.

[126] The Piazza dell'Unità was renamed Piazza Unità dell'Italia by order of the municipal council on 21 Apr. 1955: Trampus, *Vie e piazze*, 644.

tion between Yugoslavia and Italy.[127] The prime minister's visit to the city coincided with the celebration of the 'redemption' of 1918 and the feast of San Giusto honouring the city's patron saint. Despite the pomp though, Trieste remained on the margins of the nation. The port offered little benefit to Italy. The city held but symbolic importance on the edge of the iron curtain.

Two months after Trieste's return to Italy, Guido Piovene, on assignment for the Italian Broadcasting Corporation RAI, observed that the city could not 'be administered with an ordinary mentality, [as] nature and history make [Trieste] exceptional. A special yardstick is needed to measure situations, needs, and special intentions'.[128] The yardstick marked the need for aid and assistance that would become a staple of relations between Rome and Trieste. At the same time, it measured the distance between Trieste and Rome, the continuing isolation of the periphery from the centre.

[127] Novak, *Trieste, 1941–1954*, 443, 467–8.
[128] G. Piovene, *Viaggio in Italia*, Milan 1957, 57.

2

The 'Natural Order' and the Economy of Trieste

The fog began to descend on Trieste, no longer a noble and mercantile city amidst its veils in the twilight – a slow but calculated degradation from market city to provincial southern or Levantine city: Carolus Cergoly[1]

Today my kingdom is a no man's land.
The port lights for others its lamps: Umberto Saba[2]

In 1882 Giosuè Carducci asked, 'In the end, will Trieste content herself to be the Hamburg of the south for commercial leaders and German interests?' 'No, she will want to become an Italian port', was the famed Italian nationalist's answer.[3] The depiction of Trieste as an Italian stronghold played to the political sympathies of irredentists and captured the imagination of those hoping for unification with Italy. Carducci clearly called for the Adriatic port's 'liberation', the freeing of an 'Italian' centre trapped within the confines of the Germanic empire and playing second fiddle to Hamburg. Less apparent in the statement, but perhaps more important, was an economic assumption. Trieste's fame rested first and foremost on its reputation as an international commercial port. Many Triestines were convinced that prosperity under Habsburg auspices stemmed from a 'natural' position in an 'organic' order of commerce and European trade. Those advocating annexation to Italy assumed that political change would not alter the 'natural order'. They believed, as the chamber of commerce bulletin suggested in 1920 after the 'redemption', that Trieste could simply 'open its door and salute those from every part of the world who want to contribute to the growth of honest trade'.[4]

Although it was not yet clear in 1920, the economic reality of annexation was quite different. Trieste's fortunes declined steadily after 1918. Reconstruction proved a dismal failure. Trieste's location, political circumstances and changes in the nature of international commerce made the port obsolete.

---

[1]   C. Cergoly, *Il complesso dell'imperatore: collages di fantasie e memorie di un mitteleuropeo*, Milan 1979, 207 (after annexation to Italy).
[2]   U. Saba, 'Ulysses', in *The dark of the sun: selected poems of Umberto Saba*, Lanham, MD 1994, 99 (after the Second World War).
[3]   'Giosuè Carducci per Guglielmo Oberdan' (1882), in *Il diritto d'Italia su Trieste e l'Istria*, Milan 1915, doc. 497,690.
[4]   'Museo Commerciale', *BCCI* i/9 (1920), 235.

In Italy, other ports including Mestre, Bari and Genoa already catered to Triestine markets or could be easily outfitted to do so. Italian interest in Trieste resided in the political utility of the city's Habsburg relationships. Trieste's ties to Austrian lands validated Italian economic intervention in the successor states of the empire and the western Balkans. Rome needed to maintain the illusion of the port's international importance, but not to invest in its economic future.

Habsburg development

Intending to challenge Venetian domination, Charles VI extended free trade privileges in the Adriatic in 1719. From 1731 to 1775 Trieste functioned as the administrative centre of the Adriatic commercial zone. Habsburg policies fostered commercial expansion overseas. In 1835 the navigation firm Lloyd Austrian was founded. In 1836 the Austrian government granted the steamship line a charter initiating close co-operation between the private venture and the government. The marriage of government and trade fostered a sense of privilege and entitlement on the part of commercial interests in the city. By 1851 Lloyd had become the largest steamship company in the Mediterranean.[5]

By 1857 the Südbahn rail connection from Vienna to Trieste provided the Austrian capital with a direct link to the Adriatic. Barely ten years later, Austria lost Venice to Italy, and the monarchy was forced to abandon trade facilities on the western shore of the Adriatic Sea. In 1867 the Austro-Hungarian compromise that split the Adriatic coast between the two separate administrative units enhanced Triestine prospects. The compromise eased competition between Trieste and Fiume and allowed Trieste to capture trade from the more industrialised and developed areas of the Habsburg empire, including Austria proper and Bohemia. Fiume processed Hungary's largely agricultural product. Establishment of the Dual Monarchy also created an atmosphere in which Fiume and Trieste pitted Budapest against Vienna in the competition to capture maritime trade. These particularly propitious political circumstances, combined with the opening of the Suez route in 1869, fostered the expansion of trade through Trieste to the Near and Far East. In the first five years of the canal's operation, Austrian merchantmen ranked third after the British and the French in their use of the waterway.[6] The Habsburg monarchy promoted imperial monopolies on trade in Near Eastern products and differential duties on tea, coffee, cocoa, spices and rubber. The benefits of maintaining Trieste as an alternative to northern German maritime routes could not be denied. The Trieste route lay entirely in Austrian hands, allowing the monarchy to avoid relying on outlets in

5 Sondhaus, *The Habsburg empire*, 94–8, 183.
6 Ibid. 266.

potentially unreliable German hands. In addition, accommodation of trade interests in Trieste foiled Italian expansionist ambitions aimed against Austrian territories in the upper Adriatic region.[7] Trieste blossomed in the service of Vienna.

Vienna remained Trieste's overlord, but local affairs were generally peripheral to Habsburg concerns. Even after 1867 Austrian officials tended to dictate policies only insofar as they affected the port's service to the empire. Maritime trade trained Trieste's attention abroad, and international relationships remained the focus of Triestine life. The headquartering of Assicurazione Generali, Cosulich Shipping, Lloyd and other international firms signalled international recognition of the city in Europe and further afield. Still, Trieste remained in the shadow of northern ports, and even Vienna continued to favour the northern route for its efficiency and economy.[8]

By the turn of the twentieth century, technological developments brought changes in communication and transit that allowed traders to bypass commercial middlemen and local port exchanges. Like other international ports, Trieste gave up autonomy in exchange for state protection and support. Trieste's market exchange, banking infrastructure and commercial houses became entirely dependent on imperial industry and finance.[9] Viennese oversight increased and direct ties to the capital were strengthened. In 1891 the free port status of Trieste and Fiume was abrogated.

Heightened tensions in the international arena due to Germany's increasingly aggressive naval policies diverted Vienna's attention. After 1894 the responsibilities of the Magazzini Generali, an organisation founded in 1880 by the local chamber of commerce to share administrative authority with Habsburg officials, were expanded. The authority took over responsibility for policy implementation and made independent decisions regarding the day-to-day management of port facilities and related financial matters.

The city's constellation of commercial, industrial and financial elites had remained largely aloof from pedestrian political concerns and the currents of nationalism stirring in the empire. However, they could not turn a blind eye to the increasing necessity for accommodation with Vienna, particularly after the abrogation of free port status. By 1913 trade with imperial regions accounted for more than 80 per cent of Trieste's commercial rail traffic.[10]

The First World War revealed the weakness of the Austrian empire and

---

[7] For a typical nineteenth-century assessment of Trieste's position see F. Rziha, *Sull'importanza del porto di Trieste per l'Austria: relazione letta il 2 maggio 1873 nel consorzio politecnico in Praga*, Trieste 1874, 3–4.

[8] G. Montemuliano, *Venezia Giulia: italiana ed europea*, Rome 1945, 77, points out that from 1850 to 1910 the volume of commerce in Hamburg increased 24 times, while that of Trieste increased only 2.5 times.

[9] Sapelli, *Trieste italiana*, 27.

[10] BCCI i/6 (1920), 125. Figures for 'total traffic' through Trieste indicate that in 1913 of 26,975,452 total quintals shipped by rail, 21,598,177 went to the Austrian lands.

the precariousness of Trieste's position. Prior to the Armistice, with political winds pointing toward Italy, leading commercial families took measures to protect their holdings. In August 1918 the president and leading share-holders of the Triestine Commercial Bank declared their willingness to co-operate with Italian political authorities and economic institutions that would probably inherit the Adriatic provinces. Strong ties between Vienna and leading Italian institutions, including the Italian Commercial Bank and Credito Italiano, both of which were founded with German capital in the nineteenth century, facilitated the transfer of assets from Austrian to Italian hands. Businessmen in Trieste arranged for the transfer of capital and assets to the control of sister institutions based on the peninsula.[11]

Reconstruction and integration in Liberal Italy

Triestines failed to grasp the impact that war and the change in sovereignty would have on the city's fortunes. After the First World War, damaged trans-portation and communications networks could be rebuilt, but the city faced graver difficulties. The discrediting of the traditional political order hastened the transition of international ports from commercial *entrepôts* to transit centres.[12] The collapse of the Habsburg empire compounded this more gener-alised problem in Trieste.

A 'general programme for the economic reconstruction of Trieste', prepared for the Italian delegation to the Paris Peace Conference, rested on Triestine assumptions that under Italian authority their city would simply resume its former privileges and trading status. The programme's primary request was for the re-establishment of the free port. Other recommendations included currency regulation, facilitation of communication, renovation of transportation systems and the maintenance of monopolies granted by the Habsburgs.[13]

The 1919 Treaty of St Germain extended imperial importation and customs duties for three years, protecting trade to the Austrian state. However, it did nothing to accommodate commerce between Trieste, the Kingdom of the Serbs, Croats and Slovenes and other former imperial lands outside truncated Austria. Triestines hoped to extend the general Habsburg Adriatic tariff that had reduced the per kilometre charge on articles imported through the Adriatic corridor, but this was clearly not in Italy's interests.

To meet the economic challenges, Italian authorities reconstituted the chamber of commerce. The Museo Commerciale, an organisation linked to

11 Millo, *L'élite del potere*, 232–4.
12 J. Konvitz, 'The crises of Atlantic port cities, 1880–1920', *Comparative Studies in Society and History* xxxiv (1994), 293.
13 'Programma generale per la ricostruzione economica di Trieste', undated, CGCVG (ag), busta 8.

the chamber of commerce and the Austrian Commercial Institute in Vienna prior to the war, resumed its activities as a sort of public relations agency for economic activities. The Central Warehouse Authority regained many of its pre-war responsibilities. These included transport of merchandise within warehouses, management of facilities and co-ordination with railways. The authority oversaw customs and insurance payments on traded merchandise, allocated space for traders' offices and handled labour issues in the port.

Representatives of the authority lobbied furiously in support of the normalisation of trade, but made little headway with officials in Rome, who were distracted by other pressing matters. In January 1919 the director of the authority complained that military occupation of several key piers and customs facilities made it difficult for the port to process American aid shipments bound for Austria and Bohemia. Delays in trans-shipment, he suggested, could be 'embarrassing' to the Italian government.[14] His complaint fell on deaf ears. Port facilities remained clogged and customs regulations confused.

Dismantled during the war, Trieste's stock market information service received no support from Rome after annexation. Triestines resorted to costly, unreliable and uncoordinated private services. In response to the pleas of the Retailers' Association, the city established a committee to fight loan sharking. However, it lacked authority and policing powers.[15] Black marketeering, which had flourished during the war, continued unabated. Materials hoarded during wartime became available, but only at highly inflated prices. Where the government employed security forces, they were often insufficient to deal with local problems. In April 1919 the director of the Central Warehouse Authority begged the new government to provide plainclothes detectives for surveillance of the port and to help monitor waterfront activities and trade. The government contended that the manpower was simply not available.[16]

The end of Habsburg subsidies and increased competition hit hard in sectors of commercial specialisation. In the coffee sector, a Habsburg monopoly, preferential tariffs and special duties had nurtured the trade, preparation and export of coffee beans in pre-war Trieste. By the turn of the century, the coffee interests' co-operative association included sixty-six firms. Four major processing companies prepared raw coffee beans for the consumer market. Lloyd's regular shipping service fostered international trade. In 1913 the city ranked second in Europe in the transport of coffee.[17] After the war, Habsburg advantages were eliminated and political instability hurt shippers

14 'Magazzini Generali', ibid. busta 15.
15 D. Viatori, 'Il commercio a Trieste nell'arco dell'ultimo cinquantennio', in Camera di commercio, industria, artigianato e agricoltura di Trieste, Cinquant'anni di vita economica a Trieste, 1918–1968, Trieste 1968, 399–401.
16 'Magazzini Generali', CGCVG (ag), busta 15.
17 Associazione caffè Trieste, Cent'anni di caffè, 1891–1991, Trieste 1991, 22.

trading in raw beans. Continuing hostilities in the Near East devastated trade in processed coffee markets in the Levant.

Trade in wood, lumber and wood by-products also suffered. Prior to 1914, trade privileges and imperial subsidies promoted the shipment of hardwood and conifer lumber from Austrian, Czech and southern Slavic provinces through Trieste. After the war, the elimination of these commercial advantages combined with an economic downturn to cause a collapse in the trade in wood products. In the general climate of instability, the supply of exotic hardwoods from tropical and equatorial regions could not be relied upon. The war also ushered in a change in artistic tastes. Simple and austere styles, exemplified by the Bauhaus, replaced the preference for ornate ornamentation of the Liberty Style or *Belle Époque*. The demand for luxury goods and artisanal products produced with rare species of wood was severely curtailed.

The end of imperial co-operation diverted international traffic from Trieste. Firms headquartered in newly independent countries owed no allegiance to Italian Trieste. Austrian, Bohemian, Hungarian, Polish, Croatian and Slovene companies preferred to conduct affairs from their own capitals. In 1913 600 foreign firms had offices in Trieste; in 1927 there were 480. By 1930 only 330 remained.[18]

In the city, military occupation and issues related to the transfer of sovereignty compounded economic difficulties. Italian censorship and the intermittent suspension of postal and courier communication hampered commercial relations. Italian authorities closely monitored couriers between Trieste and Vienna, Bucharest, Belgrade and other centres. The Italian censorship commission's guidelines required that Italian translations accompany all business correspondence, including that written in German and exchanged with the former capital of Vienna. Communications confined to one sheet of paper could be directed to only a single agent. Only matters of 'urgent commercial character' could be discussed; no new initiatives could be proposed.[19]

Without subsidies, Trieste could not compete with German and Dutch ports. Even during the Habsburg period, for southern regions of Austria, the northern river route had offered advantages over the southern route. The ports of Hamburg, Bremen, and even Stettin and Rotterdam benefitted from superior river access and rail facilities. Although Trieste was only 345 kilometres from Vienna, 490 kilometres from Prague and 450 kilometres from Budapest, the trip to each city by rail was considerably longer at 553, 828 and 607 kilometres, respectively. Although nearly equidistant from Prague, Hamburg was nearly 200 kilometres closer than Trieste by rail.[20]

[18] G. Palladini, 'Il commercio triestino con l'estero', in Camera di commercio, *Cinquant'anni*, 438–9, and 'Industrie e commerci a Trieste', *Il Piccolo*, 5 Dec. 1930, 3.

[19] Commissione di censura to governatorato della Venezia Giulia, 28 Jan. 1919, CGCVG (ag), busta 61.

[20] C. Jangakis, *Le Port de Trieste: avant et après la dissolution de la monarchie austro-hongroise*, Lausanne 1923, 33–4.

Political separation from Carinthia and southern Austria necessitated the construction of border facilities, negotiation of passage rights and the co-ordination of railway and other transportation and communication policies. Trieste's major links, including the Tauri railroad connecting the city with Bavaria, ran through lands that now belonged either to Austria or to the Kingdom of Serbs, Croatians and Slovenes. By the end of 1920, prices for the shipment of goods from Czechoslovakia to Trieste by rail were nearly four times the cost of shipment along the Elbe to Hamburg. In terms of time, rail shipment between Trieste and Prague that took approximately sixty hours in 1913 required between 144 and 168 hours by 1931. From Hamburg the trip to Prague took between forty-eight and fifty-two hours.[21]

Political pragmatism prompted smaller states arising from Habsburg Austria to seek co-operation with Trieste and Italy. In November 1921, in the small city of Portorose in Istria, representatives of Austria, Hungary, Czechoslovakia, Romania, Yugoslavia, Poland, Italy, Great Britain and France, along with an American observer met to assess commercial relationships. They also discussed import-export policies and postal and telegraphic relations in the upper Adriatic and Danube regions. Subsequent negotiations at Graz resulted in the formation of the Adriatic League, a co-operative arrangement including Italy, Austria, Czechoslovakia and Yugoslavia. The agreement's benefits accrued to Venice. The Danube Sava Adriatic Company, a co-operative association formed among the various railways of the southern provinces of the former imperial lands, had only limited success.

A series of Italo-Czech conferences, convened in 1921 and 1922, explored options for the reduction of tariffs. Italy's major aim on entering into the talks was to combat the dominance of Hamburg.[22] However, Italian ports, including Trieste, simply could not compete. Prior to the First World War, Hamburg handled three times as much Czech trade as Trieste. The Treaty of Versailles guaranteed Czechoslovakia access to port facilities at Trieste, but it also cleared the path for trade through Hamburg, Stettin and Danzig. Hamburg capitalised on its pre-war advantages.[23] A note to Igino Brocchi from the Italian Legation in Prague emphasised Trieste's marginal position: 'In industrial and commercial circles the Triestine question is of secondary importance. Hamburg is more convenient and that is enough.'[24]

After the 1920 Treaty of Rapallo, Mosconi, the civil commissioner, promoted trade with the new Yugoslav state as 'natural and necessary' to the development of Trieste's economy.[25] However, Fiume's internationalisation placed Italian-controlled Trieste at a competitive disadvantage in the upper

[21] L. Furlani, 'I commerci di Trieste e la concorrenza nordica', La Porta Orientale iii (1933), 390–2.
[22] 5 Jan. 1922, Brocchi papers, busta 11, fasc. 95.
[23] W. O. Blanchard, Economic geography of Europe, New York 1931, 299.
[24] Italian legation, Prague, to Brocchi, 1 Dec. 1922, Brocchi papers, busta 11, fasc. 95.
[25] Sapelli, Trieste italiana, 53.

Adriatic. In addition, without a major investment in rail infrastructure, Trieste could not handle Istrian traffic diverted from independent Fiume. The Trieste–Pola rail spur was only a single track.

Disruption caused by the sequestering of the merchant fleet compounded Trieste's difficulties. A former Austrian territory, Trieste was required to cede all assets to the reparations committee. Triestine merchants claimed that the seizure of their ships constituted 'the plucking from Trieste of elements vital to her existence'.[26] For nearly two years after the end of the war, Italy fought to gain possession of Trieste's fleet. Italian authorities offered certificates of registration and other documents written in Italian and filed under Austrian authority to support claims that the city's maritime infrastructure was Italian even under Austria. They also attempted to demonstrate that Italian hands held the financial and managerial reigns of the shipping firms. The Spa Conference on Reparations of July 1920 secured most of the Austro-Hungarian Adriatic fleet for Italy, and Triestine ships returned to their local 'Italian' owners wherever possible. However, the delay exacerbated the already difficult and expensive task of collecting and refitting ships and locating equipment and cargo scattered across Europe and beyond. Of sixty-nine ships owned and operated by Lloyd, the largest company working out of Trieste in 1914, forty-six were under requisition (thirty-three by the Austrian government, seven at the port of Prokljan in the new South Slav State, four in various stages of construction or refitting, one in Amsterdam and one disarmed in Trieste). Eleven had been sunk and five were sold. Of the remainder, three were sequestered by the Chinese government, two by the English and one each by the Portuguese and the French.[27]

On the eve of its entry into the First World War, Italy possessed a merchant marine of 1,471,710 tons. Austria-Hungary had 1,052,346. By 1922, with the break-up of the Habsburg empire, Italy amassed 2,866,335 tons.[28] However, this was of no help to Trieste. On the Adriatic's eastern shore, with rail links oriented towards the northern and eastern European interior, Trieste's integration into the Italian network was difficult. The elimination of the border between the Trieste and Friuli, that might have been expected to improve access to northern Italy, instead siphoned trade away from the city. Prior to 1866, the Austrian monarchy had constructed rail lines through Friuli to facilitate interchange between Venice and Vienna. After the First World War the Friulian link offered an economic alternative to shipment through the mountainous eastern Adriatic coastland. It diverted traffic to the western Adriatic and ports on the Apennine peninsula. Padua continued to act as Italy's clearinghouse between the Danubian regions and

---

[26] Commissariato generale civile, memorandum, 14 May 1919, CGCVG (ag), busta 17.
[27] S. Cirrincione, 'Il contributo della marina mercantile giuliana all'economica nazionale', in Camera di commercio, Cinquant'anni, 220ff.
[28] Jangakis, Le Port, 102.

the Venetian provinces, and Venice functioned as the catalyst for the trade of north-east Italy.

In the Adriatic, Trieste also faced stiff competition from the growing port of Bari. Continuing political and economic crisis in the Middle East foiled Triestine plans to rejuvenate trade in the eastern Mediterranean. Turkish displeasure with the Treaty of Sèvres, unrest in Greece and Albanian nationalist agitation in Asia Minor led to violent clashes. Uprisings throughout former Ottoman lands hindered attempts to resume trade along coastal commercial routes and the Suez corridor. By November 1922 violence had abated and the Treaty of Lausanne and the Turkish nationalists' victory brightened prospects for trade, but the delay had made it difficult for Trieste to capitalise on pre-war relationships. Bari enjoyed superior rail links for processing traffic from the Mediterranean and along Suez routes. Before the First World War trade from these markets comprised nearly 20 per cent of Trieste's maritime imports.[29]

Trieste also competed with Genoa. Nineteenth-century unification around Piedmont had nourished the expansion of Genovese trade facilities. By 1918 the Genovese held a near monopoly on international sea trade bound for the peninsula. Late in 1922 Triestines challenged Genovese legislative advantages. Italian trade law differentiated between agents engaged in commodities trading and those engaged in currency exchange. Genoa had exclusive rights to engage in international arbitrage in maritime trade networks. Habsburg law had accustomed Triestine agents to handling all types of international exchange. Triestines sought an extension of the Italian legislation to include agents in the Adriatic city.[30] Rome refused.

Not only was the city's infrastructure suited to serve the interests of Vienna and its position to trade with lands east of the Adriatic, but the city had relied on German capital invested through Viennese banks. Italian bitterness after the war and suspicion of German designs prompted the Italian minister of the treasury, Bonaldo Stringher to advocate the immediate liquidation of German-run institutions. Italy had 'no interest that they continue to function'. They represented potential competition with Italian banks and threatened the development of commercial relations in Italy's new territory. On 24 February 1919 German-controlled banks in Trieste ceased daily operations. Italy prohibited them from contracting new business. Recognising that the flight of international capital would only cause a further drain on the already shaky economy, the government responded differently to Slavic institutions. Stringher recommended 'Italianisation' rather than dismantling. As of 24 February Slavic banks were subjected to the control and surveillance of the Italian state. They were forced to operate in accordance with Italian banking provisions.[31] In the following years, Italian Liberal and early Fascist

---

[29] For traffic in quintals see 'Movimento complessivo', *BCCI* i/6 (1920), 124.
[30] A. Segrè to Brocchi, n.d., Brocchi papers, busta 11, fasc. 100.
[31] 'Banche austriache – liquidazione', CGCVG (ag), busta 21.

policies forcibly suppressed all Slavic influences in these institutions and integrated them into the Italian system.[32]

The cosy relationship between heavy industry and the Italian government also placed Trieste at a disadvantage. Heavy industry lobbied intensively and successfully to negotiate restrictions on the inflow of foreign goods and to win incentives for the export of Italian finished products. These latter had been Trieste's speciality. After the war Triestines requested that traditional free zones, or *punti franchi*, through which transit shipments passed duty-free be maintained. The zones created by the Austrians after the 1891 abrogation of free port status had no clear equivalent under Italian law. Triestine commercial leaders also called for the construction of a new seaside duty-free zone in which manufactured products could be produced from locally imported primary materials without incurring Italian customs obligations. The Italians procrastinated over permitting the continued operation of the trade free zones and refused to allow them to be expanded. In 1921 the Triestine chamber of commerce was still waiting for a decision from the Italian minister of finance on *punti franchi* regulations.[33] By 1927 the legislative status of the zones had been resolved with local power and privileges being severely curtailed. Triestines, including Alberto Cosulich, as the head of the Shipbuilders Federation, continued to plead with Rome to loosen the restrictions, but to no avail.[34]

Generally, Italian authorities welcomed local commercial leaders.Under the Habsburgs, the economically privileged had not simply constituted a predominant 'corporate class', but functioned as a 'ruling' or hegemonic class. Their emphasis on the prosperity of the port had resonated with the interests of subordinate groups across the political and social spectrum.[35] With the transfer of sovereignty, the influence of pro-Italian professionals and civil servants from the peninsula increased. Trieste's commercial and economic elite held the keys to the port's prosperity, but they shared power with political elements. Rejuvenation of commercial networks remained the joint goal of local economic policy. Italy accommodated commercial leaders who were willing to support, or at least accept, new governing authorities. Rome took advantage of the elites' market contacts and the income generated by their wealth and management of Triestine assets.[36] She encouraged Trieste to maintain ties with the lands of the former empire for propagandistic purposes and to strengthen Italian claims to Austrian assets.

To assuage commercial interests angered by Italy's failure to grant special

---

[32] Sapelli, *Trieste italiana*, 55.

[33] CCIA to ministero delle finanze, Rome, 1 Dec. 1921, CCIA, busta 4065.19.

[34] A. Cosulich to Brocchi, 4 June 1927, Brocchi papers, busta 22, fasc. 209.

[35] Millo, *L'élite del potere*, 11ff. Gramsci differentiated between the 'corporate class' and the 'hegemonic class': C. Buci-Glucksmann, 'Hegemony and consent: a political strategy', in A. Showstack Sassoon (ed.), *Approaches to Gramsci*, London 1982, 119–21.

[36] Millo, *L'élite del potere*, and Sapelli, *Trieste italiana*, focus on the expansion of elite circles after the First World War.

concessions, Italian authorities allowed Trieste to sponsor a national congress of commercial leaders, industrialists and shopkeepers in September 1921. Promoted to ease the city's introduction into national circles and speed assimilation, the conference was of little economic benefit. In fact it highlighted conflicts brewing over the process of Triestine integration. Representatives at the congress proposed the improvement of port and rail facilities, clarification of governmental regulations and support for such trade initiatives as trade fairs to remedy the economic crisis, but there was little discussion of the practicalities of financing such programmes. In 1922 Trieste hosted the Italian eastern and colonial congress, convened to examine possibilities for Triestine leadership in the expansion of Italian trade to the Near East, the Balkans, eastern Europe, Russia and the colonies. Not only did the conference overlook Italy's limited involvement in these regions, but it also ignored Italian networks that already served the needs of these markets. Where other relationships were clearly established, Rome foiled Trieste's plans. Officials rejected a proposed meeting between Czech and Triestine representatives as superfluous in the light of talks scheduled in Rome and Portorose.[37]

Rhetorical emphasis on Triestine ties abroad encouraged Triestine delusions of international economic grandeur. In early 1919, recognising the need for local initiative, and at the prompting of the technical committee for national publicity in Milan (a committee dedicated to integrating the economies of the New Provinces), the Museo Commerciale proposed a standing trade samples exhibition.[38] The plan evolved over the next year into sponsorship of an international trade samples fair. Local leaders planned and oversaw the organisation of the fair, but avoided taking official responsibility for the initiative. The president of the chamber of commerce, Vittorio Venezian, declined to serve as president of the fair, claiming he was too preoccupied by other matters. He argued that if the event failed, his association with it might 'compromise the good name of Trieste'.[39] Mosconi agreed to act as fair president. His acceptance lent credence to claims that Rome was interested in stimulating Trieste's economy, but his speech marking the establishment of the fair committee emphasised local involvement. He suggested that the government welcomed the event with 'sympathy and interest' as an 'important citizens' initiative'.[40]

Government-sponsored publicity appealed to major Italian industries to participate in Trieste's 1920 fair for political rather than economic reasons. The ministry of industry and commerce urged participation 'not only as a

---

[37] Brocchi papers, busta 11, fasc. 95, passim.
[38] P. Polidori, 'Le origini della fiera campionaria internazionale di Trieste', in A. Suttora (ed.), La fiera campionaria internazionale di Trieste, 3–18 settembre 1922, Trieste 1922, 8.
[39] 'Seduta dep. Borsa', 23 Mar. 1920, CCIA, busta 4065.19.
[40] A. Mosconi, I primi anni di governo italiano nella Venezia Giulia, Trieste 1919–1922, Bologna 1924, 199.

manifestation of national solidarity in favour of the redeemed city, but also as an affirmation of the rebirth of the Italian economy'.[41] The Italian union of chambers of commerce called attention to the trade fair in Trieste 'reinvigorated by the awareness that it is no longer alone, but an integral part of our Italy'.[42] The inscription etched on the frieze of the building housing the administrative offices of the fair optimistically proclaimed 'for the recovery of the marketplace'; absent were references to the specific benefits participating firms or individuals could enjoy.[43]

Clever and eye-catching advertisements for the fair emanated from optimistic local sources. A poster depicting 'exalted Mercury' dressed in the clothes of 'Gulliver the traveller' testified to international ambitions. Gulliver stood over the harbour shepherding a line of ships from around the world into the Gulf of Trieste. In another cartoon, a laughing personification of the fair atop the roof of the Church of San Giusto, beckoned to flocks of birds attired in exotic foreigners' garb. The birds eagerly swooped down into the port.[44]

The fair planned for 1921 was cancelled after local strikes and unrest caused it first to be postponed from the early summer to the autumn. The dates Trieste then picked in September were reserved for Naples in the fair calendar. The Italian minister of commerce and industry urged Trieste to avoid competition with the 'major city of the South' and to respect the schedule set by the Italian chambers of commerce.[45]

By 1922 it was clear that the fair's purpose was primarily political. Oscar Cosulich, a local shipping magnate, served as acting president for the initiative to provide a valence of economic importance. His opening speech stressed the economic importance of Trieste proving 'that traditional energies have not died'. He touted the fair as the city's opportunity to 'extend her arms . . . to all foreign friends'. It was Mayor Giorgio Pitacco's speech, however, that underlined the true aims of the fair and its value for Italy and the city: 'an act of courage and faith in the name and under the auspices of the Fatherland and the King'.[46]

While many commercial leaders and those serving in local institutions,

---

[41] Alessi (Rome) to CCIA, 24 Aug. 1920, CCIA, busta 4065.19.

[42] 29 June 1920, and 'Seduta dep. borsa,' 2 July 1920, ibid.

[43] G. di Biagio Cobol, 'Attraverso la fiera triestina', *Fiera Campionaria Internazionale Trieste* (Sept. 1922), 5 (photograph). Ironically, the San Andrea site on which Triestines sought to affirm the city's economic importance to Italy was developed for an Austrian agricultural and industrial exposition held in 1882 to commemorate the 500th anniversary of Trieste's union with Austria: 'L'esposizione di Trieste', *L'Illustrazione Italiana: rivista settimanale degli avvenimenti e personaggi contemporanei* ix/33 (1882), 107.

[44] These are pictured in Azienda autonomo di soggiorno e turismo, *Dudovich & C.: i triestini nel cartellonismo italiano*, Trieste 1977, 156, and Francesco Babudri, 'L'arte e la fiera triestina', *Fiera Campionaria Internazionale di Trieste* (May 1922), 20–1, respectively.

[45] Alessi to CCIA, 17 June 1921, CCIA, busta 4065.19.

[46] 'La fiera campionaria inaugurata solennemente', *La Nazione*, 5 Sept. 1922, 1–2.

including the chamber of commerce, proved willing to co-operate or at least compromise with Rome, some resented interference in Trieste's economy. Eduardo Schott, formerly an irredentist and leading supporter of the moderate post-war Social Democratic party, resigned from the advisory council of the chamber of commerce and the local tourist board in 1920.[47] This influential financier was protesting against the 'imposition of certain political tendencies' by those organisations. He charged that the Triestine chamber of commerce collaborated with the Italian government. This co-operation, 'no matter how elegantly veiled', obstructed local reconstruction.[48]

Italy, like much of Europe, suffered under the strain of large public debt incurred to finance wartime spending. Traditional liberal remedies proved insufficient to check rampant inflation, and government machinations were inadequate to deal with complex economic problems arising from debt obligations. Between 1914 and 1919 wholesale prices more than quadrupled in Italy. By 1920 the overall cost of living had tripled.[49] Even the conclusion of the post-war peace agreements, heralded as a return to normalcy and stability, failed to stem the tide of inflation. Between January 1920 and January 1922 the cost of living rose by an estimated 19 per cent in such major Italian cities as Genoa, Rome, Milan and Venice. In Trieste the increase was 13 per cent. But this was measured in terms of lire. Transfer from the Austrian crown to the Italian lira aggravated the city's plight. In 1914 the lira and the crown had traded at near parity. After the war the Austrian currency was officially devalued by 60 per cent against the Italian, and by 1922 the crown held only 10 per cent of its pre-war value. The transfer of political sovereignty and the imposition of Italian economic policies cost Triestines an estimated 50 per cent of their accumulated wealth in terms of credit, pensions and individual stock shares.[50]

Triestines hoped for special accommodations to offset the economic burdens imposed by the peace and the transfer of sovereignty. In particular, economists, intellectuals and commercial leaders emphasised the importance of return to free port status, arguing it would 'have great moral and psychological significance . . . inspire a new energy and offer economic incentive'.[51] Trieste's recovery, they argued, would serve the interest of greater Italy. Triestines hastened to assure national officials that the request for free port status did not indicate a lack of local allegiance to the Italian nation. Nor,

---

[47] For more information on Schott see A. Visintin, *L'Italia a Trieste: l'operatore del governo militare italiano nella Venezia Giulia, 1918–19*, Gorizia 2000, 67ff.

[48] 'Seduta Dep. Borsa,' 15 June 1920, and Schott's letters of resignation, 8 June 1920, CCIA, busta 4065.19.

[49] V. Zamagni, *The economic history of Italy, 1860–1990*, Oxford 1993, 213.

[50] A. De'Stefani, *Documenti sulla condizione finanziaria ed economica dell'Italia*, Rome 1923, 152–3, and Ziller, 'Le nuove provincie', 247–8.

[51] 'Memorandum', CGCVG (ag), busta 15.

they argued, would it 'create a barrier between the new and old provinces'.[52] The Democratic party of Trieste even suggested that the granting of a free port would decrease the potential for animosity between the city and the rest of Italy by clearly delineating Trieste's sphere of influence outside the country's borders and placing it in Central Europe.[53]

Triestines failed to recognise that Rome's reticence was not based on political or nationalist concerns, but on pragmatic economic assessments. Italy relied on import revenues and tariffs tied to international port activities in Trieste. Perhaps more important, Rome was unwilling to set a precedent that might lead to demands for exceptional privileges elsewhere. Critics charged that free port status had not been responsible for Triestine prosperity. Trade networks had continued to expand and the volume of trade traffic through the port had continued to increase even after the 1891 abrogation of the free port.

Local leaders, including chamber of commerce officials, saw Trieste as a centre for Italian economic activity and simply equated their interests with those of the entire Italian nation. In May 1920 they urged Triestines not to be 'too preoccupied by the political point of view'.[54] They attributed the decline in traffic to a general slowdown, but the deepening crisis in Trieste was not echoed in the experience of Italian business elsewhere, particularly in Central Europe. The conclusion of a commercial treaty between Prague and Rome in February 1921 cleared the way for an increase in Italian exports to Czechoslovakia, and Italy's relationship with Austria and the new Czech state, two of Trieste's most important imperial markets, actually improved.

Decreasing international participation in the Triestine trade samples fair between 1920 and 1922 testified to Trieste's decline. In 1920 the city attracted foreign clients despite competition with numerous events in the Danubian trade sphere. Fifty-four per cent of exhibitors represented Central European firms including 241 from Austria, 103 from Hungary, 73 from Czechoslovakia, 62 from Germany, 2 each from Yugoslavia, Fiume and Poland, and one from Switzerland. Fifty-eight per cent (511 of 878) came from outside Italy and the disputed Istrian and Dalmatian regions. Only 25 per cent of the participating firms hailed from the Italian peninsula with an additional 17 per cent from Trieste and the city's immediate surroundings.[55] By 1922, however, 91 per cent or 1,060 of the participating firms were Italian. Only 64 of the 1,171 firms came from Central Europe.[56]

---

52 'Relazione della Commissione di studio al porto franco', 6 May 1922, Brocchi papers, busta 13, fasc. 117.
53 S. Muratti, 'Parte I', in Partito democratico di Trieste, Per il portofranco a Trieste, Trieste n.d, 7–10.
54 'Museo Commerciale', BCCI i/9 (1920), 235.
55 F. Babudri, 'La fiera campionaria internazionale di Trieste del 1920', in Suttora, La fiera campionaria, 20.
56 Fiera campionaria internazionale di Trieste, Statistiche della seconda fiera campionaria internazionale Trieste, 3–24 settembre 1922, Trieste 1922, 30–1.

The shift from a product-centred presentation in 1920 to a regional-based exhibition *schema* in 1922 also illustrated the increasing influence of domestic Italian politics. In 1920, to facilitate economic interchange and encourage commercial rivalry, firms were grouped by type of product exhibited – agriculture and foodstuffs, gold and jewellery, industrial raw materials, etc. With the exception of special pavilions for Hungarian and Austrian samples, exhibitors' stands stood with those of their competitors. By 1922 pavilions dedicated to Istria and Dalmatia, the Soviet Union, Sardinia and the colonies and geographically-oriented exhibits sponsored by Piedmont, Lombardy, Sardinia, Emilia-Romagna, Bergamo and Padua stood next to such non-trade-oriented exhibits as the sports palace, book fair and tourism pavilion. Commercial activities centralised in an economic zone, described as the 'heart of the fair', were relegated to a small area.

Fascist organisation and restructuring

At the exit of the Liberal government in 1922 the Triestine economy remained a shambles, but early Fascist policies seemed to offer some hope. The Fascists promoted the standardisation and integration of economic networks but proved flexible enough to accommodate a wide range of economic strategies consistent with the movement's anti-leftist stance. In 1923 commercial representatives from all over Italy met in Trieste to discuss Italian economic prospects abroad and to hammer out strategies for the development of international trade.[57] Rome acknowledged that failure to help Trieste and the 'immiseration of Venezia Giulia' would be unacceptable, but not for economic reasons. The 'lands for which Italy spilled so much blood' were politically too significant.[58] By 1924, at the national congress of accountants, Fulvio Suvich emphasised the irredentist function of the city as 'the custodian, the vigilant guardian of the . . . Italian civilizations abandoned in foreign seas'.[59] Trieste established a branch of the Rotary Club, an international organisation of businessmen dedicated to international exchange and the promotion of national, commercial and industrial ties through personal contacts. Trieste's club was the second established in Italy.[60] Its foundation acknowledged the influence of commercial interests, but did nothing to improve Trieste's economic prospects in Italy.

By the late 1920s those favouring internationalist solutions squared off

[57] See *Ordine dei lavori e regolamento del congresso nazionale per l'espansione economica e commerciale all'estero*, Trieste [4–8 Nov. 1923], Naples 1923.

[58] 'Memorandum: commercial and geographic hinterland of Trieste', [1922/3?], 70; Brocchi papers, busta 12, fasc. 107.

[59] 'La funzione economica di Trieste e gli interessi nazionali', *Il Piccolo*, 4 Nov.1924, 3.

[60] M. Cecovini, *Cinquant'anni di storia: il Rotary a Trieste, 1924–1974*, Trieste 1974, 27–9. The Milan Club was the first.

against local nationalists who advocated patriotic sacrifice in the name of Fascist Italy. In 1927 the economist Vittorio Segrè, a delegate to the Triestine chamber of commerce, recommended a three-pronged plan to increase Trieste's share of trade in Central Europe. First he suggested tighter control of expenditure in the port and market. Second he advocated independent tariff agreements with neighbouring states. Third he emphasised rail construction. His first recommendation required local action, but the second and third points demanded national intervention. His proposals failed to take into account national interests and constraints.

Squabbles among the larger European powers frustrated Italian attempts to regulate tariffs and turn competition in the Danube Basin to Trieste's benefit. Italy experienced considerable economic growth in the mid-1920s, but Italian economic strength and influence in Trieste's former markets in Central European remained marginal. Between 1922 and 1925 the value of Italian exports nearly doubled, and the trade deficit remained high. Italian industry failed to diversify, the exchange value of the lira fell and the commercial sector proved unable to tap new markets. Of particular importance for Trieste was Italian competition with Germany in Central Europe. Both Germany and Italy refused to sanction any preferential Danube agreement to which they were not a party. The small states could not hope to achieve independent agreements for fear of incurring the wrath of the larger powers. In 1925 Germany introduced a preferential tariff for use of the *Reichsbahn* to Central Europe from the ports of Hamburg and Bremen. Rome was unable or unwilling to grant comparable concessions to Trieste. By 1928 the Triestine monthly review complained that the Danube basin resembled 'a battlefield among competing ports'.[61]

Mussolini's attention turned towards countering French designs, particularly the spread of French influence through co-operation with the countries of the Little Entente (Yugoslavia, Czechoslovakia and Romania). With Czechoslovakia, Italy negotiated a treaty of friendship in 1924 and commercial accords in 1925. For a short time, the southern route through Austria and Italy became more reliable than the northern route when German industrial crisis, strikes and stoppages impeded the flow of commercial traffic. Nature helped the Triestine cause as well. The Elbe froze during the winters of 1924 and 1925, forcing traffic to use the southern route. From 1925 to 1927 Italian traders, and Triestines in particular, were better able to compete against their German rivals due to temporary reductions on transport and warehousing tariffs for sugar, metals, paper and other exports bound for Czechoslovakia.[62] Trieste did not derive any long-term benefits from the agreements of the mid-1920s. In the late 1920s an Austrian campaign in favour of economic union with Germany spelled disaster for Trieste. Although the *Anschluss* was

---

61 'Trieste all'esposizione portuale di Vienna', RMCT i/2 (1928), 11–13.
62 G. Roletto, *Il porto di Trieste*, Bologna 1941, 92, and 'L'azione della camera di commerico per l'incremento del nostro porto', *Il Piccolo*, 27 Mar. 1925, 3.

a decade away, co-operation between Germany and Austria strengthened Germanic domination of Central Europe.[63]

Trieste's role in expanding Italian influence in the Adriatic led Italy to emphasise the city's relationship with Yugoslavia. The 1924 Treaty of Rome and consequent Nettuno Accords, ratified in 1928, decreased political tensions with Yugoslavia and offered hope that Trieste's trade to interior regions of Slovenia and Croatia might increase. However, economic opportunities failed to materialise. Trieste could not compete with arrangements that favoured internal traffic and use of Yugoslav ports. In addition, the accords eased tensions, but did not erase Yugoslav suspicions of Mussolini's political designs in the Adriatic. In October 1930 a series of Italian economic accords culminated with the enactment of the Brocchi system, which established mutual trade advantages between Italy, Austria and Hungary.[64] The triumvirate aimed to check German expansionism. Co-operation was foiled by the international economic crisis.

Segrè's arguments in 1927, that the modernisation of rail links would make Italian markets more accessible to Trieste, meshed superficially with Fascist priorities for integration and centralisation, but Italy as a whole would derive little benefit from the rail improvements advocated for Trieste. Improvements on the Santa Lucia–Tarvisio line and direct links from Trieste to Fiume and from Trieste to Monfalcone would benefit the eastern Adriatic corridor alone. A proposed line running roughly along the forty-fifth parallel from Bordeaux through Turin, Trieste, Belgrade and Bucharest to Odessa, would compete with established German routes for trans-European traffic.[65]

Investment in Trieste's infrastructure held little promise of payoff for Rome. Prior to annexation, Italian irredentists had criticised Austrian contributions to Trieste as poor and, comparing them to Italy's investments in Genoa, had implied that under Italy the Adriatic city would fare better.[66] This rhetoric bore no relation to Italy's economic interests or intentions. Between 1922 and 1936 the Italian ministry of finance granted Genoa over 425 million lire for improvements. The Central Warehouse Authority in Trieste received only 110 million lire to repair its infrastructure.[67]

The Italian economy benefited from a general growth of industry from 1923 to 1925. Although Trieste received a reconstruction loan of 138 million lire to support heavy industry, the situation in Venezia Giulia did not improve. Even substantial capital investment by the Triestine insurance

[63] Sapelli, *Trieste italiana*, 143.

[64] G. Ranki, *Economy and foreign policy: the struggle of the great powers for hegemony in the Danube valley, 1919–1939*, Boulder, Colo. 1983, 65; M. Macartney and P. Cremona, *Italy's foreign and colonial policy, 1914–1937*, New York 1938, repr. New York 1972, 195; Rusinow, *Italy's Austrian heritage*, 196–9, 206.

[65] V. Segrè, *Il problema nazionale del porto di Trieste*, Trieste 1927, 4–22.

[66] See, for example, G. Pattini, *L'Italia irredenta*, Milan n.d., 5, and G. Castellini, *Trento e Trieste: l'irredentismo e il problema adriatico*, Milan 1918, 98.

[67] G. Cobolli-Gigli, *Opere pubbliche: panorama di vita fascista*, Milan 1938, 41–5.

sector did little to ameliorate poor economic conditions.[68] Calls for industrial expansion focused on the textile and mineral oil industries which would make use of the port facilities. But, plans came to naught.[69] Rome promised to finance new construction and assist in the technical organisation of the Zaule industrial port zone. Zaule, modelled on similar projects in Naples and Venice, would enjoy a ten-year exemption on customs duties for materials and machines as well as various manufactures.[70] A site in the St Andrea quarter of the city was cleared, but construction plans came to nothing. The site, previously a park and promenade, stood as a vacant reminder of Rome's neglect of the provincial capital. Trieste's participation in Italy's imperial economic expansion was limited to theory and political semantics.[71]

Two Fascist administrative changes in the late 1920s compounded Trieste's economic difficulties. First, the resignation of Salvatore Contarini, secretary-general at the foreign ministry since 1920, signalled an administrative shake-up in the ministry. Contarini's departure in 1926, ostensibly over disagreement on policy for the Alto Adige, was, in fact, indicative of deeper antagonisms between Mussolini and 'old guard' diplomats. Contarini had advocated restraint and a careful balance of Italian interests. Trieste had benefited, albeit in a limited fashion, from his efforts and experience in promoting cordial Italian relations with Yugoslavia, Czechoslovakia and Austria after the First World War. His participation, and that of other career diplomats, in foreign policy helped to build international trust in Mussolini's government in the early 1920s. Contarini's resignation roused European suspicions and signalled a shift on the part of the Italian government to a more nationalistic and aggressive foreign policy.[72] An economic shake-up followed closely on the heels of the reorientation of foreign policy. The 'quota novanta', announced in late 1927, revalued the lira at an artificially high level. Designed as much to bolster Italian prestige as to stabilise the Italian currency it caused the price of Italian exports to increase drastically. International trade suffered; workers and small industries were impoverished.

Local nationalists blamed economic failures on Triestines' lack of patriotic enthusiasm. In 1928, in a letter directed to Rome, Attilio Tamaro complained of a Triestine 'myopia' that precluded any broader perspective on the local commercial situation. He chastised Triestines for their inability to accept the primacy of Genoa, especially in western Italian markets.[73] With regard to the competition in Central European markets, he charged, 'One of the Triestines' specialities (and one of the causes of much misfortune) is that

68 Apih, *Italia fascismo*, 240.
69 L. Ragusin-Righi, *Interessi e problemi adriatici*, Bologna 1929, 22.
70 B. Coceani, 'L'acesa industriale', in Camera di commercio, *Cinquant'anni*, 312.
71 Apih quoted in Sapelli, *Trieste italiana*, 110.
72 A. Lyttelton, *The seizure of power: Fascism in Italy, 1919–1929*, Princeton 1987, 424–7.
73 Tamaro to C. Ciano, 17 Dec. 1928, and Tamaro to [Nard?-Saldini], 21 Dec. 1928, Tamaro papers.

they presume to carry on the battle against an adversary of which they are ignorant. . . . Question our Triestine friends and see how many have been to Hamburg and of them who has stayed there more than 48 hours.'[74] In 1932 he complained of 'excessive Triestineness' and the lack of local will and vision.[75]

Few commercial leaders stepped forward to exercise political leadership, but many proved willing, if not eager, to co-operate with the Fascists to maintain economic privileges and guard positions of prestige. By 1926 consolidation of the Italian economy and co-ordination under the ministry of corporations ensured the Italian state's control and co-ordination in all economic sectors. The amalgamation of employers' organisations fundamentally altered the structures of the Triestine banking, commercial and transport sectors.

However, many traditional commercial leaders found themselves accommodated in privileged circles. Rome relied on commercial leaders to assist in the reorientation of the Triestine economy and to confront 'the dynamic situation that calls for constant vigilance, ready intuition, rapid execution, and flexibility'.[76] Leading figures were singled out as local 'heroes' who contributed to the success of Fascist programmes. By 1927 Oscar Cosulich had already demonstrated that he 'understood the new road of struggle'.[77] Assuming a managerial role within the Fascist framework, the Cosuliches successfully protected their personal interests in the public economy. Lionello Stock was among those at the head of medium-sized firms who accepted political accolades for their services to industry. Headquartered in Vienna prior to the First World War, the Stock firm expanded along two axes after Trieste joined Italy. In Central Europe, the firm acquired additional plants in Czechoslovakia in 1919, in Poland in 1921 and in Budapest in 1922. In recognition of the new political circumstances in Italy, over the course of the 1920s production extended to include plants in Tuscany and Piedmont. Stock's facilities in Istria and Dalmatia reopened as canneries. The firm even demonstrated support for Italian colonial policies by expanding to Alexandria in 1928.[78]

Insurance firms would prove to be the most successful arbiters of compromise between the local and national economy. In this sector, heavily infused by international capital with diverse interests and investments, industry leaders were able to help guide the 'distinct and special economy'. Insurance escaped the effects of general decline in Trieste and even expanded during the Fascist period.[79]

Colonial trade resonated with Fascist nationalist ambitions. In 1929 a

[74] Tamaro to L. Federzoni, 4 Sept. 1930, ibid.
[75] This is quoted in Sapelli, *Trieste italiana*, 137.
[76] Ragusin-Righi, *Interessi*, preface.
[77] Alessi to Tamaro, 21 June 1927, Tamaro papers..
[78] L. Stock Weinberg, *L'Anello: the link between past and present*, Trieste 1988, 187–230.
[79] Sapelli, *Trieste italiana*, 72–6, 138–142, 293.

Gold Coast exhibition testified to local efforts to increase Trieste's participation, or at least prestige, in Italian trade to Africa. Nearly half the world's cocoa came from the Gold Coast, and the area produced other goods including gold, foodstuffs, rubber, animal skins, and such minerals as manganese, important to the British, Dutch, German and French markets. The Gold Coast initiative received a great deal of local attention, but the exhibition proved little more than a propaganda ploy. It did nothing to counter competition from other ports and had little effect on Trieste's trade.

The crash of 1929 dealt a severe blow to Trieste. By 1929 centralising policies had effectively eliminated possibilities for individual and local initiative. The inflow of capital to Italy virtually stopped. With the crash of international markets and the collapse of international commercial investment, the private fortunes of Trieste's elite evaporated. A nationalist, Fascist political elite stepped in to take over power and control in the economy, replacing the commercial and internationalist elite. Local shipbuilders were hit particularly hard by the economic downturn and the depression. Attempts to avoid competition with other Italian yards had led Giulian shipbuilders to rely heavily on foreign contracts. From 1924 to 1929, 60 per cent of commissions for yards in Monfalcone, exclusive of warships, came from foreign clients. In 1930, 84 per cent were from abroad.[80] International economic hardship reduced the flow of international contracts to a trickle. In 1930 Triestine shipbuilding enterprises merged with the major Italian shipbuilding firms located along the eastern Adriatic shore from Monfalcone to Muggia. In 1932 the infusion of Italian capital and further consolidation of the United Fleet ended the segregation of Triestine shipbuilding firms from others in Italy. The Cosuliches took the leading role in managing the United Adriatic Fleet. Upon the death of Admiral Cagni in 1932, Francesco Giunta, Fascist zealot and former squad leader, was nominated to the presidency of the Adriatic shipbuilders, sealing the marriage between government and shipbuilding interests.[81] In 1933 the establishment of the Institution for Industrial Reconstruction (IRI), made it possible for industrialists throughout Italy to abandon bad investments to government and turn their energies to more profitable ventures backed by government capital. This Fascist consolidation hastened the end of the 'reign' of the cosmopolitan commercial elite.[82]

National contracts for grandiose vessels designed to satisfy Fascist political appetites took the place of lucrative contracts for commercial vessels. The *Vittoria*, christened in 1930, was hailed as a symbol of the Triestine 'rediscovery of trade' and the 'expansion of Italianness to the Near East'.[83] The ship's fame rested on its shattering of the world speed record for motorised

[80] Coceani, 'L'acesa industriale', in Camera di commercio, *Cinquant'anni*, 314.

[81] Sapelli, *Trieste italiana*, 116–17.

[82] Ibid. 319.

[83] G. Pitacco, *Avvenimenti di vita triestina: discorsi podestarili, 1923–1933*, Rome 1935, 74–5.

passenger ships, rather than on its contributions to commerce. The *Neptunia*, launched in 1931, demonstrated the unity and equality of all passengers in Fascist Italy by providing accommodation in only one class. In 1932 *Il Piccolo* devoted an entire page to the *Neptunia*'s maiden voyage to the Americas.[84]

Armed with government subsidies, in particular long-term credit provided by the Credito Navale, and spurred by the opening up of opportunities for American investment that followed Italian settlement of its First World War debts, shippers had turned their attention to American markets after 1925 to compensate for losses in Europe. Between 1925 and 1929 American involvement in Italian ventures soared; Americans spent 316.5 million dollars in public and private concerns in Italy.[85] In 1930 Cosulich Shipping announced reduced fares aimed at increasing traffic in goods and passengers between Italy and the United States.[86] By 1938 the United States was Trieste's third largest trading partner in terms of quintals of cargo shipped by sea and rail, trailing only domestic traffic to Italy and foreign shipment to Austria.[87]

Maritime exhibitions in Trieste in the mid-1930s emphasised the city's relationship with markets overseas. Large shipping firms and commercial enterprises with local headquarters marshalled their influence to promote the expansion of Italian economic influence abroad. Displays emphasising Fascist refurbishment and modernisation of the port and facilities and other public works projects did little to stimulate local trade. They did demonstrate the shift from autonomy to integration. A dizzying array of Genovese, Neapolitan, Triestine and Venetian routes drawn on a huge white globe at the Maritime Station demonstrated the integration of Triestine shipping routes with those of other Italian ports. In the exhibition, new port installations in Genoa, Naples, Bari, Venice and Trieste received equal attention. In 1934 an exhibition on 'Ships over Time' acknowledged the technological improvements made in Trieste during the 500 years of Austrian sovereignty, concentrating attention on local initiative. The exhibition emphasised the importance of the growth of naval and maritime organisations under Fascism. Materials demonstrating the expansion of the Italian Royal Navy occupied a prominent position.

By the time Italy invaded Ethiopia in 1935, Triestine commercial elites had been enveloped by the Fascist system. Lloyd's centennial celebrations in the autumn of 1936 highlighted the firm's participation in the 'founding of the Empire'.[88] Emphasis on imperial expansion reflected national designs and

---

[84] 'La Neptunia della Cosulich inizia oggi il suo primo viaggio per l'America', *Il Piccolo*, 5 Oct. 1932, 2.

[85] Zamagni, *Economic history*, 213, 249, 268, 294, 362.

[86] 'Viaggio a piacere e di studio', *Il Piccolo*, 16 May 1930, 4.

[87] CCIA, 'I caratteri economici del territorio libero di Trieste zona anglo-americana', *Sintesi Economici* lxxxix (Sept. 1949), 14.

[88] E. Marcuzzi, 'La mostra centenario del Lloyd Triestino', *Sul Mare: rivista di viaggi del*

highlighted the consolidation of major shipping concerns under the IRI. The celebration of Lloyd's national contributions helped to mask a reorganisation that drained from Trieste what was left of the company's holdings. Under government pressure, Lloyd shareholders liquidated their stock and surrendered the firm to public management, affirming their 'disengagement from particularism . . . and . . . desire to function as an instrument of expansion in the service of imperial Italy'.[89] Triestine firms transferred their headquarters and assets to Genoa, the centre for all Fascist administrative functions related to the merchant marine.

In October 1937 a supplement entitled, 'Commercial imperialism', attached to Commercio, the organ of the Fascist Confederation of Commercial Leaders, featured Trieste's historic ties to the Levant and the Far East, and highlighted them as a road for the expansion of imperial Italy.[90] Emphasis on the port's role in this area proved empty rhetoric. By the early 1930s Rome had already begun to invest in Bari's expansion along Asian routes. Bari hosted an official Levant Fair designed to spur Italian commercial development and strengthen trade ties with the countries of the Near and Far East. Triestine ambitions took a back seat to national commitments to the southern city which had better rail links to centres on the Apennine peninsula.

Trieste and the German question

In the mid-1930s, although Fascist policies were diverting assets from Trieste, aggressive Nazi policies provided a temporary boost to Triestine trade. In 1933 and 1934 Trieste acted as a conduit between Vienna and Rome when the Austrians, wishing to protect themselves from German political intrigues, were eager to distance themselves from German failures during the depression. For Czechoslovakia, anxious to avoid reliance on Nazi Germany, Trieste served as an alternative to northern ports. An agreement reached in Vienna in August 1933 offered tax advantages to Czech shipping through the Adriatic corridor. According to Triestine sources, the Czechs pronounced the route through the Adriatic city 'the natural road . . . [that] corresponded to the logical preferences of the Czechoslovak economy'.[91] The use of Czech steel by Giulian shipbuilders laid the basis for a reciprocal relationship.

Lloyd Triestino xii/8 (1936), 22–7; 'La mostra del centenario alla stazione marittima', Il Piccolo, 18 Oct. 1936, 6; Mostra del centenario del Lloyd Triestino: catalogo, 1936 – XIV, Trieste 1936, 20–2.

[89] 'La missione imperiale di Trieste illustrata da Alberto Pirelli', Il Piccolo, 7 Nov. 1936, 4.

[90] G. Roletto, 'Funzione imperiale dei porti italiani: Trieste', Commerciale Imperiale ii/12 (Oct. 1937), 8.

[91] 'Trieste sbocco della cecoslovacchia: un interessante articolo dell "Prager Presse" ', Il Piccolo, 20 June 1935, 3.

However, the Trieste route was still inconvenient and Triestines competed for Mediterranean-bound traffic with ports in Greece and south-eastern Europe.

At Vienna's trade fairs in 1933 and 1934, Triestines participated in Italian exhibitions. Models of new facilities advertised the increased power of the port and underlined the efficiency of the Central Warehouse Authority and the recently consolidated Italia–Cosulich–Lloyd Triestino lines. The president of the Viennese initiative commented specifically on 'the special importance of Trieste for Austria'.[92] In 1934 Austria had a strong presence at the Triestine maritime exhibition. Diplomatic exchanges at the fairs warmed the political atmosphere and facilitated the negotiation of trade accords ratified in Rome in 1934.

The protocols of 1934 between Italy, Austria and Hungary aimed to strengthen Italy's economic and political position in the Danube at the expense of the French and the Little Entente. They came into effect on 1 July 1934 and were renewed each year until 1937. The agreements addressed tariff and customs difficulties and provided for preferential subsidies, transport facilitations and liberal credit. Negotiations in 1937 confirmed and expanded the tariff concessions, but the system was already beginning to weaken. The Italo-Yugoslav Pact of April 1937 broke down the exclusivity of the system. *Anschluss* in 1938 resulted in the abrogation of the preferential agreements.[93]

Passenger traffic through Trieste increased in the mid-1930s as a result of Nazi racial policies. From 1925 Trieste had functioned as a staging point for Jewish emigration. Triestine lines, which historically linked British possessions in the Near East to the continent, assisted with direct service to Palestine. In 1932 more than 8,000 Jewish emigrants passed through the port. By 1934 the number had risen to more than 17,000 and in 1935 it peaked at 26,000.[94] Refugee traffic on this scale probably drained rather than contributed to local resources. Emigrants did not invest in the local economy, and Jewish philanthropists provided aid to those journeying through the port.

In 1938 Fascist racial policies struck a severe blow to the Jewish community in Trieste. Restrictions on Jewish property-ownership and participation in certain occupations disrupted commercial life and caused a constriction of elite economic circles already narrowed by Fascist consolidation. In 1937 Jews had headed seven of the twenty-four industrial syndicates in the province of Trieste. Jewish families oversaw the management of the two largest insurance firms in the city, and Jews held the reins of management in twenty-six major commercial firms and banks.[95] *Il Piccolo*, the major daily

[92] 'L'importanza del porto di Trieste', *Il Piccolo*, 4 Sept. 1934, 3.

[93] A. Basch, *The Danube basin and the German economic sphere*, New York 1943, 159–65.

[94] E. Serra, 'Il ruolo internazionale della società e la politica estera italiana', in Lloyd Triestino, *Il Lloyd Triestino, 1836–1986: contributi alla storia del cinquantennio*, Trieste 1986, 79–84, and 'L'emigrazione ebraica attraverso Trieste', *Il Piccolo*, 9 Jan. 1932, 3.

[95] On Jewish management of Riunione adriatica de sicurtà see G. Sapelli, 'Riflettendo

publishing in the climate of Fascist censorship, admitted that restrictions on Jews in commercial and industrial activities were hurting the city's economy.

While surprising at some levels, racial discrimination was not unanticipated in business circles. Insurance companies operating within the corporative system had already begun to replace Jewish personnel. Edgardo Morpurgo gave up the presidency of Assicurazione Generali to Conte Giuseppe Volpi di Misurata. Within that same company racial restrictions forced twenty-six Jewish directors and department heads, including general director Michele Sulfina, as well as thirty-nine employees of the total 436 to leave. Fulvio Suvich, the former under-secretary of foreign affairs whose anti-German stance had contributed to his dismissal from inner government circles, took over the management of the insurance company Riunione Adriatica di Securtà from Arnoldo Frigessi. Racial laws compelled a further twenty-five of the firm's 283 employees to resign.[96] Withdrawal of the city's Jews from the international activities of the local stock exchange resulted in an estimated reduction in trade to 40 per cent of its previous level.[97] While significant for Trieste, the loss constituted a minor setback for Rome and had little impact on the city's relationship with the capital.

Commercial activities in Trieste limped along, closely controlled and subject to priorities set in Rome. Unrealistic Triestine appraisals of the city's economic value led the Triestine committee for trade traffic to propose infrastructure improvements to bolster the city's participation in a new trade plan involving Italy and Germany. A report of the committee, issued in the wake of Italian entry into the Second World War, called for an accord between Germany and Italy that would, in effect, reinstate the privileges Trieste enjoyed under the Habsburgs including the free port, special Adriatic tariffs and transport costs calculated by distance. Other proposals included a highway to link the upper Adriatic region to Salzburg through Tarvisio, abolition of discriminatory legislation affecting the relationship between German ports and Trieste and an eventual guarantee regarding quantities of traffic to be processed through the port of Trieste.[98] The plan was unrealistic from both the Italian and German perspectives. The only sector that could claim a role in the emerging economy was the insurance sector. Massive

---

sulla "presenza ebraica" nel ceto dirigente della Riunione adriatica di sicurtà', in G. Todeschini (ed.), *Il mondo ebraico: gli ebrei tra Italia nord-orientale e impero asburgico dal medioevo all'età contemporanea*, Pordenone 1991, 491–515.

[96] E. Ginzburg Migliorino, 'Jewish emigration from Trieste to the United States after 1938, with special reference to New York, Philadelphia, and Wilmington', *Studi Emigrazione* xxviii (1991), 371–2, and S. Bon, *La persecuzione antiebraica a Trieste (1938– 1945)*, Udine 1972, 58, 73n.

[97] S. Bon, *Gli ebrei a Trieste, 1930–1945: identità, persecuzione, risposte*, Gorizia 2000, 99, 129.

[98] Comitato triestino dei traffici, *Esame della nuova situazione dell'Europa centro-orientale, in relazione agli interessi italo-germanici, con particolare riguardo ai porti di Trieste e di Fiume*, Trieste 1940, 41.

international investments throughout Central Europe and abroad justified these firms' continuing function in the interests of Italy and Germany.[99] Increasing insurance investments did not require infrastructure improvements.

Trieste's political role in the expansion of Italian influence rather than its contributions to trade governed the city's relationship with the centre. The national committee for geography insisted in 1941 that 'Every ton of commodities handled by Italian ships, Italian insurance, and Italian markets from foreign production, shipped through the Italian Triestine emporium causing consumption abroad, constitutes a precious and quite sought-after affirmation of the political and mercantile power of the Italian flag.' But, as the committee's report reminded readers, 'special attention and legislative provisions of all particulars' remained necessary for Trieste to fulfil its 'unmistakable political function'. An editorial published in the Milanese *Il Sole* pointed to the failure of Trieste's economy. The city had once been a grand port on the scale of 'London, Antwerp, Rotterdam . . . a centre for commercial investment offering extensive facilities and opportunities'. Now, the port 'had practically none of this'.[100]

Port of the *Reich*

Nazi occupation in 1943 and the inclusion of Trieste in the *Reich*'s Adriatic coastland meant a further diminution in Trieste's international status and involvement. The ironic effect of Trieste's separation from Italy was the strengthening of pro-Italian sentiment among economic elites. Fascist integration had been far more palatable than Nazi domination. Fascist racial measures had already ostensibly removed the city's Jewish elite from positions of power, but Jewish influence and local respect remained. Nazi policies struck deep into the heart of the remaining commercial community. Respected members of the Morpurgo family, with large holdings in banking and financial circles, were deported. Michele Sulfina and Arnoldo Frigessi, like many others, escaped into hiding in Rome.[101]

German interference caused resentment among commercial leaders and prompted some to co-operate in resistance. Many participated in the local branch of the Committee for the Liberation of Upper Italy. This organisation, with its headquarters in Milan, forged unlikely partnerships with economic enemies, including socialists and communists active in anti-Nazi

---

[99] L. Sanzin, *Aspetti, carattere e funzione della espansione assicurativa italiana all'estero: relazione presentata alla viii riunione della Società italiana di demografia e statistica tenutasi in Milano,* [10–11 Jan. 1942], n.p. 1942, affirmed the importance of Trieste's insurance sector to Italian interests.

[100] Sapelli, *Trieste italiana,* 166.

[101] Ibid. 13, 277–8.

circles. In the eastern Adriatic provinces it even sought co-operation with the Slovenian Liberation Front. The broad range of political interests and primacy of political needs made it difficult to agree on economic policy. A pact of 9 December 1944 between Giulian representatives of the Action, Italian Socialist, Christian Democrat and Liberal parties mentioned the need to address the economic problems of the region, and underlined the necessity for the participation of the city of Trieste, public entities and private economic interests to promote free trade and the abandonment of autarchy.[102] However, no specific plans were formulated.

Even before hostilities ceased influential businessmen were seeking to increase ties with western economic interests and to promote a western-oriented peace. Pecuniary interests, including fear that the Germans would blow up port installations, led them to take part in surrender negotiations. A member of the Cosulich family helped to persuade the German troops to wait to surrender to the British rather than to the communist partisans.[103] Cosulich's intervention strengthened the position of the western European powers in the region, and his position at the head of the Committee for the Liberation assured him a firm footing in the post-war western order.

The Free Territory

The creation of the Free Territory of Trieste offered the promise of local control over economic policies. However, the division of the territory into two zones complicated commercial relationships. The Duino Agreement of 20 June 1945 called for an open border and free exchange across the zones, but authorities operating under opposing ideologies could not co-operate. Economic leaders in Trieste were forced to rely on the Allied military government.

Shipbuilding firms, united under the Fascist umbrella, split to form separate entities. Yards in Monfalcone and Muggia fell under western Allied jurisdiction in Zone A. The Yugoslavs gained control of shipyards in Pola located in Zone B. Italian manufacturing facilities were cut off from sources of raw materials in Yugoslavia. Yugoslavia inherited Italian mining equipment used to extract bauxite and building stone from mineral-rich regions of Istria. The Italians had experience of working the stone.[104] Italians argued unsuccessfully for control of bauxite mines and electrical plants located in Zone B, claiming that they served coastal plants for steel production and oil refining located in Zone A and were necessary to maintain the integrity of local ties to Vienna.

---

[102] 'Il atto del 9 dicembre 1944', *Trieste: rivista politica giuliana* (May/June 1955), 11.
[103] Cox, *Road to Trieste*, 196.
[104] Mostra di Trieste, *Mostra di Trieste 1947, stazione marittima, 11–26 ottobre*, Trieste 1947, 17–18.

Yugoslavs countered that such arrangements would be protected in the territory under international oversight.[105]

Local businessmen and industrialists had to cope with the results of wartime destruction and dislocation as well as economic irregularities arising from Trieste's uncertain political position. The Nazis had dismantled local facilities. Allied bombardment from January to June 1944 had left much of the Aquilinia industrial zone in ruins. The port facilities and the San Sabba and Aquila refineries had been military targets. Reconstruction of the fleet and of the shipbuilding industries was a high priority for both Allied officials and Triestine commercial leaders. The Triestine port had suffered heavy damage. In June 1945, 102 wrecked merchant and warships, including the 45,000-ton battleship *Impero* and the 28,000 ton battleship *Conte di Cavour*, clogged the heavily mined harbour.[106] Vessels and explosives had to be cleared before the harbour could be used. Local agents concentrated on the recovery and refitting of sequestered ships and salvaged ships, and on completing construction contracts on ships already begun.[107] Liberation came at a high cost, with fighting in pockets throughout the city and on the surrounding hillsides. Those in the city with economic interests were also left shell-shocked by Tito's troops brief occupation of Trieste.[108]

The Italian peace treaty of 1947 promised the Triestine port 'free' status, to be supervised by a representative chosen by the governor of the Free Territory and approved by the United Nations. Failure to secure a governor for the Free Territory meant that the economic representative could not be appointed. As a temporary political authority, the Allied military government hesitated to institute wholesale changes in local structures and administration. Italian Fascist laws, except where modified to meet post-war exigencies, continued to govern economic life. In efforts similar to those undertaken by Italian authorities in 1918, Allied officials revived local organisations to assist in recovery efforts. The Central Warehouse Authority once again took control of port facilities. The chamber of commerce re-emerged as a leading economic institution in the city. Political confusion should have allowed the local chamber a good deal of autonomy: it was not bound to the commercial policies of the Union of Italian Chambers in Rome, and the Allied military government hesitated to assume responsibility for the details of local economic decisions. However, the dire need for assistance from the western Allies, and from Italy, limited independent prerogative. Triestine commercial leaders remained clear in their support for western economic principles but pragmatic in their support for the political authorities ruling on the basis of

---

[105] A. Bebler, *Equilibrium or justice? Speech delivered, September 3, 1946 in the political and territorial commission of the peace conference*, New York 1949, 12–14.

[106] Allied military government British/United States Zone, Free Territory of Trieste, *Trieste handbook*, Trieste 1950, 46.

[107] Cirrincione, 'Il contributo', 254.

[108] Sapelli, *Trieste italiana*, 209–12.

temporary, *ad hoc* arrangements. Economic expertise became their currency, traded for influence in civic affairs and economic assistance from the Allies. The Allies responded with aid in the form of loans, grants, special arrangements and subsidies.

Those advocating independence for the region seized upon links with Austria as a justification for the perpetuation of the Free Territory. Pointing out that the city enjoyed its heyday when not under Italian rule, they equated the continued existence of the Free Territory with the maintenance of free trade without regard to political or ethnic affiliation. Free trade could provide a basis for a unified European market, 'the only alternative to assure a peaceful life and prosperity for the Continent'.[109]

Misplaced faith in the potential for the renaissance of international commercial relationships provided the basis for unusual alliances. Entrepreneurs, commercial leaders, businessmen and industrialists found themselves in a strange agreement with socialists and communist workers' groups looking for a means to ensure the internationalisation of the city. The precedent for co-operation set by united resistance efforts formed a basis for unified action, but the various groups could not capitalise on the opportunity. Vague commonalities in economic aspirations could not erase the history of ethnic enmity and the legacy of Fascist and Nazi persecution. Triestine commercial leaders, who had co-operated with Fascism, collaborated with the Allied military government and Italian officials in recovery efforts. Support for Italian nationalism and evidence of opposition to Nazi intervention generally facilitated their acceptance into respected post-war trade circles. The west protected Trieste and Zone A as a border territory, safeguarding democracy and defending capitalism. Not only was Italy a decidedly 'modern' state in political and economic terms as compared to Yugoslavia, but Austria and, more important, Vienna, also adhered to western models.

Despite their commitment to pro-Italian circles, the Allied authorities remained confused regarding the status of some local businessmen. Arnoldo Frigessi was arrested by Allied forces in Florence and incarcerated from May to July 1945. Both Frigessi and Sulfina, who had been persecuted under the Fascist racial statutes, attempted to return to their management positions in the insurance industry after the war. The Allies prohibited them from serving in any managerial capacity due to the taint of Fascism. Not until 1947 were they permitted to return to their duties.[110]

Allied economic arrangements forced Trieste into a debtor relationship with the Italian government. The IRI framework governed Trieste's biggest industries. Lloyd Triestino enterprises, Ilva steel, the United Fleet of the Adriatic and several banks remained subject to Italian control. In 1947 the chamber of commerce reported that 'in practice, Trieste continued to be an

---

[109] 'Nazioni con 1200 espositori alla quinta fiera di Trieste', *Tribuna dei Lavoratori*, 1 July 1953, 1.
[110] Sapelli, *Trieste italiana*, 277–8.

integral part of the Italian economy and continued to benefit from the involvement of the Italian Government'.[111]

Under the terms of the general financial agreement of 9 March 1948, the lira became the official unit of currency in Zone A. In April 1948 an international agreement granted Italy control over Triestine imports and exports. The following September the Italian government gained the right to process currency exchanges of Allied funds earmarked for the reconstruction of Trieste. Trade with the peninsula was regularised. At the request of Italy in October 1948, Zone A became eligible for recovery aid through admission to the Organisation for European Economic Co-operation, and a 17.8 million dollar grant for reconstruction was approved. Financial arrangements were used, in a circular fashion, to support claims for increased Italian political control in Zone A, a territory described as 'very closely related to Italy from an economic standpoint'.[112] In 1949 Allied officials advocated Trieste's return to Italian sovereignty claiming that recovery depended upon the regeneration of ties 'cut off . . . by political or trade barriers'.[113] Rome's apparent willingness to assist in the region's recovery justified Allied decisions to turn over to Italy responsibility for the distribution of Allied aid monies. Such aid helped to enrich firms on the peninsula.

The Allied military government stopped short of granting Italy full economic control.[114] The unsettled fate of German ports forced the western Allies to rely heavily on Trieste as the primary entry point for European Recovery Programme shipments to Austria and southern Germany. Maintaining powers of taxation and responsibility for customs levies allowed the Allies to protect their interests.

Some in the city resented the American intrusion and paternalism that was part of the post-Second World War political and economic landscape. While dependent on American aid, some were suspicious of politically-motivated American 'philanthropy'. They saw the Marshall Plan framework as a form of American 'political currency'. To ensure compliance with American political agendas, the west concentrated more economic funds and incentives in western Europe than the Soviets could ever hope to.[115] In the local press, particularly *Trieste Libera*, supporters of independence complained that American promotion of Italy, western prejudices and Allied machinations hurt the local economy. Allied military government statistics compared the

---

[111] Camera di commercio, industria e agricoltura, 'Quadrimestre: gennaio-aprile 1947', in *Relazione annuale 1947: sull'andamento economico nella provincia di Trieste*, Trieste 1947, 2.

[112] D. De Castro, 'Trieste and the Italian economy', in Peter Thorneycroft (ed.), 'Italy: an economic survey', *The Statist* [supplement], 25 Oct. 1952, 36–8.

[113] Economic Co-operation Administration, *Trieste: country study, European recovery program*, Washington, DC 1949, 8, 13.

[114] Ufficio importe e tasse to CCIA, 15 Apr. 1951, and Direzione superiore di dogana, to CCIA, 18 Apr. 1951, CCIA, cat. XXVIII .

[115] D. W. Ellwood, 'Italy, Europe, and the Cold War: the politics and economics of limited sovereignty', in Duggan and Wagstaff, *Italy in the Cold War*, 36.

standard of living and rate of recovery in Trieste favourably to that of cities on the Italian peninsula. An Economic Co-operation Administration report of 1949 maintained that real wages in Trieste stood 'at about the same level as in Milan, Turin, and Genoa, and somewhat higher than in Venice'.[116] The transport of cargoes linked to Allied recovery programmes and direct Allied assistance enabled Triestine trade to surpass its 1913 volume. Shipping totals looked impressive, but Allied assistance masked an actual decline in lucrative commercial traffic.

In 1950 *Il Lavoratore*, the revived socialist organ, charged that the European Recovery Plan was merely a means by which the United States could exercise 'stringent control over what . . . people eat, produce, import, and export'.[117] By 1951 the tone of the workers' newspaper had turned hostile. The paper referred to the Recovery Programme as an agent of American propaganda. The programme's pavilion at the Triestine trade fair was labelled a 'Trojan horse', that provided a 'hiding place' and jumping-off point for American infiltration into Trieste.[118] *Trieste Sera*, a more moderate organ, suggested merely that the pavilion occupied space that could be better used for displaying merchandise. The paper cited the decline in international presence at the Triestine fair from 1951 to 1952 as proof that the irredentist spirit and Allied orientation toward Italy threatened the success of economic recovery.[119] Pro-Slavic elements claimed that Trieste would be more efficient transporting raw materials and finished products from the Slavic and German hinterlands than from Italy.[120]

The increase in international traffic and the Allied focus on ties to Austria encouraged local commercial leaders to pursue trade in areas of nineteenth-century specialisation and to hope for a revival of Austrian networks. Rodolfo Bernardi, general director of the Central Warehouse Authority, recommended revitalisation through rail construction, echoing the plan put forward by economists in the late 1920s. He called for the construction of a more efficient double-track rail line from Trieste to Tarvisio on the Austrian border and improvements to the rail system inside Trieste to facilitate port transport.[121] This insistence on Trieste's importance in Austrian networks, the awkward juridical position of the city and the division of Europe into opposing camps of east and west all contributed to the further deterioration of Trieste's trade position.

In specific trade sectors, some initiatives did achieve limited success. In 1946 an Italian delegation, including Triestine representatives, visited South

---

116 Economic Co-operation Administration, *Trieste*, 10.
117 'Discorsi e padiglioni alla fiera di Trieste', *Il Lavoratore*, 28 Aug. 1950, 1, 4.
118 'Il piano Marshall contro la fiera di Trieste', ibid. 2 July 1951, 2.
119 'Sguardo riassuntivo alla fiera campionaria di Trieste', *Trieste Sera*, 9 Sept. 1950, 3, and 'Pro e contro l'economia triestina', ibid. 19 July 1952, 2.
120 F. Gabronsek, *Jugoslavia's frontier with Italy: Trieste and its hinterlands*, New York n.d. 24.
121 R. Bernardi, *I grandi progetti per lo sviluppo del porto di Trieste*, Trieste 1945, 2–8.

America to examine possibilities for the expansion of national 'industrial, commercial, agricultural, financial [links], and emigration' and emphasised the rejuvenation of networks related to the coffee trade.[122] Trieste's coffee exchange had closed in 1932, a victim of depression and corporative restrictions in Fascist Italy. From 1924 to 1938 the coffee traffic through the port had declined from 92,000 to 17,000 tons.[123] In 1950 traders in coffee, spices and colonial products met at the Triestine trade fair to discuss redevelopment of the local market. In 1952 merchants in Trieste sponsored special coffee exhibitions and hosted a meeting of the executive council of the National Federation of Coffee and Colonial Products. In 1953 thirteen of the leading coffee-producing nations, representing 92 per cent of world production, exhibited 172 varieties of coffee at the Second Annual Coffee Exhibition.[124] By 1959 new shipping and warehousing agreements concluded between Triestine and Brazilian coffee interests confirmed the revival, at least on a limited scale, of the Triestine coffee trade.

Attempts to reinvigorate trade in wood and wood by-products proved less successful. Triestine shipbuilders purchasing lumber for reconstruction projects mistook the increase in trade in wood products as a sign that the pre-First World War market might be revived. In 1952 the dedication of a special 'Wood Day' at the Triestine trade fair, aimed at stimulating interest in precious woods, lumber and other wood-related industries and at encouraging a triangular trade supported by Trieste, Austria and Yugoslavia. A concurrent meeting of the executive council of the National Federation of Wood and Cork Traders reinforced Triestine ambitions to leadership in this sector.[125] Samples of exotic wood, brought by foreign countries for display at the fair, were to remain in Trieste to become part of a permanent trade samples exhibition housed in the fair pavilions. Yet ports in Germany, Yugoslavia and on the peninsula offered more convenient and economical alternatives. Trieste could not increase its share of the wood products' market.

The Allies and Italy, sanguine about commercial prospects, moved forward with plans to shore up Trieste's flagging economy through the promotion of local industry. Plans for the development of the Zaule industrial port were revived. The earlier proposal for construction in the San Andrea quarter was scrapped in favour of a larger site in Trieste's suburbs. The Allied military government contributed heavily to work on the five million square metre site. Support for this project was consistent with the Italian approach to revamping industry throughout the country. Government leaders adopted

[122] Comitato per le relazioni economiche Italia-America Latina, 1 Sept. 1946, CCIA, cat. XXVIII.
[123] Roletto, Il Porto, 232.
[124] 'La V fiera di Trieste', RMCT iv/7 (1953), 9; 30 Oct. 1952, CCIA, cat. XXVIII; Fiera di Trieste, Fiera di Trieste campionaria internazionale, 27 agosto–10 settembre 1950, Trieste 1950, and 40 anni di fiera, 40 anni di vita a Trieste, Trieste 1988, 81–2.
[125] 30 Oct. 1952, CCIA, cat. XXVIII.

the American philosophy for industrial planning, marketing and machinery, while adhering to a management style based in Italian traditions. They emphasised regional co-ordination through industrial districts rather than concentration in corporate hierarchies.[126] However, in the case of Trieste, Rome made only token contributions to signal support for recovery. By 1949 the new industrial zone was established largely on the basis of Allied and local initiative.

Locals portrayed Trieste as a 'spine for expansion of Italian trade towards the east and north-east' and therefore not in competition with Italian ports on the peninsula.[127] Emphasis on Trieste's orientation away from the peninsula smoothed relations with other Italian ports, but it doomed Trieste to further decay by delineating the city's sphere of influence in hinterlands behind the emerging iron curtain. Local commercial interests and politicians in Trieste made economic sacrifices in the name of western policies in return for Allied assistance. Couching their pleas for aid in political rhetoric spiced with allusions to communists lurking nearby, they pandered to American tastes and objectives. In 1949, in his request to the ministry of commerce and industry for recognition of Trieste's trade fair and its inclusion in the Italian national calendar, the Triestine mayor claimed that Italian recognition was imperative to 'keep the initiative solidly in Italian hands', and to prevent the enterprise from becoming an 'instrument of Slav-communist political and economic penetration'.[128]

The western Allies enforced their vision of western political and economic relations but became suspicious of continued calls for aid. Convinced that it was their duty to solve European problems after the war, the Americans resented local lack of appreciation of their beneficence. A State Department representative summed up this attitude in his observation on the situation in Greece: 'The Greeks in power will use us for all we are worth. We think we are doing them a favour; they know they are doing us a bigger one.'[129] Particularly high levels of Allied aid opened Triestines to similar charges. The American high commissioner in Vienna, Llewellyn Thompson, claimed that the Triestines courted favours from both sides:

> We, the Italians, and the Yugoslavs were all cultivating the Triestini by special concessions of all kinds. They got more bread and lower electricity prices from the Italians than anybody else. We were putting in all kinds of aid projects. In fact we were hard pressed to find things to spend money on.[130]

---

[126] V. Zamagni, 'American influence on the Italian economy, 1948–1958', in Duggan and Wagstaff, *Italy in the Cold War*, 87.

[127] Fiera di Trieste, *Catalogo ufficiale fiera di Trieste campionarie internazionale: 17 giugno–4 luglio 1954*, Trieste 1954, 35.

[128] 29 Sept. 1949, CIA, cat. XXVIII.

[129] Ellwood, 'Italy, Europe, and the Cold War', 32.

[130] Campbell, *Successful negotiation*, 30.

The Allies failed to place the local response to aid in a broader historical framework. Italy's marginal position as a great power predisposed Italians to accept American foreign aid and involvement as consistent with a historic reliance on foreign investment. Italian democrats had a propensity to rely on foreign sponsorship to shore up weak domestic governments. Since the First World War, Italian financial networks and industry had fostered cordial relations between American and Italian businessmen and politicians.[131] In Trieste, where indigenous traditions relied on patronage from afar, from Vienna prior to 1918 and after that from Rome, the acceptance of American and Allied assistance seemed natural. Local action reflected pragmatic instincts for self-preservation, not necessarily political calculations to 'milk' the American cash cow.

In 1952 General Winterton, head of the Allied military government, suggested that Trieste 'already owes a special debt of gratitude to the Italian government for its generous financial assistance which in large measure has contributed to the economic progress of the past few years'.[132] The Triestine trade fair, that celebrated the increasingly close relationship with Italy, was labelled 'indispensable for the maintenance of the Italian character of Trieste' and necessary for 'increasing trade currents and ties with the rest of Italy'.[133] By June 1954 the Italian trajectory of the economy was clear. Dependence on Allied aid dispensed in many cases by Italy had compromised the zone's independence. A heavy Italian hand controlling financial arrangements reduced Yugoslavia's duty-free import credit a few days prior to the opening of the Triestine fair, upsetting Yugoslavia's plans for participation.[134]

With the writing on the wall, disappointed supporters of independence called for 'humanitarian internationalism' rather than international oversight in the territory. Giani Stuparich suggested that Trieste should free itself 'from the hands of cynical traders' and resume its position as 'an intermediary of civilisation between the east and the west, the North and the Mediterranean'. Trieste could set an example as 'the Italian door open to everyone'. Through this door, he promised, would advance 'only good intentions and civilised men of many nations, not conquerors'.[135]

The Memorandum of Understanding of October 1954 returned Zone A to Italian sovereignty. Emphasis on the centrality of the port and capitalist commerce to local life allowed the pre-Second World War economic elite to resume its position. Trieste's political review published the lament of an

---

[131] D. Forsyth, 'The peculiarities of Italo-American relations in historical perspective', *Journal of Modern Italian Studies* iii (1998), 8–14.

[132] Prefect of Trieste to CCIA, memorandum, undated, CCIA, cat. XXVIII.

[133] 14 Nov. 1952, ibid.

[134] 'La "soluzione" del problema del contingente fieristico jugoslavo: dei 295 milioni Roma ha concesso 150 milioni di lire soltanto' dal *Primorski Dnevnik*, Astra-Trieste, serv. 135, 16 June 1954, BC, RP (Italian translations by the Astra-Trieste news service of selected local Slavic publications including *Primorski Dnevnik*).

[135] This is quoted in Arosio, *Scrittori di frontiera*, 149.

anonymous commentator: 'For a long time, the important posts [in Trieste] have in fact been occupied by the same people, who share them (and no one knows how) in scores of leading jobs.'[136] Since 1918 elite commercial circles had been shrinking. The politicisation and integration of the Triestine economy had forced a merger between Italian politicians and economic elites. Fascist policies had edged out those interested in economic autonomy, members of ethnic minorities and, eventually, influential Jews. The result was economic catastrophe. In 1938 Trieste had ranked third in Italy after Genoa and Venice in terms of commercial movement through the port. Genoa handled 6.9 million tons to Trieste's 3.4 million tons. In 1954 Genoa still held the premier spot processing over 10 million tons, but Trieste shipped only 3.6 million tons. The city had fallen behind Naples, Venice, Livorno, Savona and La Spezia. Between 1938 and 1955 local shipping co-ordinated by the IRI Finmare group in the Venezia Giulia region declined dramatically. Twenty-eight lines decreased to sixteen, ninety-one ships to forty, and 581,000 tons transported to 249,000.[137]

Overwhelmingly, the elites had relied on the political promise their commercial relationships offered and the influence their wealth afforded, not on calculations for economic success within the Italian framework. Commitment to conservative economic agendas encouraged local, national and even international confidence in commercial representatives' reliability on the local level. Rome supported elite ventures and encouraged Trieste's links to markets abroad for their utility in supporting irredentist agendas. By 1954 the cosmopolitan elite of the Habsburg period had been transformed into a regional Italian elite with a liberal commercial heritage. Triestine community life continued to centre on the port. However, it was clear that the city did not occupy a 'natural' position in an 'organic' order of commerce and European trade. Rather, it relied on patronage. Italy was best prepared and best equipped to play the role of benefactress in what was increasingly becoming an economic backwater at the edge of western Europe.

---

[136] 'La vecchia classe dirigente', *Trieste: rivista politica giuliana* ix (Sept./Oct. 1955), 31.
[137] G. Sapelli, 'Il Lloyd nel contesto dell'economica triestina e del suo hinterland', in *Il Lloyd Triestino*, 140–1, 163.

3

Marking the Eastern Boundary

[T]he politics of normalisation mean closing our eyes to reality, that is ignoring the geographic position of Trieste, forgetting that it does not exist in contact with a local market and that ninety-four percent of the province lies along the border of the state.[1]

In this speech before the Provincial Economic Council in 1958, economist Pierpaolo Luzzato Fegitz pinpointed the difficulty in defining Trieste as an Italian city from the geographical perspective. Political attachment to Italy was sanctioned in 1918. In 1954 it was reaffirmed. During the intervening decades, the city's eccentric position and proximity and economic ties to lands beyond Italy's borders fuelled competing claims to the upper Adriatic lands.[2] Efforts to cast the land as Italian arose from the compulsion Italians felt to justify Trieste's inclusion within the Italian state.

Under the Armistice agreements of November 1918, much of the Austrian Adriatic Littoral, including Trieste, passed into Italy's hands. Between 1918 and 1954 Italy's eastern border was modified eight times. In 1920 the Treaty of Rapallo fixed the Italian border in Trieste's eastern hinterlands. In 1924 the Fascists negotiated for the takeover of Fiume, extending Italy to include the remainder of Istria and some islands along the Dalmatian coast. The border shifted further to the east when Italian forces annexed much of Slovenia during wartime in 1941. The Axis alliance proved fatal to Italian Trieste when, in 1943, the Nazi high command eschewed inclusion of the eastern borderland with northern Italian provinces in Mussolini's Salò Republic. The Nazis chose instead to place the city under direct German administration as part of the Adriatic coastland territory. On the surrender and defeat of Nazi forces in early May 1945 Yugoslavia prepared for the incorporation of Trieste as a constituent republic of Federated Yugoslavia. By mid-June international pressure forced the Yugoslavs to turn over the city as part of Zone A of the Free Territory to Allied military government control. In October 1954 the Memorandum of Understanding dissolved the Free Territory, and Italy gained control of most of Zone A, including Trieste. On the 'farthest shore of Italy', Trieste was an Italian gateway to the east, a border

---

[1] Quoted in P. De'Stefani, 'Trieste e Roma', *Il Borghese* ix/13 (20 Mar. 1958), 506.
[2] Ljubljana, the Slovenian capital, is 110 kilometres to the east. The nearest Italian regional capital lies 165 kilometres to the west-southwest. Vienna, at 500 kilometres to the north, and Belgrade, at 625 kilometres to the south-east, are closer to Trieste than Rome, which lies 676 kilometres to the south-west.

town between east and west, a sentinel against invasion from the east, a marker separating the Balkans from 'Europe', or a part of Central Europe.[3] Those exercising or seeking power interpreted the natural landscape to justify claims to the contested region.

Habsburg port

Each of the three designators for the city – the Slavic 'Trst', the Germanic 'Triest' and the Italian 'Trieste' – reflected a particular ethnic or nationalist perception. Advocates of each cast Trieste's history in ethnic terms. Italians claimed that Italic peoples from the Mediterranean had founded the settlement around the twelfth century BC. Rome's establishment of a military colony at the site in about 177 BC marked the true beginning of the city's history. In Italian lore, the name Trieste derived from Tergeste, the Albanian or Illyrian word for market. It recalled the Roman market and Latin settlement.[4] Opponents of the Italian position divorced the city and its name from these Roman or Latin origins. The Romans had set up a mere frontier outpost, not a colony. Celts, Byzantines, Lombards and Franks had inhabited the region.[5] The account of the Lombard historian Paulus Diaconus placed Carnic peoples, Illyrian-Celts and not Latins in the area, including the countryside, c. 568 AD. For advocates of this Celtic-based interpretation, the name Tergeste originated in Greek references to 'gest' meaning colony or establishment and 'tur' meaning water.[6]

No matter what the roots of the city's name, by the mid-nineteenth century 'core myths' evolved to explain the city's relationship to surrounding lands and the international community.[7] Under the Habsburgs, the city's role as an imperial port predominated. The *bora* from the east-northeast and the scirocco from the south-east made the site less than ideal especially during certain seasons of the year.[8] None the less, the region's topography and the port's location proved convenient for the Monarchy. Over the course of more than five centuries, and particularly after the declaration of free trade privi-

---

[3] Umberto Saba, *Trieste et un poète*, Paris 1977, 44, 46 [Italian text of 'Il molo'].

[4] The contemporary description linking the 'questionable origin' of the name to 'the Illyrians or Venetians' (both considered Italian) testifies to the enduring appeal of this nationalist mapping: G. Queirazza, C. Marcato and others (eds), *Dizionario dei nomi geografici italiani: origine e significato dei nomi di regione, città, paesi, mari, laghi, fiume, e isole*, Milan 1992, 541.

[5] Italians did not ignore the presence of these groups, but blamed them for bringing the Slavs during their invasions 'despite vain protests by the lands' inhabitants': *Guida practica illustrata di Trieste*, Trieste 1919, 16.

[6] G. Gregorin, *La Question de l'adriatique*, Paris 1919, 6.

[7] S. Schama, *Landscape and memory*, New York 1995, 16, identifies 'core myths' revealed by landscape.

[8] Jangakis, *Le port*, 18–20.

leges in 1719, the Habsburgs adapted the natural environment to facilitate trade and commerce oriented toward Vienna and interior Central European lands. They constructed the 'Old Free Point', consisting of three quays and a breakwater, between 1868 and 1883 and built a fourth quay in 1887.[9] As the city's transportation and communications facilities developed, the population of the city swelled from little more than 7,000 in 1735 to over 240,000 on the eve of the First World War. As the urban area expanded, the city's importance and influence in the local region and Central Europe grew.

Commercially-oriented interpretations of topography illustrated official attitudes emanating from Vienna. Maps prepared in 1856 by Pietro Kandler, for presentation to the Habsburg sovereign, emphasised style over detail and mapped Trieste as an integral part of the empire.[10] In 1881 Sidney Sonnino, destined to be the ardent defender of Italian claims as Italy's foreign minister after the First World War, contended that Trieste was most appropriately a port of German commerce.[11] The proximity of Trieste to the 'Postumia saddle', or pass to interior lands between the Julian Alps and the Carso hills, supported notions that the city was naturally destined to facilitate trade between the Germanic interior and markets overseas.[12]

After the mid-nineteenth century, increasingly vociferous nationalist elements espoused political ambitions, sentimental attachments and ethnic claims. The emergence of an independent and unified Italy, and the inclusion of Venice and the Veneto in the Italian state in 1866, fuelled Italian nationalist aspirations in the upper Adriatic region. Irredentist groups harped on the area's natural Italianness, portraying it as a natural and historic link between Risorgimento Italy and lands in Istria and Dalmatia. Some maintained that the need to defend Italianness bred a 'better, more pure, intact, and austere' Italianness in the borderland.[13] Commonly-held conceptions of the Apennine peninsula as Italy supported champions of Slavic claims.[14] Slavic nationalists employed Mazzini's ambiguous statement that Italy's 'indisputable boundaries' were at the Alps and on the sea. From the Slavic perspective the River Isonzo marked Italy's eastern boundary.[15]

Italian proponents affirmed the Italian nature of urban space and touted the superiority of urban over rural culture to strengthen the Italian hand. The history of medieval and renaissance free cities in the northern and central

[9] D. Mihelic, *The political element in the port geography of Trieste*, Chicago 1969, 15–17.

[10] P. Kandler, *Albo storico topografico della città e territorio di Trieste*, ed. S. Zorzon, Trieste 1989.

[11] This was reported in the weekly news periodical *La Rassegna Settimanale*, then under his editorship. It is quoted in Gregorin, *La Question*, 5.

[12] The pass, approximately 50 kilometres north-north-east of Trieste, lies only 600 metres above sea level.

[13] Castellini, *Trento e Trieste*, 65–6, quoting the well-known irredentist V. Gayda.

[14] See, for example, Albrecht-Carrié, *Italy*, 3.

[15] This is quoted in Bebler, *Equilibrium or justice?*, 9. For the quotation and a brief analysis see Rusinow, *Italy's Austrian heritage*, 16.

parts of Italy supported notions of western cultural superiority. References to Trieste's brief stint as a centre of Napoleon's Illyrian provinces in the early nineteenth century provided links to the western revolutionary tradition. Slavs and others contesting Italy's claim pointed out that Napoleon's Illyrian provinces integrated areas of southern Austria, Slovenia and Croatia.[16]

In the late nineteenth century Italian nationalists supported cultural groups like the Società degli Alpinisti (Alpine Club) to affirm the Italianness of Trieste and the surrounding areas. Venetian-Italian versions of maps and surveys accustomed the local population to Italian toponyms in place of bilingual forms or Slavic names.[17] By the end of the nineteenth century, Trieste's municipal council, in the hands of Italian nationalists, manipulated street names to promote Italianness. Overseeing Austrian authorities blocked blatant attempts at Italianisation, including a proposal in 1909 to name a street XX September in honour of the Italian breach of the Porta Pia and Rome's annexation to Italy. But the proposal in 1902 of Attilio Hortis, a well-known local irredentist, that Via di Torre Bianca (White Tower Street) be substituted for Via di Carintia (Carinthia Street) was accepted. This change eliminated the toponymic reference to Austrian Carinthia and substituted a name that invoked the memory of a long-destroyed white tower built on the site in the fifteenth or sixteenth century. Medieval references highlighted urban topography. The renaming of the Piazza Vecchia as the Via dei Rettori in 1901 asserted traditional urban autonomy. The *rettori* or city fathers had exercised power for approximately four months at the end of the eighteenth century. The renaming of the Strada al Ferdinandeo as the Strada al Cacciatore (Hunter's Road) masked the Habsburg presence and highlighted the road's terminal point at a guardhouse and forest.[18] Toponymic changes set the stage for asserting the city's inherent Italianness or at least its autonomous urban traditions on the eve of the First World War.

Emphasis on autonomy proved a double-edged sword. Opponents of the Italian position pointed out that the population of Trieste had sought Austrian protection against the Venetians. Since medieval times the city had consistently affirmed its preference for Austria over Italy.[19] Noted scholars of the nineteenth century and at the turn of the century maintained that the port city was integrated solidly with the Austrian interior and, from an economic standpoint, was a site for rivalry between Germans and Slavs.[20] However, contradictions in Austrian policy complicated questions of the port's orientation. Vienna seemed to favour Slavic interests in its domestic

16 Gregorin, *La Question*, 8.
17 Similar initiatives were undertaken in Fiume and the Trentino: P. Parovel, *L' identità cancellata: l'italianizzazione forzata dei cognomi, nomi e toponomi nella 'Venezia Giulia' dal 1919 al 1945, con gli elenchi delle provincie di Trieste, Gorizia, Istria ed i dati dei primi 5,300 decreti*, Trieste 1985, 22.
18 Trampus, *Vie e piazze*, 111, 445, 517–18, 627, 659.
19 Gregorin, *La Question*, 9.
20 Cervani, *Nazionalità*, 31; Vivante, *Irredentismo*, 258.

policies, particularly in coastal lands where Italian nationalists threatened the monarchy. In foreign policy the Habsburgs appeared to favour Italian interests, particularly where granting Serbian access to the Adriatic was at stake.[21]

'Redemption' and the First World War

Italian nationalists saw the 'redemption' of Trieste and of eastern Adriatic lands as the final chapter in Italian unification.[22] A map serving as the frontispiece to an account of Trento and Trieste entitled 'Italy outside of [Italian] borders subject to Austria' depicted the city as a focal point for 'unredeemed' Italian communities. On it Fiume and Dalmatia as well as islands in the Adriatic almost as far south as Greece were included as lands that rightfully belonged to the Italian nation.[23] Italian nationalists insisted on this interpretation of 'natural frontiers'; Slavs and Slavic supporters used different natural features and criteria. Trieste's location on the eastern shore of the Adriatic 'geographically separated completely from Italy and absolutely included in the Yugoslav hinterland' justified inclusion of the city in the South Slav Kingdom.[24]

Woodrow Wilson's Fourteen Points of January 1918 offered little guidance for the resolution of conflicting territorial claims. Point Nine suggested that 'readjustment of the frontiers of Italy should be effected along clearly recognizable lines of nationality'. Even under the Habsburgs, the majority in Trieste had professed Italian ethnicity. But the populations of the areas surrounding the city were largely Slavic, primarily Slovene and Croatian. While not alluded to specifically, these groups were understood to be covered by Point Eleven which guaranteed the 'independence and territorial integrity of the several states' to be carved out of the Balkan peninsula for Serbs, Romanians and Montenegrins. Wilson simply assumed that relations between the Balkan states could be 'determined by friendly counsel along historically established lines of allegiance and nationality'. Points Nine and Eleven sowed the seeds for territorial dissension between emerging states; Point Ten muddied the waters further. Wilson's intention to accord the 'peoples of Austria-Hungary . . . the freest opportunity to autonomous development' justified calls for independence based on Trieste's status as a maritime outlet serving the needs of Central European lands.[25]

---

[21] These contradictions were noted at the time. See C. Galli, *Diarii e lettere: Tripoli 1911, Trieste 1918*, Florence 1951, 161–2.

[22] See, for example, Tamaro, *Trieste et son rôle*, 7.

[23] Castellini, *Trento e Trieste*, frontispiece.

[24] Gregorin, *La Question*, 9.

[25] W. Wilson, 'The fourteen points', www.lib.byu.edu/~rdh/wwi/1918/1points.html, accessed December 2000.

Wilson relied on 'scientific principles' and academic experts to determine 'just' territorial settlements. The inquiry, or panel of experts, gathered empirical evidence regarding such factors as ethnic affiliations of indigenous populations. Despite intensive studies of the region, it reached no unanimous conclusions beyond a general consensus that the area had been part of the Austrian commercial network and could potentially be used as a barrier against the spread of socialism and communism.[26]

No natural topographical features formed irrefutable boundaries for nation states emerging in the upper Adriatic area. The Wilson line proposed at the Paris Peace Conference coincided 'in general' with the principal watershed, the Carnic and Julian Alps, and 'followed the crest of the high chain that extended along Istria'.[27] However, the complex or compound boundary took into account natural, economic, ethnographical, geopolitical and strategic factors. Its definition also reflected the ideological preferences of western negotiators. Both the Italians and the South Slavs questioned the legitimacy of the border drawn as a compromise.

Italian irredentists agreed with Wilson that the watershed formed the rightful boundary, but they referred to the edge of northern Italy as encompassing the 'watershed between the Adriatic and the Danube'. The Julian, Venetian or Oriental Alps formed a 'naturally-made boundary' running east of Trieste and including the whole of Istria and parts of the Dalmatian coast in Italy.[28] This 'mountain chain' argument, which considered the range of Monte Nevoso or Monte Maggiore as the last branch of the great Alpine barrier, was traced as far back as the Roman senate of 183 BC.

Claims that territory should be divided by 'the watershed that separates the Balkans of the Drava and Sava rivers from the lands of the Isonzo and reaches finally to the Quarnero at the crest of the Julian Alps' upheld Italian views that Trieste and Istria were separate from Austria and the South Slav State.[29] More ambitious irredentists referred to the Carso region to the east of Trieste as framed by rivers beginning 'south of the Gorizia–Ljubljana line bordered by the Isonzo, Idria, Zayer de Polland and Sava Rivers'.[30] This description justified claims along the eastern shore of the Adriatic Sea. Irredentists argued that ethnic Italians in cities all along the Dalmatian coast merited 'salvation' from the Balkan menace. Even before the signing of the Treaty of London of 1915, extensive claims to Dalmatia were repudiated, but Italian co-operation in the war effort and the perception that Italy had made sacrifices for the Adriatic emboldened irredentists.

Some Yugoslav circles included Trieste in the territory of the Kingdom of the Serbs, Croats and Slovenes.[31] Descriptions linked lands east of Venice to

---

[26] C. Belci, *Quel confine mancato: la linea Wilson (1919–1945)*, Brescia 1996, 31.

[27] Ibid. 23.

[28] Albrecht-Carrié, *Italy*, 91–4.

[29] Montemuliano, *Venezia Giulia*, 13–17.

[30] Jangakis, *Le Port*, 17–18.

[31] I. Lederer, *Yugoslavia at the Paris Peace Conference*, New Haven 1963, 94.

the Balkans. These presented the Carsic plain as an extension of the Balkan system 'completely separate from the Friulian plain which is a prolongation of the Venetian plain'.[32] From this perspective, exaggerated Italian nationalist claims were a manifestation of expansionist tendencies.

Both the Italians and the Slavs marshalled traditional arguments based on military and security concerns and respect for principles of *realpolitik* in support of their assertions. Irredentists were convinced, or perhaps hopeful, that diplomatic efforts in Paris would 'resolve nothing' and possession would be the primary determinant of sovereignty.[33] Despite the presence of Germanic majorities in northern provinces as far as the Brenner, Wilson had agreed to grant control to Italy, ostensibly for defensive reasons. Italians reasoned that possession of Istria and the Adriatic coastline was equally critical. Alluding to the need to create stable and defensible states and to ensure the success of the League of Nations, Italian negotiators argued for control of the Julian Alpine and Carso passes leading to the peninsula. They highlighted the potential for German domination of the Adriatic coast and the possibility of future invasion through the Adriatic corridor.[34] Such tactical arguments suited local and Italian nationalist purposes. When Italian nationalists had suggested prior to the First World War that the entire Adriatic coast was important to Italy, they had compared its significance to that of the coast of 'Belgium for England'. Traditional 'balance of power' notions presented Italians and Slavs as two interests striking an 'equilibrium' in the Adriatic.[35]

The South Slavs and their supporters argued for 'just' boundaries drawn roughly along ethnic lines and based on the principle of 'balanced minorities', or the inclusion of roughly equivalent minority populations within each state. Since Slavs predominated except in the major cities, this formula called for the inclusion of lands on the eastern shore of the Adriatic in the new Yugoslav state. Any territorial settlement assigning these lands to Italy would include several hundred thousand Slavs in Italian territory. Even population figures cited by irredentists confirmed the sparse Italian population of Dalmatia. Trieste boasted 142,113 Italians, Istria had 147,739 and Fiume had 26,000. In all of 'Italian' Dalmatia there were only 30,000 Italians.[36]

Pro-Italian and pro-Slavic elements bickered over ethnic geography, but the economic geography of the region continued to favour links to satellites of Vienna. Vanquished Austria could make no legitimate political claim to the region. Early American recommendations called for both Fiume and Trieste to be free ports. Ports along the Adriatic, Tyrrhenian and Mediterra-

---

[32] Gregorin, *La Question*, 9.

[33] A. Dudan to Tamaro, 11 June 1919, Tamaro papers

[34] 'Italian Memorandum of Claims, February 7, 1919', in Albrecht-Carrié, *Italy*, 370–87.

[35] Giulio Caprin, *Trieste e l'Italia*, Milan 1915, 24–31.

[36] Castellini, *Trento e Trieste*, frontispiece.

nean seas already served the peninsula. Fiume and Trieste competed directly with Venice or the port at Mestre for traffic to Central Europe. From the Italian peninsula, routes proceeding through the Brenner Pass allowed the Adriatic to be bypassed altogether.

No port assigned to the South Slav state had facilities comparable to those of Trieste. The Yugoslavs claimed both Fiume and Trieste, arguing that they were integrated with other former imperial lands in the Slav-dominated hinterlands. Slavic claims to Fiume, the former Hungarian port, were greeted with some sympathy, but claims to Trieste actually weakened the South Slav case. The furore over Trieste caused disputes between moderate and extreme nationalists within the Yugoslav camp.[37] It also fuelled western fears that the Slavs aimed to dominate the Adriatic. Italian control was seen as necessary to stem the tide of Slavic irredentism.[38]

'Redeemed' city

In fact, occupation did play a large part in determining possession. Wilson expressed sympathy for small nations that had been subject to 'foreign' authority, but the American proposal would have placed approximately 370,000 Slavs in Italy. The Wilsonian line was never achieved. Negotiators gave up and left the border question open. Italian authorities remained in Trieste. In November 1920 the Treaty of Rapallo contained the settlement that largely affirmed Italian claims. Trieste emerged as the capital of the new Italian territory of Venezia Giulia and adopted the role of guardian of Italy's eastern border. Rapallo did not satisfy Italian nationalists. It marked a small section of Istria, including the port city of Fiume, for internationalisation and joined coastal areas of Dalmatia to the new South Slav state. From the irredentist perspective, Italian lands remained 'unredeemed'.

In Venezia Giulia, Italian officials set out to affirm the justice of the extension of Italian control and influence. The very name Venezia Giulia mapped an Italian topography. Ascribed to Graziado Ascoli, Gorizian glottologist and Italian nationalist, who used it in 1863 in place of the Austrian term Kustenland, 'Giulia' referred to the Roman roots of settlement in the territory going back to the time of Julius Caesar, and 'Venezia' connoted medieval Venetian control.[39] Yugoslavs generally preferred the term Julian March or Julijska Krajina to describe the territory. The Slavic designation retained the reference to Roman settlement but omitted the connection to Venice. The Slavic Julian March and Italian Venezia Giulia were not completely analogous, but both referred to the area that included Trieste, Istria and parts of the Dalmatian coast and Gorizia.

[37] Lederer, *Yugoslavia*, 103–4.
[38] See Italian claims in 'Italian Memorandum of Claims, February 7, 1919', 376–7.
[39] Queirazza, Marcato and others, *Dizionario*, 562.

Italian officials promoted Venezia Giulia as one of the Tre Venezie, or Three Venices, including the new northern territory of Venezia Tridentina, the Veneto (Venezia Propria or Venezia Eugenea) and Venezia Giulia. The designation deliberately linked the new provinces with 'uncle' (and indisputably Italian) Venice. The Italian Touring Club's *Three Venices* guide, published in 1921, helped to strengthen the link in the eyes of the public. Prior to its publication, Attilio Tamaro, well known for his irredentism, had helped to revise 'toponymastic falsifications' in the guide, or to affirm the Italianness of the provinces. Luigi Federzoni, well known for his editorship of *L'Idea nazionale* and later renowned as a Fascist minister appealed directly to Tamaro for his help in 'documenting as unfounded certain assertions . . . of the Slavism of certain important Istrian and Friulian centres'.[40]

Local officials proved eager to map an Italian geography for Trieste. Little more than a week after the landing of Italian troops, on 11 November 1918, the city council renamed central arteries. The large central square, at the core of civic life, was transformed from the Piazza Grande to the Piazza Unità in honour of the unification with Italy. Via della Caserma, named for the Austrian barracks was re-christened Via XXX Ottobre in recognition of the population's declaration of liberation from Austrian sovereignty on 30 October. National officials generally sympathised with local officials, who succeeded in nationalising the landscape. During the spring of 1919, Viale III Armata was substituted for Via Massimiliana, replacing the Habsburg Archduke Ferdinand Maximillian with the army regiment famed for First World War triumphs in the Carso and Gorizia. Via Nuova, called Via Maria Teresa for a brief time during the First World War, was transformed to Via Giuseppe Mazzini in honour of the hero of Italian unification. In 1920, on the fiftieth anniversary of Rome's entry into the nation, Via Acquedotto, a street named for its proximity to the ancient aqueduct, became Viale XX Settembre.[41] The section of the port constructed between 1901 and 1914 and dubbed Port Franz Joseph became Port Emanuele Filiberto Duca D'Aosta.[42]

A studied disregard of Trieste's debts to Austria characterised Italian nationalist accounts of the city. An article by Silvio Benco, published in *Illustrazione Italiana,* welcomed the Adriatic provinces to the nation, but neglected to mention any Austrian involvement in the construction of the port facilities or in the development of the city.[43] Local initiative was credited with spurring the political and economic successes of the Habsburg period.

Liberal officials worked to acquaint Italians with the new borderlands in the months immediately following the war. Families of the fallen received

---

[40] L. Federzoni to Tamaro, 23 June 1920, Tamaro papers.

[41] Trampus, *Vie e piazze,* 381, 610, 635, 644.

[42] Jangakis, *Le Port,* 23–5.

[43] Silvio Benco, 'Trieste', *Illustrazione Italiana: numero speciale Trento e Trieste* (1919), 23ff.

special travel permits to visit battlegrounds and war graves.[44] These 'pilgrimages' underlined the sacrifices of those in the new provinces and highlighted the eastern borderland as deserving of national recognition and support. The local tourist agency, in co-operation with the national tourist association, published a tour book and pamphlets on the Venezia Giulia for distribution on the peninsula. Special itineraries attracted foreigners and patriotic Italians to local battle sites, monuments, cemeteries and Roman ruins.[45] The national tourist organisation incorporated materials from a Triestine display into a travelling exhibition which toured Italy and abroad. At the Munich Exposition Italy's special pavilion drew attention to Trieste and Venezia Giulia.[46]

In the tense nationalist climate, even seemingly mimetic geographic descriptions affirmed Trieste's link to the Apennine peninsula and tied its destiny to the 'Italian' Adriatic Sea rather than to the interior. Propagandists approached Trieste 'from the sea by way of Venice'.[47] An early guide to redeemed Trieste, published in 1919, described the city from the perspective of the Gulf of Trieste and the water approaches, dividing the coastal environment from the limestone hills and mountains of the interior Carso.[48] These accounts played to traditional western prejudices that contrasted civilised coastlands with savage mountainous regions and affirmed the distinction between the urban, sophisticated and refined population of Italians and the rural, uncultured and primitive people of the Balkans. This viewpoint fuelled sympathy for Trieste as the saviour of Italian populations 'stranded' outside Italian borders. The 'redemption' of Trieste merely represented the natural continuation of the Risorgimento and the 'tear[ing] up of the last fragment of the Treaty of Vienna, which . . . deprived Italy of some of her children, and undermined the security of her Adriatic frontier by sea and land'.[49]

The call for 'redemption' formed a powerful component of post-war Italian propaganda and even sparked 'patriotic' military action. Gabriele D'Annunzio's attempt to extend the sovereignty of Italy by the annexation of Fiume in September 1919 excited conservative nationalists. The Italian government's ousting of D'Annunzio, reflecting the decision to enforce the Treaty of Rapallo's internationalisation of Fiume, heightened tensions between nationalists and official forces. The forced surrender of the 'poet-patriot' D'Annunzio by January 1921 angered nationalists and raised public doubts about the effectiveness of the Liberal government.

---

[44] CGCVG (adg), buste 35, 36 passim.
[45] 'Società per il movimento', 10 July 1922, CCIA, busta 4065.19.
[46] Società per il movimento dei forestieri nella Venezia Giulia, 'Industria alberghiera organizzazione turistica a Trieste', in Camera di commercio e industria Trieste, L'economia triestina nel quinquennio, 1919–1923, Trieste 1924, 231.
[47] Castellini, Trento e Trieste, 65.
[48] Guida pratica, 5.
[49] 'Italian Memorandum of Claims, February 7, 1919', 375.

Eastern gateway

The proximity of Italy's eastern border and Triestines' sense of kinship with ethnic Italians 'stranded' outside Italy's borders helped to clear the path for Fascist triumph. After the March on Rome, Mussolini set out to remedy the perceived injustices of the post-First World War settlement. Trieste became a launching point for policies aimed at the Italianisation of the Adriatic. Toponymic campaigns initiated in 1923 aimed to eradicate evidence of all non-Italian influences. Not only were street names modified, but the names of villages, municipalities and small localities were converted to Italian forms. A *List of municipalities and parts of municipalities in Venezia Giulia*, published in 1924, offered an alphabetical index of place names referencing 'foreign spelling' with 'official spelling'. Foreign names were not changed officially, merely 'clarified, converted, or corrected' to an Italian form. Relatively minor administrative adjustments mixed indiscriminately with aggressive Italianisations. Of the first four alterations listed in the pamphlet, the modifications of 'Adelsberg' to 'Postumia' and 'Aichhelter' to 'Aclete' were rather aggressive translations or Italianisation. 'Aisovizza' to 'Aissovizza' was a re-spelling to render the diction of the name more comfortable for Italians. The renaming of 'Altura' to 'Altura di Nesazio' designated the village's position within a larger administrative unit. While the patterns of modification were far from consistent, names of German origin fell prey to the Fascist pen as readily as toponyms of Slavic origin.

Translations most commonly eliminated foreign, usually Slavic, saints' names and adjusted foreign names derived from topographical features. In the alteration of Vrh Svetega Mihaela to San Michele del Carso, the Italian equivalent of St Michael substituted for the Slavic. 'Vrh', meaning peak or summit, was eliminated. The addition of 'del Carso' to the Italian version designated the zone, allowing Italian officials to differentiate this San Michele from others on the peninsula. At the same time it 'Italianised' lands to the interior. In the case of Petrovo Brdo (Peter Hill), the name and topographical feature were translated, resulting in the designation Colle Pietro. In the correction from Lom Tolminski to Lom di Tolmino, the topographical term 'lom' (break) remained curiously unaltered although Tolminski was obviously altered to a more Italophone version.[50] These Fascist designations became the standard place names.

In 1923 the National Conference for Economic and Commercial Expansion Abroad in Trieste underlined the Fascist interest in Trieste's role in the borderland. One speaker affirmed Trieste's usefulness to Italy, arguing that incorporation of Trieste, Venice and even Fiume in the same political entity would allow for a 'more economical and more perfect organisation' of ports in

---

[50] *Elenco dei comuni e delle frazioni di comune della Venezia Giulia secondo le nuove circoscrizioni amministrative e giudiziarie* [Trieste 1924], repr. in Parovel, *Identità*, 110–21.

the upper Adriatic region. Each port, he claimed, 'had a distinct hinterland, rich in the past, present, and future' that could serve the interests of the nation.[51] This optimism was by no means universally shared. Trieste's Mayor Giorgio Pitacco offered a more sober, though no less nationalistic view. He supported Italian control of Venice, Fiume and Trieste, but recognised that the three cities would have to co-operate within the Italian framework.[52]

By January 1924, from the Italian perspective, some of the perceived wrongs of the territorial settlement of 1920 had been righted. Through political wrangling and international negotiation, Mussolini had expanded Italian territory to include Fiume. The Kingdom of Serbs, Croats and Slovenes, at a disadvantage in the international arena and weakened by domestic instability, had been unable to oppose the extension of Italy's eastern border.

Formulators of national policy sought to dispel fears that the integration of Trieste and Fiume would prove detrimental to Italian maritime networks. Igino Brocchi, serving in the Italian ministry of foreign affairs from 1922 to 1924, prepared a seventy-two-page memorandum regarding relations between Trieste and Hungary that reflected on the 'Geographic and commercial hinterlands of Trieste'. The memo stated unequivocally that Triestine concurrence with Fiume posed no problem, as the markets of the two cities had been co-ordinated under Austria. Brocchi emphasised the distinctive hinterlands of the three major northern Adriatic ports. Trieste served Venezia Giulia, eastern Friuli, western Yugoslavia and southern Austria; Fiume's markets were in eastern Yugoslavia and southern Hungary; Venice's interests were in the Po Valley and included the Veneto and Alto Adige.[53] Popular propaganda, including an article in the Italian Touring Club's periodical *Le Vie d'Italia* (The Streets of Italy), picked up on widespread insecurities and hastened to assure readers that Trieste was oriented toward the former empire and posed no threat to Venetian networks.[54]

More generally propaganda communicated a sense of the inherent Italianness of Trieste as it was reflected in the area's landscape. Making free with geography and history, Corrado Moschitti, a delegate from Naples to the conference in Trieste in 1923, described Trieste along with Venice, Genoa, Naples and Amalfi on the Mediterranean, or 'the Roman lake', as ports from which 'imperial galleons and republican warships set sail to conquer the world'.[55] Waxing poetical, Attilio Tamaro contrasted the 'oppressive historic function' of 'the iron-coloured and sad beauty' of the Carso, inhabited by

[51] M. Griffini, 'Fiume integratrice di Trieste', *Congresso nazionale per l'espansione economica e commerciale all'estero: ordine dei lavori regolamento del congresso* [Trieste, 4–8 Nov. 1923], Trieste 1923.

[52] Pitacco, *Avvenimenti*, 113.

[53] 'Memorandum: commercial and geographic hinterland of Trieste' [1922/3?], Brocchi papers, busta 12, fasc. 107.

[54] P. Budinich, 'Il porto di Trieste', *Le Vie d'Italia* (Feb. 1923), 165–6.

[55] Moschitti, 'Per il disciplinamento', 4–5, 9.

Slavs, to the 'enchantment of the panorama' of local Italian shores.[56] Fascist administrator Aldo Pizzagalli described the primarily Slavic villages of Postumia and Sesana as having 'no attractions' for populations (other than the Slavs) due to the aridity and infertility of the land.[57] Emphasis on sea connections tied Trieste firmly to the Apennine peninsula across a mere 'lake'. Trieste's heritage was intertwined with historic Italian maritime power.

Nationalist propaganda attributed the city's prestige to its Roman and medieval origins.[58] In the Fascist idiom, orientation toward the Germanic regions of Central Europe arose from the tradition of Italian predominance in trade networks jutting north from the Adriatic. The city's links to Central Europe, used by Etruscan traders, were developed by the Romans and subsequent Italian peoples. Trieste 'had inherited the function from Venice, as Venice in a certain way, inherited it from the splendour of Aquileia'.[59]

Nationalist historians who exalted links to Venice and Aquileia virulently denounced the Balkans and Slavism. Throughout the Fascist period Tamaro remained committed to the crusade to 'correct errors' in the presentation of local geographical history. In a scathing letter, written in 1931, he criticised Tomaso Sillani's editorship of Dalmatian entries in the Fascist *Encyclopedia*, calling them 'an optimal work to assist in the Slav claims'. The city of Arbe was 'falsely' presented as Slavic, and Zara, 'named as the principle focus of the Slavic rebellion . . . if a centre of rebellion, was the focus of the rebellion of the Latins of Dalmatia'. He also objected to an article on the Balkan region that included all Dalmatia 'without reservation' on the Balkan peninsula.[60]

By the mid-1920s Fascist officials had introduced programmes and co-operative plans that built on the Liberal government's Three Venices. In 1924 the University of Padua introduced a one-year course on the history of the three Venetias. Throughout the 1920s the Paduan trade fair, 'an instrument of the Serenissima Republic of San Marco', highlighted the Three Venices' assimilation. In March 1924 representatives from nine chambers of commerce in the three Venetian territories outlined a strategy for regional co-operation. Guido Chiap, from Vicenza, highlighted the fair as 'an excellent occasion to demonstrate the solidarity of efforts and goals of the Tre Venezie regions'.[61] In August 1926 a 'Grain Exhibition of the Three Venices', held in Padua, became a staging ground for the promotion of the government's 'battle for grain'.[62] 'Art of the Tre Venezie' was a unifying theme for an

---

56 Tamaro to Sticotti, 13 Oct. 1931, Tamaro papers.

57 A. Pizzagalli, *Per l'italianità dei cognomi nella provincia di Trieste*, Trieste 1929, 18–19.

58 V. Franchini, 'Aspetti e momenti della funzione del porto di Trieste a traverso i tempi', *Rivista di Cultura Marinara* (Nov./Dec. 1932), supplement.

59 S. Zanetti, *Trieste e l'economia nazionale*, Trieste 1934, 10, quoting an article by F. Maratea in *Messagero* (Rome), 23 Apr. 1934.

60 Tamaro to T. Sillani, 28 Apr. 1931, Tamaro papers..

61 'Fra le camere di commercio delle Tre Venezie per trattare sulla loro adesione all'ente autonomo fiera campionaria internazionale di Padova', 6 Mar. 1924, CCIA, gruppo 16 (1924).

62 'La mostra del grano delle Tre Venezie', *Il Piccolo*, 29 Aug. 1926, 2.

exhibition at Treviso in 1928.[63] In 1928 a Paduan exhibition chronicled the damage done to the 'Venetian provinces' during the First World War and the success of Italian reconstruction in the post-war decade. It highlighted Italian 'peaceful, not military' intervention, which had promoted the assimilation of the border population. The opening of the exhibition coincided with a commemoration of the Battle of the Piave, the river over which Austrians and Italians had fought to gain control of Venezia Giulia.[64]

By 1925 the Italian Touring Club's Three Venices guide had expanded to three volumes, the third dealing primarily with Venezia Giulia. The description of Trieste's central square, the Piazza Unità, revealed the government's intention to eradicate evidence of non-Italian influence. The prefect's building at the head of the square, designed by an Austrian architect in 1904, was deemed 'pretentious'. 'Awkward' described the fountain of Maria Teresa. No description of the Lloyd building was offered; the author noted simply that the architect was Viennese and that the building dated to around 1880. The statue of Charles VI honoured the founder of the free port. The municipio, redesigned by the Italian architect Giuseppe Bruni between 1869 and 1876, was praised as lively and pleasing in appearance although of no pure architecture style.[65]

The 1928 edition of the La Patria reference work on Italian geography included three volumes devoted to the Venices. These aimed 'to reveal more completely the singular particularities and magnificence for which [the Venices] are treated as a single unified section'. Venice proper and the Veneto were labelled 'Venezia Eugenea', thus blurring any distinction between the old and new 'Venetian' provinces.[66]

By 1924 National Tourist Association publications such as Winter in Italy, Summer in Italy and The hotels of Italy included sections on attractions in Venezia Giulia.[67] In 1927, with the collaboration of the Italian Touring Club, the local Trieste association published a book describing battlefields of the Isonzo Valley aimed at 'patriots'.[68] In 1931 the Primavera Triestina (Triestine Spring), a tourist initiative mimicking such other festivals in Italy as the Primavera Siciliana (Sicilian Spring) and Estate dell'Alto Adige (Alto Adige Summer), included excursions to battlefields and other 'Italian' attractions.[69]

Public exhibitions in Trieste affirmed the landscape's Italianness. In 1928 a marine festival celebrated Trieste's ties to 'the maritime spirit of our [Italian] people who see the sea as the greatest factor in the welfare and prosperity of

[63] 'Artigiani triestini alla mostra di Treviso', ibid. 25 Sept. 1928, 5.
[64] 'La mostra della ricostruzione a Padova', ibid. 22 May 1928, 4, and 'La mostra delle Tre Venezie a Padova, disposizioni del capo del governo', ibid. 19 Feb. 1928, 2.
[65] Bertarelli, Le Tre Venézie, 238.
[66] S. Squinabol and V. Furlani, Venezia Giulia, Turin 1928, 1.
[67] 'Società per il movimento dei forestieri', BCCI v/17 (1924), 510.
[68] 'Una nuova pubblicazione sulla Venezia Giulia della società per il movimento dei forestieri', Il Piccolo, 19 Aug. 1927, 3.
[69] 'La primavera triestina', ibid. 12 Mar. 1931, 4.

the nation'.[70] Photographic competitions during the Triestine summer festivals of the early 1930s captured the natural beauty of the Julian Alps and caves of the Carso, publicising less accessible areas of the north-eastern province to increase tourism and promote a sense of Italian ownership over the more remote areas of the borderland.

In June 1933 the Fascist government, along with the Italian Alpine Club, hosted a national speleological congress in Trieste. Ostensibly centred on explorations of the Postumia and Timavo grottoes, in fact the conference served to confirm the Italianness of the area in two ways. The meeting underlined the longevity of Italian ties to the region by celebrating the fiftieth anniversary of the founding of the Triestine branch of the Italian Alpine Club. In addition, it attracted representatives from all Italian Alpine clubs encouraging personal attachments to Trieste and Venezia Giulia.

Adriatic empire

The transformation of Trieste's summer festivals to official Fascist exhibitions dubbed *Mostre del Mare*, or marine exhibitions, hinted at the increasingly imperialist bent of Fascist policy in the mid-1930s. In 1933 a nautical exhibition on the development of the port from medieval to recent times divorced the city from its political context.[71] In 1934 an exhibition traced the naval history of Trieste, dating it from the establishment of the Roman settlement 'Tergeste' on the site.[72] The winning design in the poster contest for the 1934 exhibition portrayed an elegant, stylised caravel reminiscent of Venetian ships, highlighting associations with the Venetian empire.[73] In a 'ships through time' exhibition, audiences caught glimpses of the port city through models, renderings and photographs that traced the evolution of shipping from pre-history to the Fascist era.[74] Visions of ships in the year 2000 inspired fantasies of a glorious future for Fascist Italy.[75] The message at the entrance to the exhibition reminded Triestines and visiting Italians that 'all of the history of our country is anchored to the sea, the salvation of its solid, tenacious will'. A huge map of the world delineated shipping routes from Trieste. Mussolini's message, 'Your destiny and your wealth are in the sea', underscored the importance of maritime culture.[76]

Support for Trieste as a maritime centre meshed with broader Fascist impe-

---

[70] 'Il programma della festa del mare', ibid. 7 June 1928, 5.
[71] 'Oggi s'inaugura la Settimana del mare', *Il Popolo di Trieste*, 17 June 1933, 2.
[72] 'L'odierna grande giornata marinara di Trieste', ibid. 27 May 1934, 3.
[73] The poster can be found in Azienda autonomo, *Dudovich & C.*, 122.
[74] 'Alla mostra del mare', *Il Piccolo*, 10 May 1934, 4; Museo Ente Portuale, Trieste, uncatalogued photographs, 'Trieste, IIa mostra del mare', 24 May–15 Aug. 1934.
[75] 'L'artigianato alla mostra del mare', *Il Piccolo*, 17 Apr. 1934, 3.
[76] Giugno triestino, *III° mostra nazionale del mare: giugno triestino 1935–XII*, Trieste 1935, photos 44, 46, 56.

rial objectives. The Fascist *Guide to Trieste and Venezia Giulia*, published in 1937, began with a section dedicated to the 'Roman and Italian city rising on the eastern shore of the Adriatic . . . situated along the sea on the gulf that bears its name'.[77] Mussolini's speech on an official visit to Trieste in 1938 reiterated the Roman theme. 'Rome is here. It is here on your hills and in your ocean, and here in the centuries that have passed and in those to come, here with its laws, with its army and with its King.'[78]

Although Italian nationalists and Fascists asserted Trieste's commitment to Italianness, international observers associated the upper Adriatic region with the western Balkans. In 1936, nearly two decades after Trieste's annexation to Italy, the American geographer Griffith Taylor insisted that Trieste was part of Slavic territory. He emphasised the city's reliance on economic ties to the interior through Pear Tree Pass or the Postumia Saddle.[79]

Wartime compromise and the *Reich's* port

In 1939 Mussolini warned the German ambassador in Rome that the Adriatic was 'an Italian sea and only Italian' and that Croatia was an area 'reserved' for Italian influence.[80] However, with Italy's entry into the war in 1940, it became clear that alliance with Germany would lead to accommodation and compromise. In the imagined 'new [Axis] order', the need for 'vital space' was to determine policies affecting regional economies. As the 'hinge' between the Italian and Central European markets, Trieste might lay claim to 'vital space' in hinterlands in Danubian Europe. However, the extent of the city's stake, its role in the new order, and even its national destiny would be open to question until the 'armies fell silent'.[81]

The joint invasion of Yugoslavia by German and Italian forces in the spring of 1941 allowed Italy to realise imperialistic designs on territories in Slovenia and Croatia. Coveted territories in Dalmatia were annexed, and Italy gained direct control over Slovenian provinces including Lubljana. However, Italian victory rested on German might and organisation. By the summer of 1943 Italy's inability to defend its claims was apparent. With the fall of Mussolini's Italy and the creation of the puppet Salò regime, the Nazis incorporated Trieste and surrounding areas into the Adriatic Coastland, a part of the reconstituted German *Reich* that roughly coincided with the Habsburg Adriatic commercial zone of the eighteenth century.

---

[77] *Guida di Trieste*, 7.
[78] The speech appears in *Trieste 18–19 settembre XVI – Mussolini*, Trieste 1938, a commemorative booklet published in honour of Mussolini's visit.
[79] G. Taylor, *Environment and nation: geographical factors in the cultural and political history of Europe*, Chicago 1936, 63.
[80] Apih, *Italia fascismo*, 378.
[81] Roletto, *Il porto*, 95–9, 129–30.

Reincorporation of Trieste and surrounding areas into Central European networks reflected Nazi aims to establish, or re-establish, a united economic effort and integrated political network in Danubian lands.[82]

Until the end of April 1945 Trieste remained the capital of the *Adriatisches Küstenland* of the *Reich*. However, the circumstances of war and the ambiguous position of Italy after Mussolini's fall complicated international understandings of Trieste's situation. The Allies saw the upper Adriatic region as part of a larger territory disputed between the Italians and Yugoslavs. Yugoslavia's commitment to the Allied effort was indisputable. Italy's attachment to the Allies was quite recent. None the less, western biases against the Yugoslavs were evident even in wartime. The American intelligence map of the Adriatic Littoral and *Alpenvorland* included territory as far east as Zagreb in land called 'Italian provinces annexed by Germany'. Lands, which had passed from Habsburg to South Slav control in 1918 and had remained under Yugoslav sovereignty until 1941, were labelled 'Yugoslav' in small print enclosed in parenthesis.

Western bulwark

Beliefs similar to those held during the First World War – that possession would bolster claims to territory – propelled the 'race' to liberate Trieste from German control in late April and early May 1945. Yugoslav troops reached the city first, but New Zealand regiments were close on their heels. Tito's partisans secured much of the territory, but the Germans officially surrendered to the western Allies. Geoffrey Cox, an Allied solder, acknowledged that 'If [Yugoslav] title to these areas had rested on conquest, it would indeed have been a strong one.' In addition he suggested that the Allied forward position in Trieste was precarious. 'Had it come to a battle it would in fact have been impossible for the New Zealanders to hold the western position due to the narrowness of the road and vulnerability of the rails linking the city to Italy.'[83]

International impasse over the fate of the region resulted in the creation of the Free Territory of Trieste. For nine years an Allied military government would rule the western portion, Zone A, which included the city of Trieste. Yugoslav authorities would govern Zone B. Italy and Yugoslavia would resort to diplomatic schemes and propagandistic means to bolster territorial claims.

Perhaps in an effort to appear 'reasonable' in the wake of Fascist excesses, the Italians staked their territorial claim along the First World War line proposed by Wilson.[84] Nationalists had greater ambitions. They stretched

[82] Mihelic, *Political element*, 96, and E. Collotti, *Il litorale adriatico nel nuovo ordine europeo, 1943–1945*, Milan 1974, 9–11.
[83] G. Cox, *The race for Trieste*, London 1977, 185, 208.
[84] Belci, *Quel confine*, 17.

Italian borders to include Trieste and much of Istria in accordance with the Italian geographical–patriotic tradition of nineteenth-century unification.[85] Triestine writer and irredentist Pier Antonio Quarantotti Gambini, director of the civic library, suggested the Julian Alpine border. The region to the west of the Julian Alps, he argued, 'has gravitated, for natural reasons – in fact – before even ethnic [ones], toward the Italian peninsula'. He did admit, however, that the mountains had always been 'much less imposing and inaccessible than the encircling western and northern Alpine [chain]'.[86]

The Yugoslavs focused on the Isonzo River as the natural boundary line between Slavic and Italian, or more succinctly Slovenian and Venetian, lands. Trieste was simply an 'Italian island in a Yugoslav sea'. Pro-Italian factions referred to the continuous and decisive influence of Italian political administrative frameworks in the region. They suggested that the limits of the city of Trieste from 1923 to 1947 conformed roughly to the medieval and Latin limits, inherited by Austria in 1382 and preserved by subsequent Habsburg rulers.[87] The period of Habsburg rule testified to Austria's unjustifiable expansionist ambitions along two axes 'toward the Adriatic and Mediterranean' and 'toward the heart of the Balkans along the Danube'.[88] Slavs countered that, under Habsburg rule, Trieste was 'included in Slovenian territory and remained, until 1918, under the same jurisdiction as Carniola' (the region of the Carnic Alps). The Latin population had remained on the hill of San Giusto and in the vicinity of the harbour.[89] Trieste occupied merely 'a tiny promontory of the surrounding Karst along a narrow strip of low land'.[90]

Fascist Italianisation campaigns had not significantly altered the ethnography of the region. Since the First World War, Istrians had experienced life within the borders of Italy, and Dalmatians had lived in Yugoslavia. Ethnic Italians still predominated in coastal cities, and Slavs made up the bulk of the rural population in the areas under dispute. Fascist persecution of minorities and attempts to Italianise rural populations fuelled support for Yugoslav demands to territory extending west of the pre-1918 Italo-Austrian border, but in the tense political environment after the Second World War, western sympathies were in Italy's favour.

Professional boundary-makers recognised that self-determination could

---

[85] Carlo Schiffrer, *Venezia Giulia: study of a map of the Italo-Yugoslav national borders*, Rome 1946, 95, refers to the 'Italian geographic patriotic tradition'.

[86] P. A. Quarantotti Gambini, *Primavera a Trieste e altri scritti*, [Italy] 1985, 306.

[87] G. Valussi, 'Caratteri e funzioni del nuovo confine italo-jugoslavo', in *Confini e regioni: il potenziale di sviluppo e di pace delle periferie: problemi e prospettive delle regioni di frontiera Gorizia, Istituto di Sociologia Internazionale* [Gorizia, 24 Mar. 1972], Trieste 1973, 75.

[88] F. Salimbeni, 'Tra Vienna e Venezia: Trieste', in G. Romanelli (ed.), *Venezia Vienna*, Milan 1983, 228, 236.

[89] Mihovilovic, *Trieste et son port*, 3–5, and Gabronsek, *Jugoslavia's frontier*, 5, 24.

[90] Mihelic, *Political element*, 13.

not actually define the borderline; it could only delimit a frontier zone.[91] None the less the Free Territory was divided in June 1945 with ethnic precepts in mind. Ironically, the new border, proposed in May 1945 by General William D. Morgan, chief of staff to the supreme Allied commander, Field Marshal Harold Alexander, conformed more to the spirit of maintaining ethnic divisions than did the one drawn after the First World War. The commander's intent was not to promote lofty ideals for 'balancing minorities'. Instead, Trieste's importance lay in the city's (and territory's) position on the line of demarcation between the communist and non-communist worlds. To meet western expectations and further Allied ambitions, the underlying ideological principle justifying the border split shifted from 'balancing minorities' to achieving 'ethnic equilibrium', or placing a minimum number of inhabitants under 'alien' rule. Convictions that the city or urban environment formed a cultural and social hub reinforced support for the western orientation of Trieste and upheld Italian claims to coastal regions extending well into Slavic-dominated areas.

The temporary line drawn by military authorities at the end of hostilities survived the entire Free Territory period. International negotiators deliberated over the placing of the border but were unable to settle conflicting claims. In March 1946 a commission of experts resembling the inquiry of the post-First World War period visited the territory. Even the factors to be considered in their deliberations were unclear. Yugoslavia and Italy bombarded the commission with heavy doses of propaganda. Ground level investigators encountered hostility and suspicion from both sides. The lands east of the Isonzo river seemed to form an 'unmarked but distinct frontier' for both sides, but they delineated a passage into 'no man's land', a frontier region neither east nor west.[92] The existence of this 'no man's land', or the perception of it, fuelled support for the Free Territory. Fascist Italy had silenced Slavic contestants for this 'middle ground', but repression had not erased the memory of co-operation in the Habsburg frontier zone.[93]

The traditional orientation toward Austrian hinterlands fitted best with the geographical location of the port. The Allied military relied on the port to supply occupation authorities in Vienna. The city was too far to the north-east to compete effectively for trade bound for Italy and was located too far to the north-west to serve efficiently the interests of Yugoslavia.[94] However, in the emerging environment of bi-polar opposition, the structures

[91] S. Jones, *Boundary-making: a handbook for statesmen, treaty editors and boundary commissioners*, Washington, DC 1945, 28.

[92] Cox, *Race for Trieste*, 169.

[93] R. White, *The middle ground: Indians, empires, and republics in the Great Lakes region, 1650–1815*, Cambridge 1991, introduction and pp. 51–3, discusses the frontier as a 'middle ground' or a nexus of co-operation and accommodation.

[94] The port's natural geographic orientation was a primary economic argument in favour of internationalisation: Comitato austriaco di liberazione, *Trieste: porto dell'Austria e del bacino danubiano*, Trieste 1945, 7.

of Central Europe were effaced. Contenders for control of Trieste and the surrounding region were forced to argue for total advantage; co-operation and accommodation were no longer options.

Those favouring internationalisation saw the city as 'a great pier running towards overseas [markets]' from Central Europe. They argued that nature had placed the city in a 'privileged position' for development as an 'economic nerve centre'.[95] Slavic claims rested on the placing and orientation of the rail networks and transportation infrastructure that linked Trieste to Vienna through Slovenian lands.[96] The Italians argued that Italy's maritime experience and incorporation into the western European trade framework would contribute to the reconstruction and growth of the city. Although various foreign states comprised Trieste's trade area, only Italy could provide capital for the port and offer support for commerce, banking and infrastructure.[97]

The western Allies needed little encouragement to view Trieste as a key strategic point on the edge of Italy and western Europe. In Trieste, as in other areas, a 'dominant script' guided American and British interests. 'Strategic fantasies' saw Trieste as a protector of the entire upper Adriatic region against Slavic, socialist and communist infiltration.[98] Yugoslavia's claims, at least until Tito's break with Stalin in 1948, were perceived as evidence of the imperialistic aims of the Slavic world. Western Europeans interpreted them as part of the attempt to enlarge the Soviet defensive ring.

The western Allies' prejudice led them to cast Trieste in an Italian light. Fernand Braudel's description of the location of the city, written after the Second World War, reflected the broadly held view of a Europe 'constructed in opposition to the eastern frontier'.[99] 'Philosophic geography' located Austria, and therefore Trieste, in the 'civilised' portion of Europe that had benefited from the triumph of reason and spread of western thought. Braudel placed Trieste firmly on an Italian footing, on the 'flat stretch of coastline from Pesaro and Rimini to the gulf of Trieste, where the plain of the Po meets the Mediterranean'. The Dalmatian islands and the remainder of the eastern coast of the Adriatic, which were considered Yugoslav, were seen as a separate 'string of rocky islands . . . behind which rise the barren mountains of the

---

[95] Fiera di Trieste, *Catalogo ufficiale*, 35; Centro sviluppo economico Trieste, *Appunti sull'economia di Trieste: funzione e particolarità della VI fiera campionaria internazionale*, Trieste 1954, 1.

[96] Sluga, *The problem of Trieste*, 98, claims that the Yugoslav-led Liberation Front saw the boundary region as an integral space, while the western Allied military authorities saw it as a fault line.

[97] See, for example, Livio Ragusin, 'L'avvenire del porto di Trieste', *Esteri: quindicinale di politica estera* (Rome) iv/23 (1953), 34.

[98] On the fantasies associated with the 'dominant script' see Tuathail, 'Foreign policy and the hyperreal', 156–8.

[99] G. Delanty, 'L'identità europea come costruzione sociale', in L. Passerini (ed.), *Identità culturale europea: idée, sentimenti, relazioni*, Florence 1998, 57.

Balkan land mass'.[100] Slavic domination focused inland. Trieste was oriented toward the sea and the Italian peninsula.

Slovenian factions charged Allied authorities with complicity in Italian expropriations of Slovene territory. They saw the settlement of Italian refugees and positioning of Italian orphanages in primarily Slavic districts outside Trieste as deliberate attempts to subsume Slovene minorities. Pro-Italian factions maintained that Italianisation was the consequence of natural economic development. The Zaule industrial site, developed on the southern fringe of Trieste, and new apartment houses, constructed in former suburbs, simply met the needs of the expanding urban population.[101]

Conflict over the displaying of a map bearing the Slavic names of cities along the Istrian coast by Yugoslav tourist agencies at the 1947 Trieste exhibition illustrated the emotional charge carried by Slavic claims. Italian organisers maintained (or threatened) that the map could cause 'an adverse reaction by individuals or groups' in the city. Despite promises that minorities would receive fair and neutral treatment, Allied military authorities sided with pro-Italian interests and forced the removal of the map.[102]

The Allied attitude was reflected in the Army Map Service's 1946 rendering of the upper Adriatic area. Centred on the Free Territory, the map confirmed the entire territory's position on the western side of the emerging Cold War divide. The text, in English, French, Russian and Italian, attested to the intended audience. The Free Territory was positioned according to longitude 'east of Rome'. Place names were written in their Italian form, even those in areas with acknowledged Slavic majorities located in Zone B and under Yugoslav control.[103]

In outlying areas of the city, the intervention of the Allied authorities was decisive. In 1950 residents of some rural villages near the border with Zone B reintroduced Slavic geographical designations and erected bilingual signs. In 1952 the Allied administration reneged on agreements that promised toleration. It prohibited the adoption of bilingual toponyms in Duino-Aurisino, on the northern edge of Trieste along the main rail line. Authorities insisted on the validity of the Fascist nationalist law of 1923. When the mayor of the small community protested and refused to comply with the military government's orders, police removed the bilingual signs.[104]

Not all Triestines supported the nationalist mapping of the city and region. Perhaps one of the most outspoken opponents was the historian Fabio Cusin, remembered (and in nationalist circles reviled) as a committed inter-

[100] F. Braudel, *The Mediterranean and the Mediterranean world in the age of Philip II*, Berkeley 1995, i.125.
[101] Novak, *Trieste, 1941–1954*, 408–9.
[102] Consulta economica camerale, sezione industriale, 9 Oct. 1947, CCIA, cat. XXVIII.
[103] Army map service,'The frontiers of the Free Territory of Trieste', no. 10612 (US Department of State, map division, Dec. 1946), 1:100,000.
[104] Novak, *Trieste, 1941–1954*, 405–6; Sluga, *The problem of Trieste*, 194.

nationalist and a political renegade. In his *Twenty centuries of bora over the Carso and the gulf*, Cusin used natural elements, in particular the unpredictable and destructive *bora* from the north-east, as a metaphor for the tumultuous history of the city. Buffeted back and forth between the Slavs in the Carsic interior and the Italians living along the shores of the Gulf of Trieste, Cusin saw the city as belonging to neither side.[105]

Even pro-Italian elements were forced to acknowledge that the strip of Italian-dominated territory along the coast was narrow. A cartoon that appeared in the satirical Triestine periodical *Cittadella* lampooned the situation. It featured a gentleman on the balcony of an apartment describing the vista before him: 'From this side one sees a magnificent view of the Adriatic Sea, from all the others a magnificent view of the Marshall [Tito].'[106] Those favouring independence or autonomy were defeated by the widely-held conviction that the east/west divide, which had arisen with economic modernisation in western Europe and was sharpened by the bi-polar schism of the Cold War, in fact existed as an intrinsic feature of the European landscape.

Local administrators, many of whom were career civil servants who had kept positions they occupied under Fascism or even the nationalist-oriented administration prior to 1922, shared and promoted the view of Trieste as organically Italian. Changes in toponyms in the city reflected the attempt to erase the excesses of Fascism while maintaining the nationalist Italian element in the city's history. In 1946 a thoroughfare named 'Via degli Squadristi' (Fascist Action Squad Street) returned to its traditional Via del Teatro. Via Arturo Zanolla, named in 1941 for a Fascist war hero, reverted to Via degli Artisti.[107] The local landscape was painted in familiar Italian tropes. The local tourist organisation's guide, published in 1950, offered a particularly lyrical description of the city 'with all the suggestive and melodious accents of the nearby Venetian lagoon'.[108]

Visions of Trieste's inheritance of trade networks dominated by 'Venetian galleons' permeated discussions of the role of Trieste and the upper Adriatic region. Under Aquileia, Trieste and Istria had been tied historically with lands to the north and west. Friuli and Istria had formed part of the same administrative unit. Trieste, which linked the two, was therefore naturally and indisputably included as part of the Italian entity.[109]

Rhetoric promoting the Three Venices receded into the background during the Free Territory period, but public initiatives continued to emphasise historic links between the Free Territory and northern Italian provinces. In 1953 an exhibition on irredentism in Vicenza, sponsored by the

---

[105] F. Cusin, *Venti secoli di bora sul carso e sul golfo*, Trieste 1952.

[106] R. Kollmann, *Trieste, millenovecento 5, cronache dei poveri amanti*, Trieste 1956, n.p.

[107] Trampus, *Vie e piazze*, 605, 672.

[108] Ente per il turismo di Trieste, *Trieste*, Trieste 1950, 1.

[109] Montemuliano, *Venezia Giulia*, 10.

Nationalist Association, highlighted the 'old and proud Italian traditions' of the five provinces previously under Austrian rule. The 'redemption' of Lombardy and the Veneto during the Risorgimento was not distinguished from the annexation of Venezia Giulia and Venezia Tridentina after the First World War. By identifying some of the 'redeemed' regions as 'now dismembered anew and in part languishing under the domination of Yugoslavia' the exhibition raised the spectre of a threat to the whole of northern Italy and, by extension, western Europe.[110]

Despite the inflammatory tenor of Italian nationalist rhetoric, by late 1953 it was evident that Allied concerns for the fate of the area had decreased. Pro-western prejudices still held sway, but defence of the entire Free Territory as a western outpost was no longer a priority. The placing of the borderline between Yugoslavia and Italy remained a matter of overwhelming importance only to the two interested states and those living in the border region. The Army Map Service rendering of the Free Territory in 1954 demonstrated the overall decrease in the level of alarm over Trieste as a centre of the Cold War. Based on a Viennese-printed Central European road map prepared by Anstalt Freytag-Berndt in 1950, it included Trieste but did not emphasise the city or provide any strong visual cues linking Trieste to Italy. Venice, for example, barely made the map. The first language of the map was English, the second German and the third French. Most toponyms appeared in the language of the majority in the area, acknowledging the Slavic presence and Yugoslav predominance in parts of Istria. For major centres of mixed ethnicity, alternate names appeared in parenthesis, such as Rijeka (Fiume) and Opatija (Abbazia). Most areas in Zone A of the Free Territory were labelled with Italian names but the commitment to Italian politicisation seemed absent.[111]

Eastern borderland

The re-annexation of Trieste to Italy in 1954 arose from a complicated inter-action of political, cultural and economic factors. Trieste remained on the peripheries of Italy and at the gateway to Istria and Dalmatia. It still stood as a bulwark against eastern aggression. The demise of Central Europe and the division of Central European networks between eastern and western spheres, separated by the iron curtain, eliminated the possibility for expansion of trade along Trieste's former routes. The city became merely a 'terminal port' or a 'cul de sac' at the head of the Adriatic, easily bypassed through use of ports further south on the Apennine or Balkan peninsulas.[112]

[110] 'Fierissima e gloriosa testimonianza a sfida dei secoli e degli uomini', *Il Giornale di Trieste*, 12 Sept. 1953, 2.

[111] Army map service 'Map of Trieste, Free Territory of Trieste; Italy; Yugoslavia; Austria; Central Europe Road Map', no. m405 (series), 2nd edn 1954, 1:300,000.

[112] Mihelic, *Political element*, 3, 17; Sapelli, *Trieste italiana*, 183.

In 1956 an article published in the *National Geographic* captured the subliminal tone of Slavic threat to the area in its description of 'the world of the Slav' that '[a]long the eastern Adriatic loom[ed]' beyond Trieste.[113] Despite the international agreement on the extension of Italian sovereignty over Zone A of the Free Territory, Italy was unable to paint the territory as indisputably Italian. Underlying instabilities reflected in the inconstancy of state borders in the region from 1918 to 1954 manifested themselves in recurrent ethnic and national conflicts that continued even after the return of Trieste to Italian control.

---

[113] H. Kane, 'Trieste – side door to Europe', *National Geographic Magazine* cix/6 (1956), 825.

4

Fashioning Italian Triestines

Trieste is 'a place of transition – geographically, historically, in culture, and in commerce – that is [a place] of struggle. Everything is in duplicate or triplicate in Trieste, beginning with the flora and ending with ethnicity', wrote Scipio Slataper in 1912.[1] By the turn of the twentieth century, the multiplicity of affiliations had manifested itself in competing currents of Italian irredentism, Slavic nationalism and internationalist socialism. In the wake of the First World War, the decision of the international powers to uphold Italian claims to the city and surrounding areas signalled a triumph for irredentist forces. Pro-Italian groups attempted to promote ethnic affiliation as equivalent to national allegiance.[2] However, in the commercial port this equation was false. Multiple, overlapping and sometimes seemingly oppositional associations – Trieste's duality or triplicity – persisted. After 1918 various groups vied for political recognition and acceptance in a complicated, painful and in some aspects incomplete process of assimilation and accommodation within the confines of the Italian state.

Imperial subjects

In the Habsburg maritime city administered by Vienna, overriding economic concerns and reliance on imperial administrative structures and commercial privileges generally held ethnic antagonism in check. 'Official nationalism', based on political, imperial identification, did not preclude cultural, ethnic or social loyalties. A pictorial history of the Adriatic Littoral published in 1842 described 'men of every race, of every language, Friulians, Venetians, Istrians of Venetian dialects, Istrians with Italian dialects all their own, Germans, Carniolans, Morlachs, Croats, Wallachs, gypsies, mixed races, races who have abandoned their native languages' sharing residence and the Italian language in the port city. The account noted 'the disparate elements, the one and the other with none prevalent'. At the same time, it suggested that Trieste marked 'the border of two great nations', not a political boundary, but a frontier between the Slavic and Italian worlds.[3] As the nine-

---

1   S. Slataper, *Scritti politici*, ed. Giani Stuparich, Verona 1954, 134.
2   Rokkan and Urwin, *Economy, territory, identity*, 122, discuss ethnic affiliation and national allegiance in the context of the United States.
3   A. Selb and A. Tischbein (eds), *Memorie viaggio pittorio Littorale Austriaco*, Trieste 1842, n.p.

teenth century progressed, debates over the parameters of these colliding cultural worlds and heightening awareness of the implications of cultural and ethnic divides formed the bases for ethnic and nationalist antagonism.

In 1848 revolutionary challenges to Habsburg authority throughout Central Europe included a nationalist component. In Italian-speaking lands the early phase of nationalist awakening was characterised by a Mazzini-inspired commitment to coexistence and co-operation among free nations. It included an element of sympathy for the Slavs as fellow victims of Austrian oppression.[4] However, increasing suspicions among minority groups vying for recognition in the Habsburg structure counterbalanced this sympathy. In 1848 Vienna pitted troops of different ethnic backgrounds against one another. Although the Adriatic Littoral was not a centre of major disturbances, the use of Croatian troops to put down the insurrections in the Veneto provoked enmities between native Italians and Slavs, particularly Croats, in the upper Adriatic provinces.[5]

The creation of the Dual Monarchy in 1867 reflected the compromise of Germanic and Hungarian elements. Italians and Slavs in the upper Adriatic region were among the imperial minorities encouraged by reforms afforded to the Hungarians, but they did not aspire necessarily to separation from Vienna. Like other minority groups, Slovenes, Croats and Italians relied on the protection of the Habsburg state. Italians and Slovenes (the largest ethnic Slav minority in Trieste) were relatively small groups concentrated in the Austrian lands of the Dual Monarchy. Italians in the Trentino and the Adriatic Littoral accounted for less than 3 per cent of the total imperial population and Slovenes, concentrated in Carniola and parts of Styria, Carinthia and the Adriatic Littoral accounted for less than 5 per cent.[6] Their influence was naturally limited.

The association of ethnic identity and political allegiance was problematic throughout the empire. Clearly, Germanness was not a defining characteristic of allegiance to the monarchy.[7] Particularly during and after the unification of Bismarck's German state, Austria looked on questions of Germanic unity and brotherhood with suspicion. Vienna relied on the loyalty of a multitude of small ethnic groups. Habsburg authorities were at times heavy-handed or callous in their treatment of minority groups, especially if 'foreign' affiliations manifested in beliefs or actions considered threatening to

---

[4] See Rusinow, *Italy's Austrian heritage*, 15–22. Mazzini's words (quoted in Lederer, *Yugoslavia*, 10), 'Istria is Italian and as necessary to Italians as Dalmatia is to the Slavs', justified later Yugoslav claims.

[5] R. Wörsdörfer, 'Zwischen Karst und Adria', in Robert Streibel (ed.), *Flucht und Vertreibung: zwischen Aufrechnung und Verdrängung*, Vienna 1994, 97.

[6] M. Cattaruzza, 'Slovenes and Italians in Trieste, 1850–1914', in M. Engman (ed.), *Ethnic identity in urban Europe*, New York 1992, 189–90.

[7] I would like to thank Pieter Judson of Swarthmore College for his observations on the relationship of Germanness to Austrian identity.

the imperial order, but non-Germanic associations were not uniformly or resolutely suppressed.

In the eighteenth and early nineteenth centuries Trieste had attracted immigrants from Europe and the Near East who relied on personal wealth to establish commercial ventures and contacts in the city. These newcomers, including Greeks, Jews and Swiss Protestants, tended to assimilate into extant local commercial circles where trade interests, promoted and protected by the imperial authorities, were paramount.[8] Economic pragmatism manifested itself in a commitment to cosmopolitanism based in visions of local civic identity or 'municipalism'. In 1863 the Prussian poet and politician Giulio Rodenberg noted with irony that in Trieste, 'one speaks, one sings and one swears in all the languages of the world, but not in German'.[9] The association of the urban environment with Italianness, the use of the Italian language and the general adherence to Italian customs created an impression of Italian predominance. The link between cultural Italianness and urban identity was not limited to the bourgeoisie of Trieste. It had deep roots in Italian commercial and bourgeois culture and was common to Italian understandings of the Unification.[10] Ethnic Italianness went hand-in-hand with a western-oriented commitment to principles of economic liberalism and international trade. The adherence of the city's commercial classes to cultural Italianness was more an embrace of the reigning bourgeois ethos than a commitment to precepts of Italian nationalism. Trieste's multi-ethnic commercial elites were among the Habsburg monarchy's most steadfast supporters.

Influential commercial elites generally eschewed participation in ethno-nationalist politics. Marriage networks, family alliances and friendships, conceived outside the boundaries of political affiliations, served as the bases for traditions rooted in common ethnic origins or economic concerns. The marriages of the Economo brothers, members of a commercial family of Greek origin, testify to the balance struck between affiliation to a 'foreign' ethnic community and association with the Habsburg monarchy. Demetrio Economo married Eugenia Ralli of the Greek commercial community in London. His brothers married into the Habsburg nobility. Leonida chose Princess Wilhelmina von Windisch-Graetz. Constantino, who forsook commerce for a university career in science, married Lili von Schönburg-Hartenstein. Educational choices for the sons of Callisto Cosulich, the scion of the shipping family noted in later generations for pro-Italian sentiments, also demonstrate the attachment to commercial over political or nationalist pursuits. Three sons Antonio, Callisto and Augusto, went to maritime profes-

---

8 On the experiences of these specific minority groups see Millo, *L'élite del potere*, 43–74.
9 This is quoted in L. Gasparini (ed.), *Impressioni su Trieste, 1793–1887*, Trieste 1951, 97.
10 A. Lyttelton, 'Creating a national past: history, myth and image in the Risorgimento', in A. Ascoli and K. von Henneberg (eds), *Making and remaking Italy*, Oxford 2001, 27–74.

sional schools. Oscar went to an Italian gymnasium, Ulisse to a German one.[11]

For Jewish elites cultural association with Italianness may have been stronger than for elites of other origins. Austrian experimentation with liberal policies inspired by the Enlightenment had fostered a comparatively welcoming environment in the port. Antisemitism in Trieste lacked the virulence it displayed in other Austrian centres deeply affected by currents of Pan-Germanism and Christian Socialism. The local Jewish community's compromising and pragmatic attitude toward Austrian authority set the stage for co-operation and assimilation. Deeply committed to bourgeois liberalism, Jews of the commercial classes tended to be assimilationist, aligning with social peers rather than co-religionists.[12]

Yet Italy, unified under democratic auspices, offered an attractive cultural alternative to Vienna.[13] Professional and intellectual circles tended to support irredentism. By the second half of the nineteenth century Italian irredentism, spurred by the nationalist revolutions of 1848, but more directly by the unification of the Italian state, formed the strongest current of popular nationalism in Habsburg Trieste. As in other Italian-speaking lands, the rhetoric of Italian unification appealed most to the educated middle classes and intellectuals.[14] The pro-Italian National Liberal party, founded in 1868, held the majority in the local diet from 1882 to 1914. By the 1890s the municipal council of Trieste was in the hands of staunchly pro-Italian members of these upper-middle and professional class groups. Through control of the local political framework, Italian factions institutionalised discriminatory educational and social policies. The National League, founded in 1891 ostensibly to promote Italian education, furnished a 'patriotic liturgy' and rallying point for pro-Italian elements.[15]

After 1848 Slovenes too had begun to establish cultural institutions in the city. In 1874 the Slovene political party Edinost was founded.[16] The various Slavic groups represented in Trieste constituted distinct minorities, but institutional establishments were generally centres of Slavic culture. Failure to differentiate between Slavic groups reflected the notions of a somewhat ignorant west, but was promoted also by the various groups of Slavs themselves.

---

[11] Millo, L'élite del potere, 49, 191.

[12] L. Dubin, The port Jews of Habsburg Trieste, Stanford 1999, and T. Catalan, La comunità ebraica di Trieste (1781–1914): politica, società, e cultura, Trieste 2000, explore the development of Trieste's Jewish community under the Habsburgs.

[13] Millo, L'élite del potere, 333.

[14] Lyttelton, 'Creating a national past', 28.

[15] E. Maserati, 'Simbolismo e rituale nell'irredentismo adriatico', in Salimbeni, Dal litorale, 129.

[16] In addition to the Slovenes, a small number of ethnic Croats, primarily from Istria and Dalmatia, lived in Trieste. Although they formed a separate ethnic community and were generally associated with the Hungarian lands of the empire, they were usually considered simply as part of the city's Slavic population.

The particulars of alignments within the Habsburg empire, Pan-Slavic sentiments and turn-of-the-century rumours regarding the possible creation of an
autonomous south Slav entity in the empire nurtured Slavic brotherhood.
Various Slavic interests saw unity as the key to establishing legitimacy and to
strengthening political demands.[17] In Trieste the Narodni Dom hosted
Slovene, Croatian and even Czech associations.

By the 1880s the increasing wealth of the city had quickened the pace of
migration to the urban centre. This altered Trieste's ethnic character. Many,
who came in search of employment, were unskilled or semi-skilled Slovene or
Croatian workers from nearby regions. Improved rail and communication
between the city and its hinterlands helped workers to maintain cultural and
familial ties and social networks. Austrian authorities tended to ignore
economic competition between recent immigrants of differing origins. This
allowed ethnic enmities to fester.[18]

Uneasy Italian supporters interpreted the increasing pace of migration and
the growing influence of Slavic elements as an Austrian-inspired assault on
Italian influence in Trieste. The increasing Slavic presence evident in two
sectors associated with the Habsburgs – the civil service and the Church –
heightened suspicions that the Austrians were transplanting Slavic and
German people to the Trieste area. In 1907 Carlo Galli, assigned to the
Italian general consul office in Trieste, captured the mood of Italian officials
and nationalists. In a letter that conceded that the Slavic population of the
city was increasing as a result of natural migration, Galli charged none the
less that the Slovenes were 'powerfully aided by the Austrian government
that favoured their residence the city, preferring Slovenes in the railway, in
the postal service, and in all the civil services because they saw them as
loyal'.[19] Particularly in outlying districts, small cities and rural areas
surrounding Trieste, Slavic civil servants were eager to occupy lower level
administrative posts seen as tickets to social advancement. Urban Italians
generally eschewed such positions.[20] Galli claimed that Austrian prejudice
forced Italians to pursue careers in private commerce and navigation. In fact,
these private opportunities were easier to obtain for Italians and more lucrative.[21]

The Church too offered a social ladder. Many priests serving the city and
the diocese of Trieste were of Slavic, in particular Slovene, descent.[22] Reli-

---

[17] See, for example, references to the Serbs, Croats and Slovenes as a single race known by
three different names, as 'one people – the Yugoslavs', and as constituting 'a compact population of exceedingly pure race' in Committee of emigrant Jugoslavs in London, *The South
Slav programme*, London 1915, 5ff.

[18] Cattaruzza, 'Slovenes and Italians', 194.

[19] Galli, *Diarii e lettere*, 8–10.

[20] Rusinow, *Italy's Austrian heritage*, 28–9.

[21] Galli, *Diarii e lettere*, 10.

[22] By 1912, of 290 priests in the diocese of Trieste 190 were Slovene. Twenty of the seventy
in the city were Slav: Rusinow, *Italy's Austrian heritage*, 27.

gious politics intertwined with ethnic and nationalist ambitions. Most Triestines, including Italians and Slovenes, shared the bond of Catholicism with Austrian Germans. From a broader European perspective, adherence to Latin Christendom distinguished Slovenes and Croats as well as Italians from the 'less civilised' peoples of the east.[23] In the local context, the programme of the Italian National Liberal party rested on the extension of liberal political and economic freedoms constructed outside religious attachments. Edinost included both clerical and liberal members, but those with clerical leanings tended to link Slovene Catholic identity with opposition to the liberal 'ungodliness' of Trieste's 'Italian' bourgeoisie.[24] The tendency to equate Italian liberalism with anti-religious attitudes also reflected the clash between the traditional rural populations and the urban middle classes.

Despite the rise in tensions, nationalist passions generally remained in check in Habsburg Trieste. Popular affiliation with Italianness did not necessarily entail support for Italian statehood. In the urban centre imperial trade privileges formed the nucleus of life and allegiances to Vienna remained strong, especially among the influential commercial elite.

Locally-elected representatives to the Austrian diet included many ultra-loyalists professing primary allegiance to Habsburg Austria.[25] Triestine writer Bobi Bazlen observed that 'there were, it is true, nationalist struggles, but within limits'. The famous Triestine *bora* 'caused disasters much more serious than those caused by civic anger – it was one of those few cases in history in which the elements were more detrimental than man'.[26] James Joyce encapsulated his impression of the national disposition of those in the city in his character Leopold Bloom, created during his pre-war residence in Trieste. For Bloom, nation entailed 'the same people living in the same place'.[27]

In the first decade of the twentieth century, socialism seemed a greater threat than nationalist or ethnic strife to imperial structures and the commercial core of the city. Tensions between Slavs and Italians could be understood as a consequence of the jockeying of various groups for influence within the imperial structure. Socialists agitated for a new political order. Bolstered by electoral reform in the Austrian empire, in 1907 the socialists emerged as a strong political force.[28] Despite strong participation and even leadership by

---

[23] Wolff, *Inventing eastern Europe*, and M. Todorova, *Imagining the Balkans*, New York 1997, explore European perceptions of the split between east and west.

[24] Cattaruzza, 'Slovenes and Italians', 199.

[25] For a breakdown of the affiliations of representatives in the late nineteenth and early twentieth centuries see tables in E. Winkler, *Wahlrechtsreformen und Wahlen in Triest, 1905–1909: eine Analyse der politischen Partizipation in einer multinationalen Stadtregion der Habsburgermonarchie*, Munich 2000, 342–58.

[26] R. Bazlen, *Scritti*, Milan 1984, 242.

[27] This is quoted in McCourt, *Years of Bloom*, 73.

[28] For a detailed account of the intertwining of socialist and ethnic politics see Winkler, *Wahlrechtsreformen und Wahlen*, 89–209.

ethnic Italians, the socialist ascendancy in the Adriatic Littoral was perceived to have a Slavic cast. Italian workers hailing from the peninsula could align with socialism, but many were enticed into supporting Italian nationalist factions by irredentists' promises of employment in place of Slavs. Slovenes and Croats in rural districts tended to sympathise with Catholic politics. Urban Slavic workers found a political home in socialism.

Traditionalist notions held that Slavs were an 'ahistoric' people who would easily be assimilated into a culturally advanced Italian majority. By the turn of the century, these vague assumptions gave way to social science theories of racial and demographic hierarchy that identified the Slavs as biologically and politically inferior. Corrado Gini, for example, postulated in his 'cyclical theory of population' that differing reproductive capabilities explained how Italians, as a 'wealthier, more intelligent race with a glorious past, should be unable to expand in the face of an intellectually and economically inferior one'.[29] The propagandist Gualtiero Castellini remarked on the 'whiteness of the Istrian citizens on the coast' as a measure of the 'marvellous *italianità*' of Italy's 'extreme borderland'.[30] Racial prejudice equated 'whiteness' with the beauty and purity of Italian civilisation. Association of ethnic identity with nationalist politics and concomitant social and economic prejudices curbed Slavic assimilation into the urban Italian majority.

Increasing nationalist differentiation was reflected in census data.[31] In 1900, using 'customary' language as an indicator of nationality, the Austrian census showed that 65 per cent of the inhabitants of Trieste and surrounding areas spoke Italian as their primary tongue. Those registered as Slovene made up 14 per cent and less than 0.5 percent were Serbian or Croatian. This contrasted with the entire Illyrian coast where 42 per cent registered Italian, 34 per cent Slovene and 15 per cent Serbian or Croatian.[32]

By 1910 the percentage of Slavs had increased dramatically. The pace of Slavic migration to the city, heightened Slavic national awareness and a decreasing propensity or ability to associate with the predominantly Italian urban environment altered the city's ethnic make-up. Nationalist debates were so heated in 1910 that the findings of the census were contested.[33] To appease those who complained that local officials had underestimated the Slavic population in favour of the Italian in urban areas, Austrian officials agreed to a reassessment. The recount raised the number of Slavs in the

---

[29] Ipsen, *Dictating demography*, 221.

[30] Castellini, *Trento e Trieste*, 65.

[31] Austrian assessments based on primary or customary language were particularly problematic. Officials recorded linguistic orientation on the basis of a voluntary statement. Critics charged that officials manipulated declarations to promote nationalist aims. Corruption may have poisoned census findings, but bilingual individuals probably responded with pragmatism to government inquiries, perhaps shaping their own declarations in the hopes of deriving personal benefit or enhancing personal security.

[32] ['Sator'], *La populazione della Venezia Giulia*, Rome 1945, 44.

[33] On the retaking of the census see Cattaruzza, 'Slovenes and Italians', 193–4.

region substantially, from 38,499 to 59,312. The Italian population registered a coincident decline from 142,113 to 118,959, provoking accusations of foul play from pro-Italian factions. Using the recount figures, Italians accounted for 52 per cent, Slovenes for 28 per cent and Serbians and Croatians for 1 per cent of the population of Trieste. Italians remained in the clear majority, but the Slovene minority was significant. Important too was the assignment of some 22 percent of the population to the category of 'others'. Austrian censuses were concerned primarily with Austrian citizens. Those living in Trieste who held foreign residence or citizenship fell into the category of undifferentiated others, no matter what their politics or proclivities. Slovene or Croat immigrants were native to the empire and unlikely to hold foreign citizenship or residency. Italian residents might be foreign citizens.[34]

At the outbreak of the First World War, Italian and Slavic nationalists saw Austria-Hungary's involvement as an opportunity to assert their claims. They shared a common interest in countering Austro-Germanic dominance. Italy's entry into the war in 1915 fuelled Italian irredentists' hopes and encouraged Slavs who saw the defeat of Austria as a ticket to statehood. Belief in Slavic inferiority and assimilability allowed Italians to disregard Slavic claims that competed directly with their interests. As Carlo Galli wrote in 1915, 'If we leave the Slovenes and Croats free to conserve their language, their customs, and so on, without doubt, after one or two generations at most have passed, even those who are today in Trieste will inevitably be absorbed by the Italian culture.'[35]

Wartime propaganda hearkened back to mid-nineteenth century calls for Italian and Slovene fraternity. The Committee of Emigrant Jugoslavs' [sic] *Southern Slav programme*, published in London in 1915, lauded the 'great Italian Mazzini, that far seeing statesman and true friend of our [Yugoslav] people'.[36] The Pact of Rome in April 1918 testified to the united front advanced by minority nationalities committed to 'joint struggle against the common oppressors'. It included mutual pledges by the Slavs and Italians for the recognition of national minorities' rights to 'have their language as well as their culture and their moral and economic interests' respected within new national states once post-war borders were drawn.[37] The spirit of fraternity lingered even after the war in some cases. A Yugoslav pamphlet of 1919, intended for international consumption, enumerated incidents of Yugoslav and Italian wartime co-operation.[38]

---

34 Schiffrer, *Venezia Giulia*, 45; ['Sator'], *La popolazione*, 27, 40, 42.
35 Galli, *Diarii e lettere*, 252–3.
36 Committee of emigrant Jugoslavs, *South Slav programme*, 7.
37 'The Pact of Rome, April 10, 1918', in Albrecht-Carrié, *Italy*, 347–8.
38 Z. Moravec, *Italie et les Yougoslaves*, Paris 1919, 32, 48.

Italian citizens

Triestines bore no mark identifying them as Italians, Austrians or Slavs. Belief that the essence of a nation could be discerned in the complex mixture of 'physical and mental characteristics that distinguished one nation from others' did not resonate with the experience of those in the port city.[39] The principles of ethnic nationalism and self-determination appealed to American leaders and others dreaming of a peace based on democratic ideals, but these principles proved unworkable in practice. Self-determination required that some authority clearly delineate just who was entitled to determine the fate of an area. In many areas the right to decide was hotly contested. In the upper Adriatic region it proved impossible to divide Italian and Slavic populations along 'clearly recognisable lines of nationality'.[40]

Of the three potential claimants to lands at the head of the Adriatic – Austria, Italy and Yugoslavia – only Austria bore the taint of defeat. The victorious Italians asserted the predominance of the Italian language and the cultural affinities of urban dwellers in Trieste. Slavs based their case on the language and culture of the population of small towns and rural areas. They were, however, divided among themselves. The Serbian government saw itself as representing the interests of all South Slavs for whom centralised statehood was an overriding concern. Groups in former imperial lands, particularly Slovenes and Croats, saw the creation of Yugoslavia as a federal project.[41]

At the Paris Peace Conference, the Big Four, or perhaps more appropriately the Big Three (Italy being noticeably absent for part of the negotiations and in a comparatively weak position), fashioned the political arrangements that placed Trieste under Roman control. The motivation for assigning the city to Italy was unclear.[42] The decision was probably based, at least in part, on western pro-Italian prejudices. A comment in the diary of George Louis Beers, Paris-based American expert on colonial affairs, suggested that assigning Italians to the South Slav state would mean sacrificing them 'to people whose cultural value was infinitely less'.[43] None the less, negotiators' support for Italian claims fell short of Italian aspirations. The position of Italy's eastern border remained open for further discussion. International negotiators were not disposed to deal with complex issues of national identity and ethnicity on the local level. They defined requirements for citizenship that set the parameters for national political allegiance, but abrogated

[39] In 1924 Otto Bauer identified the nation in these terms: 'The nation', in G. Balakrishnan (ed.), *Mapping the nation*, London 1996, 40–1.
[40] Albrecht-Carrié, *Italy*, 63.
[41] Lederer, *Yugoslavia*, 4–5.
[42] Rusinow, *Italy's Austrian heritage*, 41–50, offers a succinct discussion of negotiations. Book length analyses include Albrecht-Carrié, *Italy*, and Lederer, *Yugoslavia*.
[43] This is quoted in Albrecht-Carrié, *Italy*, 119.

responsibility for delineating standards for Italianness to Liberal Italian authorities.

Much has been made of Massimo D'Azeglio's purported statement of the need to 'make Italians'. His desire to uncover points of convergence around which the collective national character of Italians could form and be recognised grew from an understanding that unification through an 'artichoke policy' of agglomeration had meant the inclusion of individuals with widely varying conceptions of Italianness in the state.[44] The legacy of vague or ambiguous expectations of the characteristics of Italianness was particularly salient to questions regarding the assimilation of the new provinces after 1918.

The power of the Italian nationalist professional classes and the association of Italianness with the higher ranks of local society meant that Italian ethnic affiliation appeared dominant in the city. However, as critics were quick to point out, those in Trieste were undeniably of mixed origins and, from a linguistic perspective, the city was merely an enclave within a larger Slavic territory. Post-First World War settlements linked ethnic identity with national allegiance, forcing local populations to choose between loyalties that had coexisted in the Austrian empire. Uncertain and shifting bases for personal identification revealed a constellation of characteristics that could be associated with adherence to the nation and ethnic Italianness.

From the perspective of the Italian government Trieste was an Italian city. Most of its inhabitants spoke Italian and, if pushed to define themselves, identified themselves as Italian. In stark contrast to the Austrian findings of 1910, the Italian census of 1921 recorded Italians as the vast majority of Triestines, at 85 per cent. The Slovene minority registered at a comparatively insignificant 8 per cent. No Serbs or Croats were identified. No doubt Italian officials set the geographical limits of the city to exclude those living in outlying, predominantly Slavic districts.[45] Data might also have been corrupted. However, the picture was more complicated. In 1910 of the population of Trieste 22 per cent had appeared in the category 'others'. In 1921 only 8 per cent appeared thus.[46] At least some had been Italian citizens living in Habsburg Trieste and the Italian census of 1921 did not distinguish 'new' citizens from 'old'. In addition, an avowed preference for Italy or even acceptance of Italian citizenship could not be equated with commitment to Italianness. It may have reflected individual pragmatism or unwillingness to accept minority status within the confines of the national state.[47]

---

[44] R. Sarti, response to H-Italy query by P. Cannistraro, 8 Feb. 1997 on the origins of the phrase, 'We have made Italy . . .' http://www.h-net.msu.edu.

[45] Historians have argued the justice of such practices. For example Schiffrer, *Venezia Giulia*, 48–9, justified the exclusion of the suburbs of Barcola (pop. 1,900 Slavs, 1,000 Italians) and Servola (pop. 3,200 Slavs, 2,200 Italians) from the 'urban complex' of Trieste in 1931 on the basis of 'national and topographical individuality'.

[46] ['Sator'], *La populazione*, 40, 42.

[47] Sapelli, *Trieste italiana*, 322–3, observed that for the Slovene middle classes, Italy was

Migration, too, contributed to the population shift. Although Venezia Giulia's official annexation to Italy was not celebrated until 1921, the processes of drawing new national borders and working out residency and citizenship requirements, begun in November 1918, prompted a flood of 'ethnic' refugees into and out of newly created borderlands. Slavs migrated to take up residence in the emerging Kingdom of Serbs, Croats and Slovenes. Italians migrated from inland districts in Slovenia and coastal districts of Dalmatian Croatia to take up residence in lands under Italian control. By June 1919 between 400 and 700 persons were passing through Trieste each day. Nearly 4,000 refugees in the city were reported homeless.[48]

Effectively, in the new provinces of Venezia Giulia, the German-speaking minority was eliminated. Carlo Galli, reassigned to the city after the war, noted in his diary on 13 November 1918 that '[We have] nothing to fear from those who were Austrophile. Austria no longer exists. Therefore, Austrophilism can no longer be a preoccupation.'[49] Those who wished to maintain their Germanic identity left or were dismissed by Italian authorities. Ethnic Germans, who had transferred to the city to occupy civil service positions, found it expedient to return to Vienna or relocate to regions within the confines of the truncated Austrian state. Liberal Italian authorities facilitated the emigration of Austrian rail and postal workers as well as customs and tax agents, along with their families.[50] Those of Germanic background who chose to stay in Trieste were well entrenched in Italian-speaking bureaucratic or commercial circles and were disinclined to associate openly with a Germanness associated with states that had been so recently enemies of Italy.

Policies for repatriation and the granting of Italian citizenship exacerbated problems related to the more or less voluntary ethnic migration. Immediately upon the cessation of hostilities in November 1918, Italian authorities were forced to deal with a flood of wartime refugees, internees and prisoners who sought repatriation. Those seeking to return to the territory acquired by Italy were not simply returning to an abandoned homeland; they were electing to live within the new boundaries of the Italian state. In 1919 Italian authorities adopted criteria limiting access to the new territory on the basis of suspicion of insurgent political tendencies or uncertain financial standing.[51] The social and political biases of officials often intertwined with ethnic prejudices to affect determinations of suitability for repatriation.

Denials were most often justified by a petitioner's purported hostility to Italy. A local woman's petition for the repatriation of her boyfriend Francesco

transformed from the 'wicked stepmother' to a nation 'with which it became profitable to identify oneself'.

[48] 27 June 1919, CGCVG (ag), busta 41.
[49] Galli, *Diarii e lettere*, 324.
[50] 'Rimpatrie', CGCVG (adg), busta 36.
[51] 'Criterio per regolare il rimpatrio e l'accesso a Trieste', 12 Feb. 1919, CGCVG (ag), busta 41.

Glaser, the father of her four-year-old son, was turned down on suspicion that Glaser, formerly an Austro-Hungarian policeman, harboured 'hostile' political sentiments. A student wishing to return to the city to continue his studies was denied permission, because officials judged him to be a propagandist and a 'dangerous Yugoslav'.[52] A captain in the Austrian army was refused repatriation on suspicion of 'hostile sentiments toward Italy'. He had reputedly denounced Italy while serving aboard Lloyd's mercantile ships before the war. Another man, deemed an avid pan-Germanist and a political reactionary who favoured the Austrian government, was not only refused permission to return to his native city of Pisino, but authorities took the further step of prohibiting him from crossing the Armistice line. They identified him as a shady character who had fled his post in Pisino on the defeat of the Austrian army and carried away local funds earmarked for distribution to the poor.[53]

The criteria for repatriation outlined in February 1919 sanctioned economic prejudice by calling for the adoption of 'severe and prudent' criteria for dealing with small firms, itinerant tradesmen and workers who wished to return to the city. Although Giuseppe Fumis, a labourer, was required to prove means of support, and Antonia di Venceslav Zamanova, a Czech woman seeking employment, were denied permission to come to the city, economically-based rejections appeared rarer than politically-based ones.[54] The repatriation guidelines even advocated sympathetic consideration of those who found themselves completely impoverished by the war and suggested that exceptional provisions might be adopted for poor returnees.[55] None the less, repatriation took on an ethnic cast. Provisions hit recent immigrants, among the poorest elements of the urban population, hardest. Many affected were Slavs.

Those with economic influence, regardless of past affiliations, had little difficulty in being repatriated. Eugenio Pollak, born in Trieste in 1864, but a naturalised citizen of Switzerland since 1883, gained permission to return to his business in Trieste. Authorities suggested that despite his appearance on a list of suspected persons, issued in March 1916, he was 'never occupied by politics, but was dedicated to commercial affairs'. In industrial circles, Pollak was reportedly 'well regarded and considered an able businessman'.[56] A request by Teodoro Gauzoni, 'much esteemed in commercial circles and uncensured', was granted despite the fact that he was identified as 'a Germanophile and Austrophile'. Officials noted that Gauzoni would no doubt begin a 'new life' within the confines of Italy.[57] Giovanni Alt relied on

---

[52] 'Glaser', ibid.
[53] 'Rimpatrie', CGCVG (adg), busta 35.
[54] CGCVG (ag), busta 41; 'Rimpatrie', CGCVG (adg), buste 35, 36.
[55] 'Criterio per regolare il rimpatrio e l'accesso a Trieste', 12 Feb. 1919, CGCVG (ag), busta 41.
[56] 'Rimpatrie', CGCVG (adg), busta 36.
[57] Ibid. busta 35.

his position with the Mobiliare bank and his relationship with Vittorio Venezian, a member of one of Trieste's most prominent banking families and president of Trieste's chamber of commerce. Despite Alt's Viennese birth and a report by the Italian national police to the effect that he was of 'good moral standing but of wicked political precedent having been a fervent pro-Austrian', he obtained permission for the repatriation of his wife, son and sister-in-law from Hungary.[58]

Official guidelines called for 'generous' treatment of important commercial and industrial firms.[59] Despite Vittorio Honigschmid's German birth and citizenship, the Cantiere Navale Triestino shipbuilding firm gained permission for his return. The firm argued that Honigschmid's expertise was indispensable in light of the need 'to sort out the multiple and complex interests that continue[d] to tie the Cantiere to the former Austrian government'. Honigschmid's wife and daughters returned from Vienna where they had fled during the war. In another case, although travel was severely restricted, Pietro Terzettu 'Yugoslav and up until the last moment pro-Austrian without limit with sons who were Austrian officials' gained permission to travel on behalf of Lloyd Triestino.[60] The firm considered his services important to reviving the local economy.

Arrangements for granting citizenship to inhabitants of former Austrian lands outlined in the 'Clauses relating to nationality', articles 70–82 of the 1919 Treaty of St Germain, encouraged population displacement and exacerbated problems of dislocation. Negotiators assumed that most former citizens of Austria-Hungary would consider themselves to be of the nationality of the new state in which they resided. Those who found themselves members of a national minority could opt for citizenship in the state of their 'national' homeland.[61] However, in lands assigned to Italy, residency did not automatically confer citizenship rights. Foreign-born persons residing in new Italian territory, those who acquired rights of citizenship in the territory after 24 May 1915 and those who acquired them as a result of government positions had to petition for citizenship. In cases where citizenship was not granted, petitioners obtained 'the nationality of the State exercising sovereignty over the territory in which they possessed rights of citizenship before acquiring such rights in the territory transferred to Italy'.[62] Subsequent Italian directives of 1920 set linguistic, residency and property requirements for those affected by

---

[58] 7 May 1920, CGCVG (ag), busta 11; 'Rimpatrie', CGCVG (adg), busta 35.
[59] 'Criterio per regolare il rimpatrio e l'accesso a Trieste', 12 Feb. 1919, CGCVG (ag), busta 41.
[60] 'Rimpatrie', CGCVG (adg), buste 35, 36.
[61] For clauses pertinent to the granting of Italian citizenship see 'Treaty of St. Germain, part III: political clauses for Europe, sec. vi: clauses relating to nationality', in Carnegie Endowment for International Peace, *The treaties of the peace, 1919–1923*, New York 1924, 292–5. 'National' affiliations were based on the vague criteria of 'race or language'.
[62] This was particularly difficult for those who held citizenship in extinct states, for example Ottoman citizens who had spent virtually their entire lives as part of the commercial community in Trieste.

these stipulations.[63] Dispositions on citizenship requests, like those on repatriation requests, were influenced by social status. A request for citizenship by Oscar Cosulich, a principal officer of Cosulich shipping, was granted only days after the diplomatic agreement on requirements. Fortunato Vivante, at the head of the Unionbank, given the title of baron by the Austrian monarchy, was also readily granted Italian citizenship.[64]

Citizenship was only one aspect of Italian identity; it indicated the state's acknowledgment of political rights. Individuals' voluntary and spontaneous actions testified to local support for pro-Italian agendas. In the first four years after annexation to Italy, almost 1,000 people, of varied origins and social backgrounds, sought to demonstrate their allegiance by the Italianisation of their surnames.[65] Some claimed to seek Italianisation to standardise their names. Roberto Caucich, who suggested that his family was known as 'Caucich, Kaucich, Caucig, Kaucic, Kavcic, Kauzizh' in various public documents, asked that his family's name be set in the Italian form of Caucchi.[66] Giuseppe Schottlik petitioned authorities asking for the surname 'Scotti'. He maintained that in official documents his surname varied so much that 'even [he] no longer knew the exact spelling'.[67]

Most who sought alterations referred simply to Italian nationalist sentiments. In a petition to the Italian authorities in March 1919 Umberto Terchig, a native of Venezia Giulia, exemplified the nationalist fervour. Claiming to have 'always fought on the part of the struggle to unite these lands to the great mother Italy', Terchig begged authorities to change his surname 'to liberate [him] from the detestable yoke of foreignness' and to 'obliterate forever the traces of the evil past'.[68] Military officials in charge of the territory from November 1918 to July 1919 generally proved willing to accommodate those exhibiting such patriotic sentiment.

Civilian officials under Commissioner Antonio Mosconi were more circumspect. Mosconi refused to grant name changes motivated simply by a desire to demonstrate patriotism. He explained:

Slowly, but generally, it is beginning to be recognised that Italianness can be manifested more by acts than by changing surnames. Our brothers in the Old Provinces, those who have intimate knowledge of the special conditions of the redeemed lands must from their historical and ethnic experience under-

[63] *Gazzetta ufficiale del regno d'Italia: parte prima leggi e decreti, 1921*, no. 14/1890 (30 Dec. 1920).
[64] CGCVG (ag), busta 11. The bulk of documents relating to requests for Italian citizenship in Venezia Giulia were incorporated into Fascist files. They therefore remain closed to researchers.
[65] Requests for name changes appear in several buste labelled 'Cambiamenti cognomi', CGCVG (ag). The form, tone and diction of the letters demonstrate the range of social and educational backgrounds of petitioners. Little information exists for each individual.
[66] CGCVG (ag), busta 97.
[67] Ibid. busta 99.
[68] Ibid. busta 82.

stand that they can no longer judge Italianness based on whether names of their new citizens are more or less exotic.[69]

Name changes were limited to cases deemed to 'merit special consideration'.[70] Among the types of requests honoured were those of women affianced to soldiers who had died in Italian campaigns. This was consistent with policy adopted throughout Italy to legitimise relationships severed by war and to recognise women's sacrifices in the name of Italy. Under the provisions, Maria Moretti changed her name from an Italian to a non-Italian one, that of her fiancé Ermano Philipp and arranged for her unborn child to bear his name as well.[71] Legitimisation not Italianisation was clearly the aim.

Just as officials sought to honour those who had made sacrifices for the Italian state, Mosconi took pride in exposing political opportunists who professed nationalist sentiments in the hope of taking advantage of the political turmoil. In a memo detailing the dangers of allowing widespread name changes, Mosconi cited as particularly 'elegant', but none the less 'characteristic', the story of an individual named 'Italo'. The man had petitioned Austrian authorities in 1915 to change his name so that, as a good Austrian citizen, he would not have a potentially 'offensive' first name. After Austria's defeat, this 'good man' came before the Italian authorities bearing a copy of his birth certificate and claiming that the 'nefarious Austrian government' had changed his name.[72]

Despite civil officials' reluctance to grant name changes, those with economic privilege or political connections were accommodated. Enrico Feriancich, a ship captain for Lloyd Triestino, received the change he requested, to Feriani in September 1919. Not only was he a high-ranking employee of Lloyd, but also his mother's family, the Hermets, were well known for their support of Italian causes dating back to 1848. Arrigo Arnerrytsch obtained permission to change his name to Arneri in August 1919.[73] No reason for acceding to the request was recorded, but Arnerrytsch was clearly linked to elite circles in the city. His name was changed along with that of Mario Arnerrytsch, who was married to Zoe Mayer, a member of a family prominent in commercial and publishing circles in the city. Antonio Gluncich changed his surname to Grillo after officials verified that he had been dubbed Grillo by the head of a local irredentist society in 1902 and that was the only name by which he was known.[74]

---

[69] Ibid. busta 97. This undated explanation by A. Mosconi is taken from a memo by L. Fels, a Habsburg civil servant assigned to head the civil affairs branch of the military government and subsequently appointed to the same post by the Liberal government. It appears in 17 Dec. 1919, ibid.
[70] The pattern for changes in small towns in the interior and in Istria is less clear. Oppressive Italianisation policies seem to have been applied more stringently in these areas.
[71] CGCVG (ag), busta 98.
[72] Ibid. busta 97.
[73] Ibid. busta 82.
[74] Ibid. busta 97.

Although these particular elites chose to reinvent themselves as ethnic Italians, for many in Trieste personal affiliations remained a complex mixture of allegiance to Italy and loyalty to ties of birth, heritage or sentimental attachment. The affiliations of the commercial elite appeared particularly malleable. The Economo family, originally of Salonika, had renounced links with the Ottoman empire and accepted Austrian citizenship in 1903 and 1904. After the war they found themselves in Italy and readily accepted Italian citizenship. Members of the family went on to be instrumental in the revival of the Triestine Commercial Bank. The Sevastopulo family, also of Greek origin, with controlling interests in Trieste's oil-processing industry and its banking and commerce, shared similar circumstances. When Italian troops entered the city on 3 November 1918, Paola Sevastopulo remembers her father, without compunction or regret, urging his children 'to consider themselves to be Italian citizens in all respects, without reservation or exclusion'.[75] The adaptability of the economic elite facilitated the merger with pro-Italian political forces and the development of a new Italian elite in the city.

Conceptions of national attachment varied even for individuals well ensconced in pro-Italian political circles. Before 1918 Attilio Tamaro had established himself as an avid nationalist through his irredentist writings and efforts on behalf of pro-Italian organisations. However, he professed membership of the Central European community, wrote on the politics of Central Europe and lived in Germany. He was frequently consulted for his expertise on Central European affairs. In 1917 he argued that Trieste was a centre for anti-Germanism and could be used by Italy as a wedge against the spread of German influence.[76] He saw no conflict in his association with Italy and with Austrian Central Europe. He would adapt readily to the vicissitudes of Italy's interwar relationship with Germany, would serve as a diplomat under Mussolini and return to his nationalist, irredentist stance after the Second World War.

Prior to the First World War, Lionello Stock, a noted Jewish industrialist, was a loyal Austrian citizen, an Italian nationalist and an avowed Zionist. Described as a 'vintage triestino' who always looked at broad possibilities on 'a European scale', family members suggested that '[n]one of [his] cosmopolitan activity however prevented him from breathing in the Italian national feelings with which the air of Trieste was impregnated'. Despite his adherence to Zionism, the Fascist government decorated him for contributions to Italy and Italian industry.[77]

The experiences of Triestine writer Claudio Magris's Uncle Otto suggest that overlapping affiliations extended even to Austrian officials. Otto was an Austrian officer in charge of supplies in Trieste during the First World War.

---

75 This is quoted in Millo, *L'élite del potere*, 234.
76 Tamaro, *Trieste et son role*.
77 Segrè, *Memoirs*, 100; Weinberg, *L'Anello*, 187–9, 194.

Impressed by his 'efficiency' and 'neatness', the Italian general Petitti di Roreto asked him to take charge of the distribution of rations during the transition period after November 1918. Otto remained in the Italian bureaucracy until the Fascist takeover, when he returned to Vienna to take up a civil service post similar to the one he had left in Italy.[78] Triestines' visions of participation in the Central European world did not imply sympathy for Germanness, but rather for an urban cosmopolitan culture tied to the city's tradition, economic orientation and relationship with Austria. For the majority, cultural identity was constructed not in opposition to Germanic Central Europe, but to the Balkans or Slavic Europe.[79]

Associations with Slavic, specifically Slovene or Croatian, identity were viewed with suspicion and interpreted as evidence of ties to the uncivilised east, of sympathy for the Kingdom of Serbs, Croats and Slovenes, and of support for socialism or communism. In November 1918 Petitti di Roreto promised that 'grand and victorious Italy' would 'watch over all its own citizens without regard for nationality'.[80] The Orlando and Nitti governments pledged liberal treatment of minorities. Foreign Minister Sforza and Prime Minister Giolitti advocated peaceful coexistence and publicly promised support for minority rights. But Italian administrations failed to match rhetoric with the passage or enforcement of protectionary legislation. Under the 1920 Treaty of Rapallo, the Yugoslavs promised to protect Italian minorities. The Italians made no such guarantees for Slavs.

State policies openly sanctioned anti-German sentiment. In Rome there was little distinction drawn between Austrian Central Europeanness and Germanness. Bitterness resulting from the circumstances of war, memories of the historically tumultuous relationship between Austria and Italy and animosities between Germany and Italy, despite periods of alliance in the nineteenth century, made association with Germanness extremely unpopular. This attitude spilled over into Trieste. Shortly after the takeover by Italy, military authorities pressured Triestine firms to replace ethnic Germans with Italians. They subjected even such large and powerful firms as Lloyd to censure. In December 1918 an official at the office of civilian affairs accused the firm of employing Germans to the detriment of Italian workers. It alleged that Lloyd had retained 100 or more Germans. However, the parameters of ethnic identity were not easy to define. Rather than quake in the face of government scrutiny, Lloyd representatives turned over employment rosters which showed no more than sixteen German workers, all playing essential roles in the transition from Austria to Italy.[81]

[78] C. Magris, *Danube*, New York 1989, 199.

[79] Todorova, *Imagining the Balkans*, 21–61, explores the various definitions and meanings of Balkan.

[80] This is cited in Parovel, *L'identità*, 17.

[81] Memorandum, 15 Feb. 1919, and supporting documents, CGCVG (ag), busta 17. The government soon cleared Lloyd of charges.

German ethnic influence was virtually eliminated in Trieste after the defeat of Austria and Germany in the war. The 1921 census recorded only Italians (202,382) and Slovenes (18,150) in the city.[82] The disappearance of the Germanic Austrians and the crystallisation of an expanded Italy alongside the new South Slav State opened the door to direct confrontation between native Slavic and Italian populations. Italians tended to elide Slavic and German identities, reflecting the transfer of enemy status from Germans to Slavs. The case of Mario Adrario, a local railroad official denounced for harbouring sentiments hostile to Italy, demonstrates this. According to police reports of June 1919, an agent overheard Adrario suggest that railway workers could communicate 'unbeknownst to Italian authorities' with Yugoslavia over telephone lines running through a tunnel near the border. Adrario's conversation, in German, had caught the agent's attention initially, but his behaviour with Slavs had formed the basis for the agent's suspicions. Adrario purportedly spoke perfect Italian and was 'very courteous and deferential with Italians', but he appeared hostile to Italy when in the company of Slavs. On further inquiry, the Italian agent learned from another railway official that Adrario was suspected of spreading propaganda emanating from Yugoslavia to local newspapers, but admitted 'nothing could be certain in this regard'.[83]

In fact, Adrario's pro-Austrian sympathies were well known. He had petitioned to cross the armistice line with his Viennese wife and in-laws to leave Trieste and settle permanently in Austria. The authorities expedited his request for an emigration visa rather than incarcerate him. They contended that rail shipments were too tightly controlled and inspected for Adrario to have aided in the import of Yugoslav propaganda and suggested that his remarks posed no real threat to the Italian government. None the less, they concluded that the man was an 'unfavourable element' and could possibly 'spread deleterious propaganda among the soldiers and businessmen'.[84]

Adrario's ties to the Slavic cause were particularly noteworthy as he was a former captain of one of the rail stations near the new border with Yugoslavia. Railway officials, like other civil servants, were noted for Austrophile sympathies. The Italian agent's association of Adrario with pro-Slavic rather than pro-Austrian sentiments probably reflected anxiety about the vulnerability of rail lines near the border. After the First World War, these were often the loci for anti-government violence. Unknown assailants shot off revolvers to intimidate passengers and crews. Several attempts to impede the movement of trains through acts of sabotage were reported. Most of the incidents

---

[82] M. Scroccaro, *Dall'aquila bicipite alla croce uncinata: l'Italia e le opzioni nelle nuove provincie Trentino, Sudtirolo, Val Canale, 1919–1939*, Trent 2000, 57. According to the 1921 census, the population of Venezia Giulia included 479,591 Italians, 258,944 Slovenes, 92,800 Croats, 50,589 Ladins, 4,185 Germans and 1,644 Rumanians.

[83] 'Rimpatrie', CGCVG (adg), busta 36.

[84] Ibid.

took place between stations or in smaller stations and were perpetrated by culprits who evaded detection by police.[85]

Railroad workers were suspect due to their strong associations with socialist organisations, assumed to be riddled with pro-Slav elements. Indicative of the high level of tension was the furore caused by a relatively minor incident, the derailment of a locomotive on a line to a mine near Trieste. On investigation, the civil authorities concluded that the negligence of a brakeman and a machinist had caused the accident and urged equanimity in the approach to such incidents. None the less, they praised the captain who had arrested the two railway workers, both of whom coincidentally had Slavic surnames. They lauded the captain's diligence in light of the hostile climate between workers and the mine company.[86]

Ethnic Slavs did not appear to constitute the primary threat in the eyes of Triestines nor of Italian government officials. The civil commissioner, Mosconi, a native of Vicenza and long-time Italian civil servant, and those serving under him, have been portrayed as eager Italianisers who supported Italian nationalist extremism. The attitude of Liberal government officials is assumed to have facilitated the early triumph of extreme nationalists and Fascists in Trieste.[87] No doubt Mosconi was sympathetic to the Italian cause. Sympathies for pro-Italian agendas allowed for official inaction, but did not institutionalise the persecution of minorities.

The attitude toward ethnic Slavs remained equivocal. In September 1919 the editor of the Triestine daily *La Nazione* admitted that Trieste's Slavic problem was 'grave', but noted that this was 'not for its own importance which is secondary, [but] for the confusion of the question that reigns among those who are called upon to decide it'.[88] Attacks against minorities and foreign-run institutions were not officially condoned, but sporadic violence went largely unpunished. The well-documented burning and looting of the Narodni Dom in July 1920 was only one in a series of incidents in which Italian troops or officials turned a blind eye to violence against minorities. The burning of the headquarters of the Croatian-managed Adriatic Bank, also in July 1920, was another such incident. Restitution was made but the attack could be counted a nationalist victory. The bank moved immediately to transfer its headquarters and assets to Zagreb.[89]

The association, real or imagined, between Slavic ethnicity and the socialist challenge to the liberal order exercised the Italian government. Official inaction or prejudice was most evident in the response to incidents involving attacks on socialists. In the autumn of 1920 Fascist squads attacked a funeral procession mourning a socialist worker killed in a general strike.

[85] 'Ferrovie', CGCVG (ag), busta 41.
[86] 'Miniere di Carpano-Vines', ibid.
[87] Rusinow, *Italy's Austrian heritage*, 95–7, and Sluga, *The problem of Trieste*, 43.
[88] C. Cesari to Tamaro, 10 Sept. 1919, Tamaro papers.
[89] Memorandum and correspondence, 20 July 1920, CGCVG (ag), busta 21.

The socialists erected barricades in the streets of Trieste's San Giacomo quarter, a working-class neighbourhood. Police levelled the undefended barricades and intimidated local residents by carrying out a house-to-house search.[90] In 1921 a firebomb exploded in the offices of *Il Lavoratore*, the local socialist newspaper.[91] Police watched the premises burn. Nascent Fascist groups and nationalist extremists were tolerated, not for their persecution of ethnic Slavs, but for their outspoken and active opposition to socialism associated with Slavs.

Suspicion of Slavs also undermined support for Catholic politics in Venezia Giulia. On the Italian peninsula, between 1921 and 1923, Catholic opposition led by Luigi Sturzo and the Partito Popolare posed one of the greatest obstacles to Fascist ascendancy. The Vatican dissociated itself from the party's political activism, but the Italian public recognised the Popolari as an alternative to socialism and a wedge whereby Catholic agendas might be asserted in political life. Fascist anti-clerical tendencies and violence against institutions and representatives of the Church alienated many. Much of the lower clergy in Italy united in opposition to Mussolini's centralisation policies, considered a threat to Vatican supremacy.[92] In Venezia Giulia the politics of ethnicity divided the Catholic constituency. Many Slavs, who might have been expected to support the Catholic party, chose instead to align themselves with socialist and Slavic nationalist parties. Priests with a history of support for Slavic nationalism championed these popular movements which offered alternatives to Fascist as well as Italian Catholic movements.

The Liberal government's failure to differentiate between Slavs, socialists and communists, and unwillingness to distinguish between their various interests undermined its already tenuous position in the multi-ethnic border region. In November 1918 Carlo Galli predicted that the Italian government's major challenges in Trieste would come from the most fervent 'Italian patriots' who would be the most critical of the new administration.[93] These observations proved prophetic. By 1921 Professor Mario Stenta, Italian nationalist and Triestine, was being brutally frank in his assertion that no one could 'ever negate the merits conferred by the Fascio, especially in our region polluted by Austrian, Slav and communist barbarians'.[94] The triumph in 1921 of the nationalist bloc, which included Fascist representatives, demonstrated the erosion of the moderate Liberals' power. Legislation passed after the elections took on a more nationalist tone. Use of Italian was required in

[90] Novak, *Trieste, 1941–1954*, 40–1.
[91] S. Ranchi and M. Rossi, *Il Lavoratore: richerche e testimonianze su novantanni di storia di un giornale*, Trieste 1986, 38–44.
[92] Lyttelton, *Seizure of power*, 33, 130–2.
[93] Galli, *Diarii e lettere*, 324.
[94] M. Stenta to Tamaro, 19 May 1921, Tamaro papers.

all capacities. Public use of a 'foreign' tongue invited discrimination.[95] Local 'patriots' adopted radical and violent strategies to promote Italianness, seen as consistent with loyalty to the Italian state.

The equivocal response of the Liberal authorities to ethnic enmities in Venezia Giulia was consistent with a reluctance to deal with nationalist extremism throughout Italy. Areas on the nation's periphery, including Trieste, were the first to spin out of the control of those preaching a moderate course. Political activism by Slav socialist workers and Italian maximalists heightened perception of the menace of the red peril spreading from the east. The Italian government was increasingly seen as ineffective. Italian policy, particularly for the upper Adriatic region, became focused on nationalist ambitions and the extension of sovereignty over Fiume and disputed territories. The Liberal government was destroyed by the violent anti-socialist elements that it had depended upon to enforce the traditional order and restore stability.

Fascist nationalism

In 1923 the Italian Fascist state began a campaign of outright persecution of ethnic and political minorities. Mussolini promoted a 'civil' or 'patriotic religion' that replaced traditional loyalties with emphasis on duty and sacrifice to the state, faith in and glorification of the leader, and mass participation in state-sponsored rituals. Trieste and Trento, 'redeemed' in the wake of the First World War, played an important part in Fascist liturgy as the blood sacrifice of the new nation.[96] Through persuasion, coercion and violence, Fascist policies for Venezia Giulia forged Triestines in the image of the ideal Fascist man, a paragon of devotion to Italy and a model for the new Italian nation.

By the time of the March on Rome, the willingness of local leaders to tolerate violence had already compromised local Slavic, primarily Slovene, political institutions and crushed political opponents in Venezia Giulia. In July 1923 persecutory policies were enacted. A law that permitted the mayor to remove and replace the editor of any periodical that had received three official admonitions resulted in the suppression of the Slavic and opposition press.[97] During the 1923 school year, authorities instituted a ban on teaching in Slavic languages in Venezia Giulia and German in the new northern provinces. They eventually prohibited secular classes in any language other than Italian. In 1927 Fascist education codes were extended to include religious

[95] E. Capuzzo, 'Sull'introduzione dell'amministrazione italiana a Trento e a Trieste (1918–1919)', *Clio* xxiii (1987), 260.
[96] E. Gentile, *The sacralization of politics in Fascist Italy*, Cambridge 1996, 15–18.
[97] Apih, *Italia fascismo*, 278.

instruction, preventing priests from conducting classes in Slovene, Croatian or German.[98]

The continued political activism of the Slavic clergy exacerbated the antagonistic relationship between Italian nationalism and the Church. It drew attention to the opposition of minority groups to the Fascist political order. The religious education order of July 1927 allowed the Fascists to invade churches with German and Slavic clerics. Priests sympathetic to minorities were beaten and intimidated.[99] The 1929 Lateran Pacts, by means of which Mussolini made peace with the Catholic Church, did little to alleviate local tensions. Nationalising articles used Roman Catholic missionary duty as a justification for jingoistic national policy.[100] In 1930, in the wake of clerics' protests against the persecution of parishioners from ethnic minorities, the government forced the Church to replace the remaining Slavic priests, who were in charge of thirty parishes in Trieste.[101]

Assumptions that the Slavic populations were uncivilised and innately brutal fed Fascist anti-Slav campaigns. In 1929 Aldo Pizzagalli, Triestine linguist and Fascist administrator, summed up prevailing attitudes, praising all Italian life 'rooted in traditions of Rome' as 'beautiful, natural and noble'. Slovenes were 'farmers of an almost barbarous cultural level'. Contempt for Slavic cultures, not foreign ethnic affiliation, was the key to Slovene and Slavic inferiority for Pizzagalli and other Fascist administrators.[102]

Trieste's cultural periodical *La Porta Orientale* harped on the Balkan, Slavic taint. It presented name modifications in the north-eastern borderland as a 'purification of the Balkan scourge which had polluted local populations particularly in recent decades'. Fascist intellectuals pointed to the ahistorical basis for Slavic and pagan names, claiming that they had been adopted in a blatant effort to disguise the Italian heritage of the Upper Adriatic lands 'civilised' by the Roman legions and the Church, in particular by the see of Aquileia.[103]

Campaigns to alter names in Venezia Giulia were perhaps the most powerful and widespread tool of Fascist Italianisation. Given names were the first to come under attack. An obscure Austrian code, renewed by Italian royal decree in 1928, forbade parents from giving names 'ridiculous, immoral, or offensive to religion and national sentiment'. The statute was invoked most forcefully at the time of baptism for newborns to prevent parents or clergy from recording 'vulgar' names. Slovene, Croat or German saints' names came under particular attack. In March 1928 baptismal names already

---

98 G. Salvemini, *Racial minorities under Fascism in Italy*, Chicago 1934, 7–24, discusses anti-minority legislation.

99 Apih, *Italia fascismo*, 285.

100 Lyttelton, *Seizure of power*, 421, and Salvemini, *Racial minorities*, 26.

101 Apih, *Italia fascismo*, 290.

102 Pizzagalli, *Per l'italianità*, 8, 18.

103 A. Scocchi, 'I nomi pagani slavi e l'onomastica romana', *La Porta Orientale* (1932), 281.

recorded in public registers became subject to official modification.[104] By 1939 Fascist law disallowed the bestowing of any non-Italian name on an Italian citizen.[105]

The campaign to modify surnames, initiated in 1927, constituted the most systematic attempt to enforce the Italian nature of the border region. From the legislation's enactment to its discontinuance under the Nazi occupation in 1943, the names of nearly 100,000 people, out of a population of approximately 400,000, were altered.[106] Based, in theory, on the practices adopted by Liberal Italian officials dealing with name changes in the wake of annexation, the campaign transformed a voluntary and spontaneous demonstration of loyalty to a coercive project aimed at eradicating evidence of foreign influences. The legislation formed part of a particularly combative border Fascism designed to assimilate Croatian and Slovene minorities, to maintain the population in a state of mobilisation tied to generic Italian patriotism, to promote cohesion in the Julian region and to widen the perception of popular consensus for the Fascist regime.

In Venezia Giulia the weight of the law fell on the Slavic population, but the oppressive policies were not a direct assault upon them. The statutes were extensions of measures that had targeted the Germanic populations of the Trentino and Alto Adige. Nowhere in the statutes, or in the supplementary instructions provided to the prefect of the province of Trieste in April 1927, was there reference to any nationality besides Italian. The legislation was to be enacted in a 'uniform and adequate' manner to ensure that the population of Trieste conformed to Italian cultural expectations.[107] German, Jewish and other foreign names fell to the Fascist pen as readily as Slavic ones.

In May 1927 the prefect of Trieste appointed a commission to produce guidelines for name revisions.[108] Headed by Pizzagalli and composed primarily of academics and teachers, the commission cast a wide net to determine which names should be affected by the legislation. Pizzagalli had been involved in the formulation of policy for name alterations in the years immediately following Trieste's annexation, and the list of alterations granted by Liberal authorities formed a starting point for administrative alterations. For example, a change from Adamich to Adami in 1920 set the precedent after 1928 for the wholesale conversion of those named Adamich to Adami. Reliance on the rosters of the previous government lent a sense of historical continuity to the re-naming project. The initial roster listed more than 2,500 surnames which were to be altered by administrative fiat. Beginning in 1929,

---

[104] Salvemini, *Racial minorities*, 10.

[105] Parovel, *Identità cancellata*, 29.

[106] This estimate is from ibid. 28. It seems consistent with a cursory count and extrapolation of the 'reductions' contained in *buste* held in AdS, PPT (rc).

[107] Guidelines, 20 Apr. 1927, AdS, PPT (rc).

[108] A. Andri, 'I cambiamenti di cognome nel 1928 e la scuola triestina', *Qualestoria* xi (Feb. 1983), 11.

sections of the list of affected surnames were published in *Il Piccolo*. Individuals received direct notification from the prefect's office.

Pizzagalli was careful to avoid tarnishing the appearance of consensus and widespread support for the Fascist nationalisation. He suggested that the surname legislation remedied inconsistencies in 'a population nationally and culturally Italian with surnames in large part of foreign character'. To avoid abuse of power, name conversion could 'not be done capriciously, it had to follow a formal administrative procedure'. Under Italian law, surnames were immutable. So, rather than changing names the legislation called only for the conversion or 'reduction' of names to their 'original' Italian or Latin forms. Hence, Slavic and Germanic names were subject to the decree, French and other Latinate or western names were not. To encourage extensive Italianisation, the statutes allowed inhabitants of Venezia Giulia with a foreign name to volunteer for conversion.[109]

Many of those who did come forward to request alterations were coerced or pressured. In March 1928 the provincial education office urged teachers to help the schools to be among the 'first in this manifestation of Italianness'.[110] Prefectural records indicate that many complied. The power of the authorities to dismiss teachers, or revoke their credentials, combined with psychological pressure upon them. Civil servants too risked censure. Many employees of the customs authority, the Central Warehouse Authority and large shipping firms dependent on state contracts, were among early petitioners for alteration of foreign names. Edoardo Weiss, a noted psychoanalyst, claimed that he was asked to resign his post at the provincial psychiatric hospital because he refused to change his German-Jewish surname.[111]

Individuals of foreign ethnic origin who wished to Italianise their names generally received permission to do so. Petitioners themselves, or the officials, noted a specific etymology of the original name, identified, for example, as Hungarian, Slovene or Croat and offered an Italianised version. However, Italianisation was not open to all. Political enemies or those with criminal records were denied permission as 'Slavs' or simply 'foreigners', implying that they were inevitably and irrevocably enemies of the Italian state.[112]

Leading families or political figures were not compelled to Italianise their names. The government minister Fulvio Suvich and members of the Cosulich family kept their names despite their obvious Slavic roots. The retention of selected non-Italian names lent credence to Fascist assertions that the general population was neither coerced nor oppressed, but complied voluntarily with Italianisation. It also avoided confusion in political and economic circles. By 1932 the veneer of Italianness spread by the national-

---

[109] Pizzagalli, *Per l'italianità*, 8, 15, 21–3.

[110] Andri, 'I cambiamenti', 11, cites circular no. 312, Provveditore agli studi della Venezia Giulia e di Zara.

[111] U. Saba, *Lettere sulla psicoanalisi*, Milan 1991, 92.

[112] PPT (rc), passim.

ising campaigns prompted Silvio Benco to comment that 'Trieste in the past has been a crucible of peoples; today it is a city which can refer to itself as having one nationality alone.'[113]

The turn towards Germany

After 1935 the Italian–German *rapprochement* changed the contours of ethnic relations and affected Italianisation policies. Fascists who did not wish to offend their Nazi allies subtly toned down anti-German aspects of the nationalist legislation. A commercial trader's request in 1936 to hyphenate the German version of his surname to the Italian form conferred by authorities in 1930 testified to the change in the climate. The man cited commercial reasons for the readoption of the German name, and officials willingly granted his request.[114]

Not only did increasingly amiable relations with Germany promote sympathies for Germanness, they also encouraged the adoption of legislation mimicking Nazi racial policy. For Trieste, where the Jewish population numbered approximately 5,000, and was widely assimilated, highly respected and powerful in economic circles, segregation and persecution were inconsistent with previous attitudes. Many local Jews had been honoured by the Italian state for their support for irredentism and voluntary service for Italy during the First World War.[115] Nationalising campaigns in Trieste had upheld the Jews as loyal citizens of Italy. Under the surname legislation, Italianisation of Jewish names had not only been tolerated, it had been compelled. The names Loewy and Löwy 'Italianised' to Levi, and Kohen and Kohn 'reduced' to Coen had appeared on Pizzagalli's list for automatic alteration.[116] Fascist authorities judged these Jews to have been 'denationalised' at some point, implying that they were an organic part of the Italian national community. In Italy as a whole, Jewish contributions to the state had been recognised. *Surnames of the Jews of Italy*, published in 1925, celebrated the fact that twenty or more of Italy's 7,600 noble families were Jewish.[117]

In 1928 Mussolini announced an anti-Zionist campaign. He distrusted the 'Jewish Masonic International movement' and seemed to believe in the existence of the international Zionist conspiracy common in antisemitic theories propagated throughout Europe. He did not, however, equate Zionism with Judaism, nor was his invective against Zionism translated to anti-Jewish or

---

[113] This is quoted in Sluga, *The problem of Trieste*, 60.

[114] PPT (rc) passim.

[115] The number of requests from Jews asking to hyphenate Italian 'noms de guerre' attests to the level of Jewish involvement in the Italian campaigns. Copies of birth certificates required to process these requests indicate affiliation with the Jewish community (comunità israelitica).

[116] Pizzagalli, *Per l'italianità*, 141, 143.

[117] S. Schaerf, *I cognomi degli ebrei d'Italia*, Florence 1925, 71–85.

even uniformly anti-Zionist policy. He recognised that international Zionism offered Italy an opportunity to increase Italian prestige in the Mediterranean and to counter British imperialism in the Near East.[118]

In an interview with the German writer Emil Ludwig, published in 1932, Mussolini denied the existence of antisemitism in Italy suggesting that 'Race is a sentiment, not a reality; ninety-five percent is a sentiment.' He said that 'Jews have acted well as citizens of Italy, and as soldiers have fought courageously. They occupy high posts in the universities, in the army, in banks.'[119] In an *Il Piccolo* editorial of 1 January 1938, its director Rino Alessi, a boyhood companion of Mussolini, spoke out in favour of Jews who had 'done their national duty' and proved their patriotism.[120] Alessi maintained that Jews could be assimilated into the Italian population. As late as September 1938, in a speech in Trieste, Mussolini distinguished between loyal Italian Jews whose contributions to Italy were 'indisputable' and Zionists and foreign Jews who were 'irreconcilable enemies of Fascism'.[121]

While some in commercial circles had anticipated the antisemitic persecution, the severity of the racial measures that took effect in October 1938 surprised the general population.[122] Triestines, including Jews hitherto considered culturally Italian, generally saw Slavs as the alien race subject to suspicion and persecution. At the time the statutes were enacted, Trieste's Fascist-appointed mayor Enrico Paolo Salem was Jewish.[123] The redefinition of alien identity tore apart the fabric of the integrated and assimilated commercial community. The lineage-based definition of Jewishness proved particularly problematic for those, like the commercial leader Salvatore Segrè Sartorio who were of Jewish ancestry but had converted and been dissociated from the city's Jewish community. Segrè Sartorio's objections revealed his own prejudices and laid bare the potential for rifts within the Jewish community. He argued that despite his Jewish heritage, he was 'different from the others . . . not a profiteer, not a Polish Jew, not a Jew by religious confession . . . made a count by the King . . . then a Senator by Mussolini . . . for forty years a Christian Catholic'.[124]

Legislation directed against Jews excepted those who could prove loyalty to the nation, through evidence of meritorious service on behalf of Italy or in the Fascist cause.[125] In 1938, from Trieste alone, almost 400 Jews forwarded pleas to Rome for special consideration. The Fascist government looked with

118 F. Biagini, *Mussolini e il sionismo*, Milan 1998, 8–9.

119 E. Ludwig, *Colloqui con Mussolini*, Verona 1950, 71–2.

120 Bon, *Gli ebrei*, 46–7.

121 Mussolini, *Opera omnia*, xxix. 146.

122 On the Jews in Trieste under Fascism see Hametz, 'The ambivalence of Italian antisemitism, 376–401.

123 Salem was relieved of his post, retired from public life, changed his name to D'Angeri and moved to Rome where he died in 1948: Trampus, *Vie e piazze*, 554.

124 Millo, *L'élite del potere*, 336–7.

125 T. Staderini, *Legislazione per la difesa della razza*, Rome 1940, 13.

favour on the requests of at least seveny-nine individuals, or nearly one in every five.[126] After July 1939 Mussolini's agents could Aryanise Jewish citizens 'irrespective of services rendered to Italy or Fascism'.[127] Many hoped that economic influence or political clout would be decisive in their bids to gain recognition as 'not belonging to the Jewish race'. Yet the transient nature of the port's population and the legacy of Habsburg rule meant that many of Trieste's Jews were among those who might be considered foreign Jews, judged loyal to their race rather than the nation.

In Trieste, the response of local officials to racial measures targeting Jews was equivocal. A report on demography and race forwarded to Mussolini in August 1940 complained of the lack of 'severity' in the application of racial measures in the Adriatic territory. It claimed that in some sectors the Jews had simply 'been left in peace to their activities'.[128] To demonstrate local zeal, Prefect Tullio Tamburini reported that officials revoked 3,000 name modifications beginning in the autumn of 1941. However, this number was greatly exaggerated, probably in an attempt to curry favour with Fascist superiors.[129]

Local officials hesitated to revoke Italianised forms of names and sought clarification before applying the racial measures. A provision of 1938 that revoked the Italian citizenship of Jews who 'took up residence in Italy, Libya or in the Aegean possessions after 1 January 1919', formed the basis for one official's inquiry regarding contradictions created by application of the citizenship and nationalist laws. Many long-time Triestines, including Jews, had applied for Italian citizenship after annexation. The Italian citizenship of approximately 1,500 Jews in the city was revoked in 1938. The name revocation statute of 1939 required that Italian citizens of the Jewish race resume their original names. Should the Italianised name be revoked for a woman whose citizenship had already been revoked? Despite his anxiety to demonstrate commitment to the Fascist cause, Tamburini ruled that since the law revoking citizenship preceded the law requiring revocation, action on all decrees restoring original surnames to Jews who were no longer Italian citizens should be suspended.[130] The ironic result was that foreign-born Jews retained Italianised names. Native-born Jews, long considered ethnically Italian, relinquished Italianised identities.

Although the state officially condoned the persecution of Jews, Slavic ethnic background seemed to carry a greater stigma than Jewish affiliation for many individuals. After 1938 few 'Aryan, Italian' women who were parties to mixed marriages and bore Jewish-sounding married names took advantage of

---

[126] Bon, Gli ebrei, 75.

[127] M. Michaelis, Mussolini and the Jews: German-Italian relations and the Jewish question in Italy, 1922–1945, Oxford 1978, 254–5, describes the implications.

[128] De Felice, Storia degli ebrei, 584–8.

[129] Little archival evidence exists to support this claim. G. Mayda, Ebrei sotto Salò, Milan 1978, 45, suggests that the total was only about 70 decrees. Decrees generally included all members of the nuclear family so this probably affected approximately 200 individuals.

[130] Staderini, Legislazione, 12; PPT (rc).

legislation that permitted them to change their names. A number who bore non-Italian maiden names obtained modifications of those names, but most chose to erase Slavic or eastern European associations, not Jewish ones. Paternalistic attitudes and familial honour and responsibility seemed stronger than antisemitic sentiment or fear of being associated with Jews.

The antisemitic codes segregated Jews on the basis of racial characteristics, but persecution did not spring from deep-seated notions of biological racial inferiority. Exempted Jews seemed to have little fear of persecution. A sea captain, 'once an Israelite' but recognised as 'not a member of the Jewish race', even challenged the boundaries of Fascist law. In 1941 he asked the authorities to add an 'i' to the end of his surname to rid it of its foreign sonance. They did not accommodate his specific request, because the form he asked for did not conform to standards for reduction or translation. However, they were willing to entertain 'Italianisation'. They offered several 'legitimate' name choices. The captain rejected them all.[131] His obstinacy rather than discrimination blocked Italianisation.

In May 1940 Italy's entry into the war exacerbated ethnic tensions. Wartime scarcities and economic dislocation contributed to a general feeling of discontent. Political realignments brought antagonism to the surface. Trieste's Greek minority suffered as a result of Italy's bitter experiences on the Greek front. Anti-Greek prejudice further splintered the Jewish community, split between 'foreign' and 'Italian' Jews. Pupils of Greek Jewish descent, whose parents or grandparents had come to Trieste at the turn of the century to escape pogroms, found their loyalties questioned. Already barred from public schools as Jews, they were expelled as enemy aliens from the Jewish Middle School.[132]

Yugoslavia's entry into the war in 1941 on the side of the Allies fuelled anti-Slav and anti-socialist sentiment. It also formed the basis for invective against Jews who were associated with socialist Slavs. Violence against minorities increased as a consequence of perceived political threats to the Italian Fascist state. In general, authorities seemed bent on tactics of humiliation and subjugation rather than the extermination of Jews. In July 1942 the Jewish synagogue and buildings of the Committee for the Assistance of Jewish Emigrants were severely damaged. By the end of 1942 the census counted only 3,521 Jews still in Trieste.[133] In early 1943 local Jews were arrested and then released after a short period. Antisemitic laws allowed for the property of well-to-do Jews to be liquidated; villas of Jewish families were seized. In May 1943 marauding Fascist bands attacked and looted stores run by Jews and Slovenes in the aftermath of the funeral of six Fascist soldiers

---

[131] PPT (rc).
[132] See Università degli studi di Trieste, *La scuola media ebraica di Trieste negli anni 1938–1943: storia e memorie*, Trieste 1999, 48.
[133] Bon, *Gli ebrei*, 249.

ambushed in the Carso hinterlands.[134] Although the attacks certainly had an ethnic component, ethnicity was not the prime motivating factor. Jews and Slavs were increasingly associated with resistance.

Citizens of the *Reich*

The Italian surrender in September 1943 and the subsequent Nazi occupation complicated political and ethnic alliances in the upper Adriatic region. Ethnic politics blurred the choice between resistance and collaboration. On the Italian peninsula, anti-Fascist partisans took to the forests or mountains. In Venezia Giulia, anti-Fascist Italians faced Slavs, who most certainly harboured resentments resulting from the oppression of minorities during more than twenty years of Fascist rule, in interior and rural lands. They also risked encountering any number of Yugoslav forces engaged in civil conflict and in attempts to defeat Fascist Italians and Germans. The result, as Piero Quarantotti Gambini suggested, was that for Triestines fighting with the partisans meant fighting against Italy not simply against Fascism. 'No Istrian or Triestine of truly Italian leanings could become a partisan', he asserted.[135]

The Nazi-appointed prefect, Bruno Coceani, Mayor Cesare Pagnini and others like them justified collaboration with the Nazis as an effort to prevent Slav and communist encroachments from the east and to ensure continued Italian control and predominance in the region. Coceani's collaboration with the Nazis certainly reflected a desire for self-preservation, and charges that he was a Nazi collaborator are certainly justified. None the less, his record indicated an attachment to the Italian cause that transcended a mere devotion to Fascist politics. In his dealings with the Nazi command, Coceani harped on the ferocity of the Slavic opposition to the German occupying forces. He claimed that the Slav 'problem' in the border territories was not dire in and of itself, but rather as a result of provocation from Lubljana and other lands 'beyond the borders'.[136] Throughout his tenure as prefect, he maintained ties with Italian nationalists involved in the resistance activities of the local committee for national liberation.

Official attitudes assisted Nazis bent on enforcing persecutory policies. At Trieste's Risiera di San Sabba, a former rice refinery, the Nazis established one of the four German detention and deportation camps in Italy. Upwards of 20,000 prisoners were detained at San Sabba, where the compound contained a prison with torture equipment, outbuildings for seized property and a crematorium, the only one constructed on Italian (or at the time former Italian) territory. The Nazis aimed at political prisoners. Slavs, socialists and partisans bore the brunt of punishment. An estimated 3–5,000

---

134 Università degli studi, *La scuola media*, 50–1.
135 Quoted in Arosio, *Scrittori di frontiera*, 146.
136 Bruno Coceani, *Mussolini, Hitler, Tito alle porte orientali d'Italia*, Bologna 1948, 73–4.

people were killed by various means, many among them Slavs active in the resistance.[137] For Jews, San Sabba functioned primarily as a holding station where those collected from the Adriatic Littoral and the Veneto awaited transport to extermination camps in Poland. Between 9 October 1943 and 1 November 1944, at least twenty-two transports departed Trieste for Auschwitz. Others went to Dachau or Mauthausen. Officially 837 Triestine Jews were deported.[138] An unknown number awaiting deportation were killed at San Sabba, executed to allow the ovens to run at capacity when there were not enough political prisoners. By May 1945 the city's Jewish population was decimated; only 4–500 Jews remained of the pre-war population of approximately 5,000.[139]

Nazi policies that took aim at minority populations heightened political confusion and exacerbated ethnic tensions. In the political realm the Nazis played feuding nationalist factions off against one another in a bid to maintain dominance. They promised the Slovenes and Croats recognition and responsibilities within the administration. At the same time, they offered guarantees of continued Italian predominance in urban centres. Nazi propaganda campaigns disparaged the Italian Fascist state and promoted nostalgia for Habsburg dominance in an attempt to foster a positive memory of Germanic rule.[140]

By 1944 the Milan-based Committee for the Liberation of Northern Italy, the parent organisation for the local branch, had negotiated with the Slovene Liberation Front to create a broad, multi-ethnic front against the Axis.[141] Allied recognition of the contributions of Tito's communist resistance prompted the Milan-based Italian leadership to accept Slovene proposals for an ethnically-based territorial settlement after the war. Such agreements were antithetical to the interests of Italian nationalists and even some socialists in the upper Adriatic area. On the local level, in the pact of 9 December 1944, Giulian representatives of the Action party, the Italian Socialist party, the Christian Democrats and the Liberal party agreed to concerted political and economic action and pledged to avoid placing obsta-

---

[137] For more on the risiera San Sabba see F. Fölkel, *La risiera di San Sabba: Trieste e il Litorale Adriatico durante l'occupazione nazista*, Milan 1979; S. Bon, 'Un campo di sterminio in Italia', *Il Ponte* xxxiv/11–12 (1978), 1440–53; Enzo Collotti, 'Sui compiti repressivi degli Einsatzkommandos della polizia di sicurezza tedesca nei territori occupati', *Il Movimento di liberazione in Italia* xxiii/103 (1971), 79–97; and G. Sluga, 'The risiera at San Sabba: Fascism, anti-Fascism, and Italian nationalism', *Journal of Modern Italian Studies* 1 (1996), 401–12.

[138] Fölkel, *La risiera*, 135; S. Zuccotti, *Under his very windows: the Vatican and the Holocaust in Italy*, New Haven 2000, 279. For more on the deportations see M. Coslovich, *I percorsi della sopravvivenza*, Milan 1994.

[139] Reitlinger, *Final solution*, 356–7.

[140] Pupo, *Guerra e dopoguerra*, 41.

[141] Sluga, *The problem of Trieste*, 65. Created in 1941, the Slovene Liberation Front originally included noncommunist members. By 1943 it had aligned with Tito's Yugoslav communist resistance.

cles in the way of Italian and Slav co-operation. They promised to respect minority rights and culture.[142] However, continuing ties between Italian nationalist collaborators and nationalist resisters resulted in an ethno-political muddle. Internecine bickering even broke out between the Italian communists and communists in Trieste over territorial and nationalist issues.[143] Ethnic politics became a tool of the various factions jockeying to position themselves for advantage in the post-war order.

Towards membership of the Yugoslav federation

By the spring of 1945 tensions between the western Allies and Yugoslavia over Trieste were palpable. At San Giusto castle, in the centre of Trieste, Yugoslav partisans who reached the city at the end of April contended that they had arranged for surrender. The Germans held out to surrender to the New Zealanders in the vanguard of the western Allied armies. Geoffrey Cox remembers the Germans simply allowing the New Zealanders to pass through the castle gates 'to the fury of the Yugoslavs'. The partisans then began 'sniping from the surrounding houses at any movement in the Castle, whether made by Germans or New Zealanders', forcing the New Zealanders to take up defensive positions. He suggested that the Germans proposed retrieving their weapons to aid the western Allied troops. While the New Zealanders refused such assistance, Cox's account implied an understanding between the Germans and western Allied troops. He affirmed this by commenting that later in the evening 'the prisoners and the New Zealanders shared a meal of mixed New Zealand and German rations'.[144] His story presaged the shift in attitudes that marked the post-war period. Seething enmities between east and west, Slav and Italian, replaced fear of Germanic domination.

The Yugoslav Liberation Front that assumed power in Trieste on 1 May 1945 pledged to promote Italo-Slovene fraternity, but it did so based on the assumption that the region would become the seventh republic of the communist Yugoslav federation. Latent hatreds, fed by wartime frustrations, exploded into ethnic conflict. Officials declared the Fascists and also the pro-Italian committee for liberation as enemies. The new government participated in anti-Italian violence. Particularly before 15 May revenge killings and extra-legal purges were carried out.[145]

The controversy over the victims of the *foibe* (limestone caves or pits) in the Carso countryside surrounding Trieste gained particular momentum during the spring of 1945. Stories of the *foibe* were grounded in nationalist

---

[142] 'Il patto del 9 dicembre 1944', *Trieste: rivista politica giuliana* (May/June 1955), 11.
[143] Novak, *Trieste, 1941–1954*, 75, 114–15.
[144] Cox, *The race for Trieste*, 187–8.
[145] Sluga, *The problem of Trieste*, 89–90.

propaganda which could be traced back to the period prior to annexation to Italy.[146] New accusations provided compelling grist to the rumour and propaganda mill. Italian supporters would identify hundreds, even thousands, as missing, presumed thrown into the pits. Such tales became the best known and perhaps the most oft-repeated charges of ethnic and nationalist persecution against the communist Yugoslavs.[147]

By 1945 western expectations and assumptions affirmed the supremacy of western political culture and democracy. Prejudice against the Slavs was institutionalised. An Allied government report of late May 1945 noted that Slavs were 'considerably below the cultural and intellectual level of racial Italians'. This inferiority was attributed 'partly' to Italian and Fascist domination of the area and oppression of the Slavs, but the writer assumed that the Slavs would 'probably reap the advantage of superior Italian education'.[148] Members of the Allied forces differentiated between Slavic groups, ranking them according to their political leanings. Cox identified the Chetniks, generically accepted as the remnants of Serbian anti-communist Yugoslav forces and therefore considered western sympathisers, as cutting a distinctly military figure. They 'looked excellent soldiers, tall, marching with disciplined ease'. The partisans meanwhile appeared to him as disorganised and rather frenzied, a rag-tag band 'grown to a national army' that 'marched . . . in a multitudinous variety of uniforms'.[149] Tito's troops were 'Mohammedans with faces as dark as Moors'. The Slavic communist troops were better suited to fraternisation with racial minorities including the Maori New Zealanders. 'From fighters they [the Maoris] turned to diplomats' establishing links with the Slavic population, considered hopelessly foreign.[150]

Inhabitants of the Free Territory

In 1945 a propagandist in Rome suggested that Trieste was 'the most anti-German city of Italy'.[151] In a letter to Joachim Fleischer, editor of the journal *Psychoanalysis*, Umberto Saba went so far as to suggest that his 'fear and horror of Germans made him forget even the little he knew of their

---

[146] C. Cernigoi, *Operazione foibe a Trieste: come si crea una mistificazione storica: dalla propaganda nazifascista attraverso la guerra fredda fino al neoirredentismo*, Udine 1997, 123–4.
[147] The debate over the victims continues to rage. Cernigoi counts only 517 people as missing in the province of Trieste and estimates that, of these, only some forty odd were *infoibiata*. Only forty-two skeletons were found. In Istria, where the accusations of ethnic genocide were even more widespread, just over 200 skeletons were discovered. Those whose remains were identified were of various ethnic backgrounds. Their murders appeared motivated by political or personal vendettas rather than ethnic enmity. Ballinger, *History in exile*, 156–67, traces the threads of this debate.
[148] This is quoted in Sluga, 'Liberating Trieste', 35.
[149] Cox, *The road to Trieste*, 202, 218.
[150] Idem, *The race for Trieste*, 209, 243–4.
[151] Montemuliano, *Venezia Giulia*, 93.

language'.[152] This loathing of Germans and Germanness would fade quickly in the environment of the emerging Cold War. The clash between east and west, understood as a schism between Slav and Italian, would bury memories of the mercurial relationship with the Germanic world.

By 1945 Italian clamour for the 'salvation' of peoples left outside national borders had diminished somewhat from the fever pitch of the era of the First World War. Decades of frustrated Fascist irredentist schemes had sated the Italian taste for acquisition of new territory in the borderland. Considered one of the defeated Axis powers, Italy could not, as it had in the wake of the First World War, claim a moral right to Trieste and disputed territories in the upper Adriatic region. Pro-Italian elements justified Italian claims to lands inhabited by Slavic peoples by reference to the security needs of the west. The Allied administration, predisposed to sympathy for Italians and fear or suspicion of Slavs, saw the maintenance of the ethnic divide between Slavs and Italians as a key to the military and cultural integrity of the west. Even such pragmatic Italian diplomats as Carlo Sforza interpreted the American presence in the Free Territory as support for Italy's position. 'With re-established ties to the mother country, Trieste is in reality, for all practical purposes, Italian by origin and by sentiments as it has always been. In sum – and this should not be forgotten – the city of Trieste, or as it is convenient to say, Zone A, is already beyond discussion', he reasoned.[153]

In March 1946 peace negotiators appointed a commission of experts to examine the Trieste situation. Ethnic considerations were not to be the basis for post-Second World War settlements. The committee was to be guided by the principle of 'balanced minorities' expressed in the Atlantic Charter of 1941. The Yugoslavs put their faith in these articles. Italian territorial claims far exceeded areas with Italian majorities. Although the committee admitted it was difficult to get a precise count of the population, the report it issued in April saw Trieste as overwhelmingly Italian. The suburbs were recorded as Slovene, but with strong Italian minorities. Information contained in the 1921 census formed the basis for the committee's recommendations.[154] There was no recognition that minority populations had been dissatisfied with the findings in 1921.

Migration also influenced ethnic politics, as it had after the First World War. In 1946 the Italian nationalist Camillo de Franceschi, director of the municipal museum, relayed his anxieties regarding migration. He suggested that if the 'exodus' continued at the present rate, it would affect 'if not the total population certainly half'.[155] The Fascists had not engaged in concerted

---

[152] Saba, *Lettere*, 17. He used this to justify his inability to correctly spell the psychoanalyst's name.

[153] C. Sforza, *Cinque anni a palazzo Chigi*, Florence 1952, 407.

[154] J. Martin-Chauffier, *Trieste: libération de la Vénétie Julienne: conférences de Londres et de Paris: le problème de l'internationalisation*, Paris 1947, 67.

[155] C. de Franceschi to Tamaro, 14 Oct. 1946, Tamaro papers.

actions to forcibly transplant minority populations in Venezia Giulia as they had in the northern provinces of Venezia Tridentina. However, Fascist nationalisation policies had promoted Italianness in the contested border-land. After the war, Istrian and Dalmatian Italians regarded Trieste as a safe haven for those fleeing Tito's Yugoslavia. Ethnic Italians who had chosen to migrate to, or stay in, previously Italian borderlands, which had been assigned to the Yugoslav sector after the Second World War, fled for Zone A or the peninsula. While Italian refugees from Zone B were able to settle in Trieste, Slovenes wishing to return to birthplaces in Zone A were not permitted to do so. In 1951 the census reported approximately 24,000 refu-gees from Zone B in the city. An order of 1950 had registered them as perma-nent residents and even allowed them the right to vote.[156]

Italian nationalist factions complained about the treatment of Italians in Zone B. Of particular influence in early 1952 were charges of religious perse-cution levelled by Bishop Santin, known for his outspoken opposition to Fascist racial measures and resistance to Nazi occupation.[157] By painting Yugoslav attacks as not only anti-Italian but anti-Catholic and anti-religious as well, pro-Italian factions played on broader western anti-communist preju-dices and implied that the populations in Zone B merited 'redemption' by the west.

Allied insistence on pro-western agendas encouraged the politicisation of ethno-national antagonisms throughout the nine years of occupation. Alfred Connor Bowman, American commander of the civilian government in Trieste from 1945 to 1947, expressed 'surprise' that 'virtually every murder or bombing, when thoroughly investigated, proved to be motivated by love, hate, greed, jealously or one of the other deadly sins rather than by political considerations'.[158] This flew in the face of his assumption that ethnic rela-tions formed the locus of local conflict. General Terence Airey, his successor as civil commissioner for Zone A, suggested that the minority problem repre-sented 'the primary reason for our presence in Trieste' and that Allied policies should be 'directed towards complete equality for the Slovene population'.[159] However, he saw the population of Trieste as 'undeniably Italian', and emphasised 'family, cultural, and economic ties to the peninsula'.[160]

Even in cases where the western Allies claimed to distance themselves from local, nationalist politics, reluctance to act decisively in defence of minorities led to *de facto* Italian favouritism. The Allied military government insisted that the trade fair held in the city in 1947 was designed to spur economic recovery and that 'after two years of dramatic daily events, . . . the two neighbouring populations [would] find themselves on grounds of moral

---

[156] Novak, *Trieste, 1941–1954*, 407.
[157] Ibid. 379.
[158] Bowman, *Zones*, 52.
[159] Quoted in Sluga, 'Liberating Trieste', 138.
[160] Airey, *Report of the administration*, 5 (1 Oct.–31 Dec. 1948), 2.

parity'. Yugoslavs and Italians would come together 'to sow the seeds of a respectable and industrious co-existence'. Yet they claimed that Trieste was 'in the end Italy'. They insisted that 'anything of a political nature [be] strictly excluded' from the fair.[161] Apolitical events were impossible. Even the language of signs, publicity and decorations became an issue of debate. Some argued for the official use of Italian since it constituted 'the most widely-used and best recognized' language in the city. Others felt that restrictions were unnecessary and claimed that regulating use of language would require too much oversight, inconvenience foreign exhibitors and unnecessarily provoke minority elements.[162] Pro-Italian publicity met with little or no opposition from occupying authorities. Italian newspapers including *Messagero Veneto* and *Voce Libera* and satiric Italian-language magazines including the Triestine *Cittadella* were openly displayed. Slavic or communist publications were banned as seditious.[163]

The western Allies occupying Trieste saw themselves as disinterested arbiters in antagonistic relations between the Italians and Slavs, but they understood the relationship between the two groups in light of their own biases. Lieutenant Colonel Armstrong, an Allied officer, compared the position of Slovenes in the region to that of the Scots in the United Kingdom. He suggested that the Slovenes should concede to Italian culture and adopt Italian as a language as the Scots and Irish had adopted English.[164] In his memoir, Alfred Connor Bowman justified the exclusive use of Italian toponyms in the territory by maintaining that the Italian was easier to pronounce. Italian names were in common use, and Trieste's history could be traced back to Roman roots.[165] Allied reports suggested that in their 'preference for the Italians Allied troops simply express their undoubted preference for the Italians whose standards of living and charm they prefer to Jugoslav standards'.[166] The official tour guide to the city published in 1950 admitted that the population of the city derived from a 'melting pot of races' but contended that pervasive use of the Italian language represented the first stage of an 'irresistible assimilating force'.[167]

Allied administrators blamed pro-Italian bias on local Slavs and communists. The British political adviser William Sullivan claimed that Slavs' 'refusal to collaborate with AMG [Allied military government] and their

---

[161] Mostra di Trieste, *Mostra di Trieste*, 1947, 15–16.

[162] Comitato camerale per la mostra di Trieste, 19 Sept. 1947, CCIA, cat. XXVIII.

[163] Allied military government, industry and utilities division, 8 Nov. 1947 and General regulations for the fiera di Trieste campionaria internazionale, regulation 6; consulta economica camerale, sezione industriale, 9 Oct. 1947; comitato camerale per la mostra di Trieste, 30 Sept. 1947.

[164] Sluga, *The problem of Trieste*, 105–6.

[165] Bowman, *Zones*, 5.

[166] 'Top secret' report from main xiii corps to allied field headquarters (Mediterranean), quoted in Sluga, 'Liberating Trieste,' 35.

[167] Ente per il turismo, *Trieste*, 1.

making constant attacks on the force the main plank of their campaign against the administration' justified the overwhelmingly Italian composition of the Venezia Giulia police force.[168] Sullivan did note that the decision to use the British model for colonial security forces favoured majority participation, but he ignored the ideological motivations for the pro-Italian choice.[169]

The Allied decision to restore Zone A of the Free Territory to the legislative status of 1939 and 1943 put Fascist laws into effect. This signified a tacit acceptance of Fascist politics. Slavs, oppressed by Fascist policies for more than twenty years, had hoped that the Allied military government would offer more equitable arrangements. Denationalisation ordinances remained enforceable. Allied military government policies protected Jews and restored property taken by the Nazis, but they failed to address Fascist expropriations from Slavs.

The reluctance of individuals to associate with Slavic groups played a role in subverting Slavic culture too. Just as members of minority groups were reluctant after the First World War to identify themselves as ethnic non-Italians, so they now hesitated to be associated with Slavic groups viewed with condescension and suspicion by ruling authorities after the Second World War. Very few took advantage of Allied provisions passed in December 1947 that allowed individuals in the Free Territory to restore surnames modified under Fascist policies. The western Allied attitude may not have inspired the confidence of minorities, and the policy did not include specific guarantees against the persecution of those who came forward.[170] However, individual decisions to retain Italianised surnames did not necessarily reflect a fear of the ruling Allied authorities or the undue influence of Italian nationalists. People were probably pragmatic, willing to accept an Italianised identity rather than stand out in opposition to the Italian majority. Italianised names had been in use for more than a decade, a generation had been born and come of age. Most petitioners who came forward to have naming orders rescinded were local Jews, seeking to recover Italianised surnames involuntarily relinquished after 1938.[171]

Silvio Benco claimed in 1952 that 'We old Triestines and our Triestine ancestors and the young generations that we see growing up around us, have never seen our city as anything but an Italian city.'[172] However, he and his political compatriots saw western overtures to Tito and improving relations between Yugoslavia and the west as signals of a weakening Italian position.

[168] This is quoted in Sluga, 'Liberating Trieste', 93.
[169] G. Rosignoli, *Uniformi e distintivi della polizia civile del governo militare alleato Venezia-Giulia* [sic] *1943–1945 e del governo militare alleato territorio libero di Trieste 1947/54*, Castelbolognese 1986, 55.
[170] Parovel, *Identità cancellata*, 30, charges the allies and Italian nationalists with collusion.
[171] PPT (rc). In Zone B Yugoslav authorities required name changes: Novak, *Trieste, 1941–1954*, 413.
[172] Arosio, *Scrittori di frontiera*, 148.

After 1948 changing political alignments and priorities fed Allied frustrations with the inability to reach an agreement over the Free Territory. The break between Tito and Stalin, as well as the increasingly volatile contest between east and west in Asia, prompted the western Allies in Trieste to seek a solution and withdrawal from the upper Adriatic. Local irredentists interpreted waves of ethnic migration from Istria and Zone B as symbolic of Italy's renunciation of the Italian borderlands.[173] Discontent the census of November 1951 was emblematic of nationalist fears. Designed by the Allied authorities in consultation with Slovene parties, the census failed to ask for any information regarding ethnicity. The Allies claimed that this was to avoid upheaval and minimise differences among the populations, but Italian nationalists interpreted the exclusion of ethnic data as an attempt to pander to minorities and as an overture to Yugoslavia. Allied neutrality was certainly spurious from the beginning of the Anglo-American military administration in June 1945, for pro-Italian sympathies were pronounced throughout the nine-year occupation. Italian nationalists were nevertheless unhappy with the *status quo*.

Of particular concern to those who favoured annexation to Italy were changes in the Allied administration and in Allied attitudes, beginning in 1951. In March General Winterton replaced General Airey as civil commissioner. Winterton was a less sympathetic character, who supported Allied disengagement from the local situation and closer relations with Zone B. In July an Italian press campaign complained of restrictions on flying the Italian flag. Disconcerting too was the Yugoslav opening of the border between Zone B and Zone A to Anglo-American troops.[174]

Increased pressure for inter-zone co-operation fuelled Italian nationalists' concerns over the influence of strong indigenous factions favouring independence. In the elections of 1949 and 1952 in Zone A, supporters of independence won the majority of votes in all areas of the Free Territory, excluding the actual city limits of Trieste. Even in the city itself ethnic affiliation could be blurred by political convictions. Some workers, irrespective of their ethnic origins or affiliations, were influenced by socialism and communism and sought independence from Italy. Ethnic Italian industrial workers purportedly sent their children to schools the Allied military government labelled 'Slav' to demonstrate that their commitment to political independ-

---

[173] The debate over the fate of these refugees or exiles fuelled controversies well past the period of the Allied military government and even to the present day: Tito Favaretto and Ettore Greco (eds), *Il confine riscoperto: beni degli esuli, minoranze e cooperazione economica nei rapporti dell'Italia con Slovenia e Croazia*, Milan 1997; Ballinger, *History in exile*. On conflict in the 1990s between Slovenia and Italy over the rights of former Istrians see M. Hametz, 'Friuli-Venezia Giulia and Italian foreign policy: local identity as a centripetal force', *Italian Politics and Society: Review of the Conference Group on Italian Politics and Society* xlix (1998), 63–70.

[174] Novak, *Trieste, 1941–1954*, 363–5, 377. The replacement was the emblem bearing the city's coat of arms.

ence outweighed their sense of ethnic solidarity.[175] Whether for economic, political or ethno-nationalist reasons, large segments of the population of Zone A saw internationalisation as a viable and preferable alternative to annexation by either Italy or Yugoslavia.

Italian citizens once again

The emerging alignments of the Cold War drowned out voices calling for independence or non-alignment. The nine-year western Allied occupation of the city amounted to little more than an ineluctable, albeit contested, march toward reannexation to Italy, and in October 1954 Zone A was joined to Italy. The Italian ethnic orientation of Trieste had been beyond real debate for several years. None the less, the British and American withdrawal and the Italian takeover spurred isolated incidents and protests testifying to continuing bitterness over ethnic and nationalist issues. The ceremony marking the Anglo-American withdrawal and Italian takeover was cancelled. Officially, the British reported that General Winterton's car could not penetrate the crowds to get to the Piazza Unità. However, a rumour spread that the change in plans resulted from an Istrian extremist threat, arising from the assignment of Zone B to Yugoslav control, to assassinate the general. In the largely Slovene suburb of Opicina, a group of over-zealous 'patriots' hanging out Italian flags clashed with local residents. Police quickly broke up the fighting and dispersed the crowd.

The political settlement glossed over ethnic issues that had spurred so much controversy in the Free Territory. Annex II to the Memorandum of October 1954 safeguarded the rights of minority populations and promised free development of cultural, social and educational institutions.[176] It outlined plans for a mixed Yugoslav-Italian committee that would deal with ethnic complaints and problems, but provided no real guarantee for minority freedoms. Geoffrey Harrison, the British negotiator, called the minorities' statute 'a very handsome, substantial facade', which enabled Italians and Yugoslavs to capture domestic support for the settlement. He claimed that negotiators realised from the outset that Annex II 'was not going to be tremendously effective in practice'.[177]

An anecdote in the National Geographic testified to the western powers' lack of concern over their failure to sort out the complexities of ethnic iden-

---

175 Sluga, 'Liberating Trieste', 108.
176 In a secret exchange of letters, the Italian and Yugoslav ambassadors outlined some specific measures to be taken in this regard. Brosio promised the establishment of three Slovene cultural centres in Trieste, two to serve the minority population in the suburbs and one in the city centre to compensate for the burning of the Slovenian Narodni Dom in 1920: Novak, Trieste, 1941–1954, 459.
177 Campbell, Successful negotiation, 51, 162–7.

tity in the borderland. The story, about two brothers, reduced cultural intermingling and ethnic confusion in the upper Adriatic territory to the level of
mere historical curiosity. 'Mr. Starec and Mr. Vecchi are brothers', the author
explained. 'Both names, in English would be the same – Olds. Each man has
been under a different influence. Sometimes it's like trying to separate the
yellow from the white in a scrambled egg.'[178] Gone was the insistence on
bi-polar opposition and allusion to the threat of violence between Slavic and
Italian populations. Trieste remained the 'place of transition' identified by
Slataper more than half a century earlier. If not in the political sphere, in the
cultural arena local life continued to be understood in 'duplicate or
triplicate'.

---

[178] Kane, 'Trieste – side door', 840–9.

5

The Culture of Border and Port

It is the affliction of the two natures – the commercial and the Italian – that collide to cancel out each other. And Trieste cannot suffocate either of the two. It is her double soul. It will kill her. Each thing of commercial necessity is a violation of Italianness. . . . [Trieste] feels the importance of the German and must combat it; it fears the Slavic banks and makes of them clients. A relentless disagreement . . . [generating] the sad compromises useless to placate it: Scipio Slataper, *La Voce*, 25 March 1909[1]

Triestine writer Scipio Slataper, killed in action in the First World War, did not live to see Trieste's annexation to the Italian state. Although he underlined the city's multiplicity, as a 'place of transition', he also saw Trieste as undeniably an Italian city 'in certain aspects, more Italian than other Italian cities because in all frontier lands national identity is not a given, but a sentiment and a choice'.[2] For him, interpretations of the city's past and perceptions of its future incorporated a complicated mixture of traditions, practices, beliefs and local institutions, but these pointed to the predominance of Italy. In short, he saw the city's community culture as Italian.[3]

If Slataper saw the 'sign posts' of his society pointing to Italy, he also recognised an anational preoccupation, sometimes referred to as cosmopolitanness, rooted in the city's economic traditions. Trieste's 'true commercial tradition' produced 'a commercial culture'.[4] This Trieste, whose 'culture was fulfilled in commerce', lacked self-consciousness, Slataper suggested, the key to its 'fairly peaceful life'. When the 'cold crust' of this disinterestedness was disturbed, 'anxious debates' were revealed below.[5] These lay at the heart of Trieste's culture as an Italian border city and a Central European port.

After the Italian takeover in 1918, the economically privileged, less constrained by the particulars of geographical political alignments and less

---

[1] S. Slataper, *Lettere triestine: col seguito di altri scritti vociani di polemica su Trieste*, Trieste 1988, 38–9.
[2] Idem, *Scritti politici*, 134, quoted in Arosio, *Scrittori di frontiera*, 148.
[3] Culture here refers broadly to understandings of Trieste's orientation based on interpretations of the daily life, customs and experiences that contribute to the communal identity of the Adriatic city, rather than to the individual identities of Triestines. 'Culture', as examined in this chapter, is not meant to represent an exhaustive study of the various aspects of the city's 'high' and 'low' culture. Rather, the aspects of community identity under examination are meant to be representative of the broad spectrum of communal associations and elements that help to shape perceptions of the city.
[4] Slataper, *Lettere*, 32.
[5] Idem, *Scritti politici*, 134.

blinded by triumphalism than irredentist professionals and intellectuals, took a leading role in maintaining the city's distinctive culture. Ethno-cultural influences of the Habsburg period remained embedded in civic practices, customs, traditions and habits. Economic links to Central Europe, a history of local irredentism and Italian nationalism, and the political circumstances of the city sandwiched between Italy and Yugoslavia formed the basis for a distinctive cultural perspective of *triestinità*. The 'two natures' Slataper identified before the war – the commercial and the Italian – continued to collide under Italian rule. Nationalists painted various aspects of the city's culture in an Italian light. The customs and traditions of the city were reinterpreted to fit Italian agendas. At the same time, the Italian state continued to emphasise, even exaggerate, Trieste's role as an international port. This sense of internationalism tied Trieste to other cities in a worldwide port community that shared anational ties to the 'open frontier' of the sea, maritime culture, a commitment to the maintenance of maritime port infrastructure and reliance on international commerce and liberal economic structures.[6]

Internationalist commercial orientation meshed nicely with the cosmopolitan attitude characteristic of the Habsburg port. Many looking in on the city interpreted local 'cosmopolitanism' as nothing more than a 'romantic localism' or provincial snobbery.[7] Yet Italian authorities read and interpreted the internationalist, cosmopolitan thread to fit national agendas and to meet national and international expectations of the Central European city in Italy. In many cases political agendas did not affect the city's cultural underpinnings. Enduring cultural influences related to Trieste's 'two natures' facilitated apparent shifts in political or economic orientation. They lay at the core of the city's cultural identity throughout the twentieth century.

The Triestine palate

The shift to Italian sovereignty did not alter the underlying flavours of the city. Throughout the twentieth century the city's cuisine continued to reflect the mixture of Germanic, South Slav and Italian influences on the turn-of-the-century Habsburg city. In Habsburg Trieste the best-known cookbook, Katarina Prato's *The south German kitchen*, featured a conglomeration of local Triestine dishes, 'Italian-inspired' recipes and specialties of German, Magyar or Slavic origin. It had aimed at the wealthy, providing a model of bourgeois Central European lifestyle in its suggestions for food preparation, comportment and table settings. First published in German in 1858, it

---

6   Konvitz, 'The crises', 300.
7   R. Wilson, 'A new cosmopolitanism is in the air: some dialectical twists and turns', in P. Cheah and B. Robbins (eds), *Cosmopolitics: thinking and feeling beyond the nation*, Minneapolis 1998, 352–8, discusses the implications of 'cosmopolitanism' and 'romantic localism'.

appeared in its fourth Italian edition by 1901.[8] After Trieste's annexation Italy, seen as lacking the tradition of a 'high transregional cuisine' due to intense regional variation, quite easily accommodated the south German-inspired culinary tradition.[9]

The effects of the undercurrent of Germanness surfaced in the late 1930s. The adoption of racial measures altered the face of Trieste's public eateries. The turn toward Germany subverted Jewish influences on the community and forced the closing of kosher establishments, including the Ristorante Ebraico that catered for the orthodox Jewish community and emigrants bound for Palestine.[10] At the same time, alliance with the Nazis promoted the city's Central European culinary traditions. In 1942 an eccentric guide to Trieste's drinking establishments listed the Dreher Tavern first among the city's watering holes. Clearly written in sympathy with, if not in support of the Italian wartime alliance with Germany, the guide called the German 'in particular the Munich style' beer hall 'unique of its kind in Italy'. The Italian influence permeated in the 'bright and festive' atmosphere attributed to the '[Italian] inflection'. The food served at the Dreher included a mixture of Italian and Central European dishes –'Friulian ham or Hungarian salami . . . Goulasch or Viennese sausage with mustard. . . . Pecorino cheese or paprika dumplings . . . plates of fish common to Italian use'.[11]

The compatibility of Italian affiliation with 'foreign' influences is upheld in cookbooks and culinary guides featuring Triestine cuisine. Giuseppe Maffioli's Cucina e vini delle Tre Venezie, published in 1972, placed the city firmly within an Italian political framework by emphasising its location in the Three Venices. At the same time, Maffioli highlighted the 'drama' of Trieste, 'joined by nature to foreign territories', with hints of 'a little Austria and a little Yugoslavia'. Emphasis on the cosmopolitan traditions of high cuisine came through ties to the sea, 'a sort of other fatherland, . . . open to their [Triestine] prestige and to their ancient vocation'. 'Ship board cuisine' provided the bases for knowledge of standards of cordon bleu, a distinctively western tradition adopted by those serving on luxury liners that originated in Trieste, as well as an international perspective won through the knowledge of many languages and interactions with many populations.[12]

Mady Fast's discussion of local desserts, published in 1989, also emphasised Trieste's internationalism. Typical dishes demonstrated the city's experience as a 'meeting point of civilisation'. They incorporated the influences of immi-

8 U. Tucci, 'Il manuale cucina di Katharina Prato e Trieste', in M. Cattaruzza (ed.), Trieste, Austria, Italia tra settecento e novecento, Udine 1996, 137, 243–4.
9 A. Appadurai, 'How to make a national cuisine: cookbooks in contemporary India', Comparative Studies in Society and History xxx (1988), 4, mentions Italy's lack of a national cuisine.
10 A. Seri, P. Covre and L. Grassi, Le insegne dell'ospitalità: due secoli di esercizi pubblici a Trieste, Trieste 1988, 44.
11 C. Ermacora, Vino all'ombra: le Tre Venezie, Pordenone 1942, 175.
12 G. Maffioli, Cucina e vini delle Tre Venezia con 638 ricette, Milan 1972, 19–20.

grants from throughout Europe and the Near East who had found fortune and assumed the language and spirit of Italy in Trieste governed by Austria.[13] Emphasis on the Triestine dialect in *Sapori Nostrani*, an exhaustive reference work and recipe collection that appeared in 1993, draws attention to the culture as regionally based and unique. Recipes for artichokes appear under 'a' for the Triestine 'articiochi', rather than the Italian 'carciofi'. Peas, 'piselli' in Italian, are found under 'b' for the Triestine 'bisi'.[14]

The unique palate of Trieste forms an underlying theme in contemporary literature. A description of a local eatery called 'Alla Lanterna' forms a background to the narrative in the epilogue to Carolus Cergoly's *Il complesso dell'imperatore* (The complex of the emperor). 'Alla Laterna was a shack somewhere between an *osmiza* style inn serving a cold buffet and a cantina with relative permanence', suggested Cergoly.[15] Patrons of Alla Laterna could choose 'fried or breaded fish with white or red wine' characteristic of the coastlands and Italy or 'smoked pork sausage with light beer or dark beer from the delicate mixture of hops and malt' reminiscent of the cuisine of interior Danubian lands. His description of offerings to the exclusive clientele at the Caffè alla Stazione was no less international in flavour. Patrons chose coffee prepared in a variety of international styles including Bourbon (French) roast, Turkish style and mocha. Austrian bread was served with 'butter from the Upper Isonzo Valley and wildflower honey from the fields of Carniola'.[16]

Eateries in the city serve the variety of foods emphasised in fiction. The continuing success of the Antica Trattoria Suban, a family-owned restaurant in business since 1865, and currently run by Mario Suban, attests to the living gastronomic traditions and the eclectic palate of Trieste. Established by a cook apprenticed in the Habsburg kitchens at the Miramare, the local residence of the Archduke Maximillan, Suban continues today to prepare 'typical regional foods' including *jota*, a hearty bean- and horseradish-based soup of Slavic origin, strudels characteristic of Germanic *Mitteleuropa* and vegetable dishes akin to those served in the nearby Italian Veneto. The combination and clash of Central European influences is ensconced in the restaurant family's lore. Tales pit Mario Suban's grandmother, who adhered to the Hungarian methods in which she was schooled, against her husband, who preferred Austrian methods in the preparation of pastry. Their lively debates resulted in a fusion of culinary traditions. Neither the political upheavals in the city after annexation to Italy in 1918 nor the social changes related to

[13] M. Fast, *I dolci a Trieste: punto d'incontro di civiltà*, Trieste 1989, 13.

[14] C. Fonda, *Sapori nostrani: manuale e completo della cucina triestina, istriana e isontina*, Trieste 1993, 34–6, 63–5.

[15] Osmizas are seasonal family-run open houses located throughout the Carso in the hills beyond the city of Trieste. Generally, the public is invited, for a modest sum, to partake of a 'cold table' of local meats and cheeses as an accompaniment to new wine produced by the family.

[16] Cergoly, *Il complesso*, 198–9, 299.

urban expansion, especially after the Second World War, altered Suban's underlying commitment to the promotion of local cuisine and its inflection of *Mitteleuropa* in Italy.[17]

Trieste's coffee house culture offers another continuity with Central European traditions. Several of Trieste's famed coffee houses trace their roots to the Habsburg city and Trieste's pre-war role in international coffee markets. Ornate furnishings and architectural adornments evoke bourgeois urban life and ghosts of the city's Habsburg past.[18] The combination of Central European influence and Italian politics is evident in the history of the Caffè degli Specchi (Cafe of Mirrors). Established in 1839, at the heart of the city's commercial district and called a 'thermometer of polite society' by the *Osservatore Triestino*, it catered to a bourgeois clientele. Between 1884 and the end of the Second World War, the establishment transformed itself according to the shifting political winds. Restored in 1918 and modernised in 1933, the café won two Fascist medals for its 'inspired artistic allegory of the Fascist decade'. *Il Piccolo* noted the coffee house's intimate ties 'to the history of long-ago battles for Italianness and those more recent for Fascist passion'.[19]

Cergoly also noted the Central European atmosphere of Trieste's cafés, but he mourned its passing. He reminisced that in 1921 the air in Trieste's coffee houses 'still carrie[d] the tempered smells of Central Europe'. They were still 'wrapped in the market atmosphere all still with the charm and nostalgia of Central European civilization'. Thugs 'with arrogance in their eyes and violence in their hands' shattered this tranquil Central European atmosphere in 1922. Fresh from looting a warehouse at the Old Port, they entered the café shouting 'Long Live Italy!', 'Long Live the King!' and 'Death to the Bootlickers!' Cergoly blamed Fascism for the destruction of the 'supra-nationalism that transcended all borders'.[20] Yet the coffee house culture remained.

In a collection of poems written between 1913 and 1915 Umberto Saba recognised the Caffè Tergeste as a popular meeting place 'conciliating the Italian and the Slav'.[21] The atmosphere in the city was not as benign as his description. In 1915, on the entry of Italy into the First World War, pro-Austrian elements, aided by Austrian police, destroyed several cafés in the city in protest against their hospitality to irredentist intellectuals.[22] The Caffè San Marco, perhaps the most noted among them, re-emerged in 1919.

---

[17] Author's interview with Mario and Federica Suban, Antica Trattoria Suban, Trieste, 14 April 2000. Mario Suban's description of Trieste furnished the title for this chapter.

[18] F. Prose, 'Trieste', *New York Times: The Sophisticated Traveler* [special section], 13 May 2001, 56, begins with a description of the ethereal imperial presence at the Caffè San Marco.

[19] G. Botteri, *Il caffè degli specchi*, Trieste 1985, 5, 30–6.

[20] Cergoly, *Il complesso*, 196–7, 201, 205.

[21] Saba, *Trieste et un poète*, 62.

[22] McCourt, *Years of Bloom*, 246.

It changed hands several times during the Fascist period to emerge from the Second World War relatively intact.[23]

Despite Trieste's history of allegiance to Vienna, the lack of support for the revolutionary elements in 1848 and failure of revolutionary movements to attract a significant following for anti-Habsburg political conspiracy, Italian and Fascist political lore associated the coffee houses with irredentist, pro-Italian conspiracy. Local coffee houses were compared to similar locales across northern Italy. Particularly in Padua and Venice, these establishments had been the meeting grounds of radical anti-Habsburg organisations. A plaque outside the Caffè Tommaseo, around the corner from the historic exchange building, recalls this association. It proclaims the Tommaseo's revolutionary tradition as 'a centre of the national movement that diffused the flame of enthusiasm for Italian liberty' in 1848.[24] While irredentists, particularly intellectuals, no doubt had met and argued in some of Trieste's coffee houses, in others the commercial spirit of the Habsburg city had reigned and continues to reign supreme.

The politics of culture

Scipio Slataper's affirmation of Triestine commitment to Italianness prior to the First World War sprang from a deep uncertainty regarding Italian perceptions on the peninsula. In the wake of that war nationalist leaders concentrated on eliminating the Slavic 'taint' or 'pollution' from local culture. Yet Slavic influences permeated all facets of cultural life. On the one hand, 'exotic' aspects of Triestine culture provided opportunities for the provincial capital to contribute to the nation. On the other hand, they kept Trieste at a distance from Rome.

Even Fascist nationalists intent on describing the city's cultural Italianness found it necessary to nod to the city's 'foreign' political past. An official Fascist guide to the city assured visitors that Trieste was a 'city Italian in language, in customs, and in artistic, literary, and theatrical traditions', underlining that 'throughout the centuries even when politically divided from Italy, [Trieste] always cultivated Italian culture'.[25]

In 1950, during the period of Allied occupation, Ernesto Sospisio, president of Trieste's fair organisation, emphasised the role of Trieste's international ties in affirming the 'utter' Italianness of the city. He painted the city's international economic ambitions as 'reinforcing the natural Italian character of the city' and contended that 'the succession of alternating invasions and migrations, of conquests and defeats, ha[d] never changed, even for a

---

[23] E. Vinci and S. Vinci, 'La storia del Caffè San Marco', in S. Vinci (ed.), *Al Caffè San Marco: storia, arte, e lettere di un caffè triestino*, Trieste 1995, 39–60.
[24] Trampus, *Vie e piazze*, 620.
[25] *Guida di Trieste*, 9.

moment, the will of the city nor changed its spirit, nor suffocated its inner flame. . . . [Italian] national consciousness functioned as the pure source of an inexhaustible spring'.[26]

Churchill's famous characterisation of the iron curtain from 'Stettin in the Baltic to Trieste in the Adriatic' simply codified existing assumptions for many who saw the upper Adriatic area as forming part of the demarcation zone between desirable and civilised Europeans and others. Although Trieste stood at the edge of the divide, the city's leadership, under the guidance of an educated, cosmopolitan bourgeoisie placed the city within the 'civilised' sphere, at least as far as the British and Americans were concerned. Triestines' cultural affiliations with Central Europe were conflated with western-oriented political and economic experiences. The city's port traditions confirmed Trieste's attachment to the west and capitalism. Trieste appeared as 'a normal enough mid-European commercial city'.[27] A description of the city in a tourist pamphlet authorised by the Allied military government affirmed the combination of Italian and Central European characteristics that promoted a western orientation. Features of Trieste were reminiscent of 'the customs of Old Europe', but the 'golden light of the sun' that 'envelop[ed] it from early Spring to late Autumn immediately recall[ed] its Mediterranean character'.[28]

By 1949 Trieste's international ties appeared more as exotic curiosities than as evidence of an ethnic or national threat. An exchange between two soldiers in the 1949 film 'Sleeping Car to Trieste' made this clear. One boarded the train for his new positing in Trieste as the other looked on:

> 'Well pal, I sure wish it was me . . . Trieste or gay Paris. I'll take Trieste. There's more variety.'
> 'Yeah?'
> 'Yeah sure, Serb, Croat, Bulgarian, Austrian, Italian, Turk, and Greek . . .'[29]

For the American soldiers, Trieste's international ties were relegated to the level of cultural curiosity most evident in the variety of 'girls'.

Although the Allied view could be associated with American cultural imperialism or the spread of the 'Marilyn Monroe doctrine', Triestines, like Europeans in other occupied regions, proved eager to accept it. Intent on renouncing associations with Fascism and committed to western economic traditions, they embraced Allied cultural visions that accompanied political and economic aid and 'ran on the psychological track of defending the

---

[26] Fiera di Trieste, *Discorso inaugurale della II fiera campionaria internazionale di Trieste pronunciato il giorno 26 agosto 1950 dal presidente dell'ente dott. ing. Ernesto Sospisio*, Trieste 1950, n.p.

[27] Cox, *The race for Trieste*, 211.

[28] Ente per il turismo, *Trieste*, Trieste 1953, 2.

[29] 'Sleeping car to Trieste', 96 min. videocassette distributed by Evergreen Entertainment, Los Angeles 1997 (video release of feature film Eagle-Lion, Two Cities, UK 1949).

Occident'.[30] Defence of the west was the city's defining role until the end of the Cold War in 1989.

The Italian cityscape

Just as nationalists supported Italian agendas through reinterpretation of natural geographical features and by casting Central European influences in a western light, so nationalist Triestines sought to prove their Italianness by manipulating, deliberately or unwittingly, the urban landscape. The city that Italy inherited in 1918 did not 'look' Italian. The Italian architect Camillo Boito, who visited Trieste in the 1880s, called the city 'a commercial place between Italy and Germany'.[31] By 1918 the architecture and urban style reflected broad European trends, including Neoclassicism, Liberty or Art Nouveau and Eclecticism.

In 1919 a special edition of *Illustrazione Italiana*, dedicated to welcoming the new provinces, reinforced the vision of historic Italian predominance in the Venezia Giulia territory. Descriptions of the port focused primarily on infrastructure and modern equipment, emphasising commercial investment over Austrian inspiration.[32] The rational urban plan and regular streets of the 'Borgo Teresiana' or Theresian city, the downtown centre that included the area surrounding the *bourse* or city stock market and central square, were attributed to the practicality of local commercial interests not to the influence of the monarchy.

Italian city life tended to centre on the square or *piazza*. In post-Risorgimento Italy, these squares typically contained statues of Italian heroes, in particular Victor Emanuele and Garibaldi.[33] The major monument in Trieste's Piazza Unità offered a sharp contrast. The fountain of continents testified to the city's devotion to commerce. Designed by Bergamesco sculptor Giovanni Domenico Mazzoleni in 1751, the romantic baroque monument originally marked the terminus of the centre city aqueduct. It contained figures representing the four continents recognised in the mid-eighteenth century and the animals associated with them. On top of the fountain an allegorical 'Trieste' perched alongside a classical figure of 'commerce' amidst packages and wrapped merchandise.[34] Political squabbles played out on the massive Piazza Unità ringed by commercial and government buildings reflected the mixed Italian and Austrian inheritance.

---

30 R. Wagnleitner, *Coca-colonization and the Cold War: the cultural mission of the United States in Austria after the Second World War*, Chapel Hill 1994, describes the impact of American cultural imperialism in occupied Austria.

31 From C. Boito, *Gite di un artista*, Milan 1884, quoted in Gasparini, *Impressioni*, 105.

32 Benco, 'Trieste', 23–40.

33 Isnenghi, *L'Italia in piazza*, 3–4, 24.

34 L. Loseri, *Guida di Trieste : la città nella storia, nella cultura e nell'arte*, Trieste 1985, 128.

The heart of Italian cultural life centred on the cathedral of San Giusto and the adjacent area on Castle Hill. Built at the behest of Frederick III of Austria in 1470 as part of a defensive network designed to protect against the incursion of the Ottomans, the castle was erected adjacent to the cathedral. The Austrians' reign and the brief period of Venetian rule in the early sixteenth century influenced the castle's architecture, but the edifice was interpreted by those in the city as a symbol of Trieste's autonomy. The cathedral was constructed on the site of a Christian basilica and above a Roman temple. After Italian unification, nationalists saw its survival as evidence of the city's undying attachment to Rome, to Christianity and therefore to Italy. Images of the cathedral and nearby statues figured prominently in the 1919 *Illustrazione Italiana*.[35]

Cathedral Hill became a shrine to local Italianness during the Fascist era. The civic museum of history and art moved to a building on its slope near the cathedral. Opened in 1925, the museum brought together the collections of the local museum of antiquities and the museum of natural history. A nearby stone garden featured artefacts collected by local historian Pietro Kandler in the nineteenth century. In 1929 the road constructed to the summit of the hill was named the Via Capitolina to commemorate the Roman settlement at Trieste and to honour Trieste's links to Rome.[36]

Fascism incorporated the melange of styles in Trieste into a rubric of urban architectural landscape 'infused and dominated' by Italian style or at least Roman tradition and Latin 'grace and pure serene beauty'.[37] Reinterpretation of the architectural influences of impressive temples and churches cast religious structures of various denominations in an Italian architectural vein. Opulent gold mosaics and statues of saints in the prominent Serbian Orthodox church were interpreted as classical rather than religious art. References to Greek heritage, while providing a somewhat mixed metaphor of eastern and western influence, tied the church to a broader history of ancient civilisation and culture linked to the Italian inheritance from ancient Rome.[38]

In 1925 the synagogue, designed by the local architect Ruggero Berlam and constructed between 1906 and 1912, was described as 'based on Syrian models with concessions to western and modern tastes'. Its decoration 'translated from the iconography of Judaism', was hailed as 'one of the important things to see' in the city.[39] In 1926 *La Grande Illustrazione d'Italia* featured the synagogue in a column dedicated to 'national monuments in the New Italy', suggesting, '[T]he rich but sober vision of the interior correspond[ed] well to

[35] Benco, 'Trieste', 23–40.
[36] Trampus, *Vie e piazze*, 123.
[37] 'Architettura', in G. Treccani (ed.), *Enciclopedia italiana*, Rome 1929, lxxii. 77.
[38] *Guida di Trieste*, 54.
[39] Loseri, *Guida di Trieste*, 316, describes the synagogue in these terms. See also G. Peterlin, *Guida di Trieste e dei luoghi più notevoli della Venezia Giulia*, Trieste 1925, 47.

the Asiatic mysticism of the exterior under the clear Italian sky.'[40] The accep-
tance and adaptation of the building's eclecticism was consistent with
Fascism's acceptance and tolerance of diverse architectural styles throughout
Italy in the early 1930s.[41]

Miramare, situated on a promontory overlooking the gulf north of Trieste's
centre was the most prominent reminder of Habsburg reign. Begun in 1856
by the Habsburg Archduke Ferdinand Joseph Maximilian and completed in
1871, four years after his death in Mexico, the castle's architecture reflected
the city's distance from Vienna and the mixture of local tastes. Designed by
local architect Carlo Junker, it was built in a 'Romantic European style'
rather than an identifiable Italian or Germanic style.[42] The Fascists studi-
ously avoided the castle's political affiliation, but took advantage of its
imposing appearance to make it a symbol of local political power. In 1931,
with a nod to its royal traditions, Miramare was transformed into a royal residence for the Duke Amadeo D'Aosta, the Italian monarchy's representative
in Trieste. He lived there until his departure in 1938 to fight in Africa.[43]

Fascist modernists dismissed modest Habsburg structures, including villas
and bourgeois homes constructed over the course of the late eighteenth and
nineteenth centuries, as 'solid and a bit gloomy'. These residences reflected
'the cold and dull style of the time of Metternich'.[44] Vaguely defined western
influences were credited with the design of the city, and urban plans said to
be based upon western styles brought in during the Napoleonic era.[45]

Throughout the 1930s archaeological investigation and restoration work
was bringing to light the city's Roman past. The remains of Roman structures
on the Capitoline Hill were unearthed. Fragments of Roman columns,
marking the site of the Roman marketplace, were reinforced and built up.
Where sections were missing, new cement columns were fashioned to copy
the Roman style.[46] Pre-war archaeological finds received new attention. In
1936 Archaeografo Triestino published a piece on the 'Arco di Riccardo', a
Roman archway uncovered during excavations in 1904.[47] In the early nineteenth century, basing his argument on the semi-circular pattern of the foundations of several houses in the city centre and historical references to the

[40] 'Monumenti nazionali della nuova Italia: il tempio maggiore israelitico di Trieste', La
Grande Illustrazione d'Italia iii (Oct. 1926), 13–16.
[41] On Fascist cultural policy and the 'selective appropriation' of foreign cultures see
R. Ben-Ghiat, Fascist modernities: Italy, 1922–1945, Berkeley 2001, 33–5 and passim.
[42] C. Ulmer and G. D'Affara, The castles of Friuli: history and civilization, Cologne 1999,
16–20.
[43] Apih, Italia fascismo, 337.
[44] Pizzagalli, Per l'italianità, 15.
[45] Guida di Trieste, 9.
[46] A. Ciana, Trieste scomparsa: demolizioni e rinnovameni, 1932–1939, Trieste 1982, photo
xxix [caption].
[47] F. Farolfi, 'L'arco romano detto "di Riccardo" a Trieste', Archeografo Triestino xxi (1936),
135–69.

site as the 'rena vecia' or old arena, local architect Pietro Nobile had identified the location of a Roman arena in the city. Fascist excavations begun at the site in 1937 did indeed uncover the remains of a Roman amphitheatre.

These excavations, together with new building, formed part of a broader plan for Fascist urban renewal, highlighting the civilising and modernising influence of Italian and Latin culture. A new building constructed in the monumental style directly across the street from the ancient Roman arena and at the base of the castle hill, housed the police headquarters, the *Questura*. The building's location highlighted the prominence of the ruins and implied continuing Italian predominance in the region from the Roman period to the Fascist era.[48]

The promotion of urban Italianness in the borderland never constituted as high a priority for Fascist officials as for local nationalists. A dispute over the location of the city's museum in the mid-1930s testified to the divergence of irredentist and official understandings of the cultural role of Trieste. In consultation with Rome, local officials proposed the transfer of the museum of history and art from its new quarters on the slopes of the Capitoline Hill to the San Giusto castle, which had been turned over to the state in 1926 and was being used as a barracks and warehouse. The opposition of Triestine nationalists to the proposed move demonstrated their inability to consider local affairs in the context of national priorities. Attilio Tamaro took up the nationalists' cause. He argued the castle's inappropriateness as a museum site and thundered that Italy must not 'transform old barracks of barbarians into bad museums!' At the same time, in a seemingly contradictory statement, he asserted that castles were residences constructed with 'will and magnificent ambiance' constituting 'museums in themselves'. The proposed renovation of the castle therefore represented an affront to both the city and the nation. How can Trieste be 'a truly Italian city if it doesn't have a good museum and if it does not honour the arts and architecture above all?', Tamaro asked. His arguments echoed the tone of Italian propaganda suggesting that Trieste served as a stepping-stone for the nation toward Central Europe, the Balkans and the Near East. But his statements assumed that the city played a real rather than symbolic role in this expansion. Tamaro's proposal, that the government invest in the building of a Fascist centre and the construction of a museum, as well as his suggestion that the Triestine mayor approach Fascist authorities in Rome with 'intelligent audacity, like all the mayors of the great Italian cities' to win support for the two projects testified to his lack of perspective. Tamaro reasoned that together these buildings would allow Trieste to present itself as a 'cultured and truly Italian city'.[49]

His perspective as a native Triestine and ardent Italian nationalist also

[48] On urban renewal see also G. Contessi, *Umberto Nordio: architettura a Trieste, 1926–1943*, Milan 1981, 71.
[49] Several letters refer to the dispute. The most important include Tamaro to the mayor of Trieste, 5 Dec. 1932, and Tamaro to Sticotti, 30 Nov. 1928, Tamaro papers.

caused Tamaro to exaggerate the implications the museum's transfer to the castle would have on Italy's image abroad. He compared the situation in Trieste to that in Ljubljana and Zagreb. Both of these cities had, in his opinion, 'resolved the problems of cultural institutions very well and suitably'. Tamaro failed to recognise that the importance of Trieste to Italy could in no way approach the position of Croatian Zagreb or Slovenian Ljubljana in Yugoslavia. Rome obviously saw Tamaro's objections as of little concern. By 1936 a part of the restored castle housed the museum's collection of arms.

In the late 1930s Trieste became a convenient site to accentuate Italian links with Germanic culture. For Rome, promotion of ties to an Austrian or German heritage in the northern border provinces including Trent and the South Tyrol, where in some instances ethnic Germans remained in the majority, carried political liabilities. In Trieste, Germanic influence was less pronounced. Austria was not a serious contender for territory. The thrust of the anti-minority campaigns had been against Slavs. The removal of the Fountain of the Four Continents from the Piazza Unità to the lapidary garden at the museum of history and art signalled the renunciation of Trieste's commercial function in favour of its political utility in promoting Italy's *rapprochement* with Germany. The fountain's 'temporary' relocation, ostensibly to make room for the crowds expected in the piazza for Mussolini's first state visit to Trieste since the March on Rome, lasted thirty years. Fascist authorities published tourist information in German which emphasised Austrian and German contributions to the local cityscape, for example the work of Austrian and German architects including Zimmerman, Pertsch and Ferstil.[50]

Trieste's architectural monuments were adapted to fit political exigencies during the Second World War too. The conspicuous opulence and dominant aspect of Miramare, rather than its political heritage, formed the bases for local associations with the property. The Nazi high command found it a suitable residence during the German occupation. After the Second World War the castle was rehabilitated. It maintained its political function as a trapping of power, continuing as the seat of the 'foreign' authority ruling over Trieste. First it housed the Allied commander's headquarters and then the headquarters of the Trieste United States Troops serving in the Allied military government.

While under Allied military control, Trieste was associated with Italian rebuilding and reconstruction efforts. Monies for reconstruction were funnelled through Rome. Trieste's participation in the regional convention for building reconstruction held in Venice in 1946, and in the exhibition for the restoration of monuments and works of art in the Tre Venezie, promoted cultural ties between those in the Free Territory and those on the peninsula.

---

[50] Azienda autonoma, *Das Triest der Touristen*, 1ff.

It reflected the perception that Trieste fell within the Italian architectural idiom.[51]

None the less, the approach of the Allied military government and the local authorities to local landmarks disappointed irredentists. In a letter written in 1946, Attilio Tamaro harped on the importance of the 'hallowed Italian space' of the Capitoline Hill. He reminisced about a meeting prior to 1918 with Attilio Hortis, a fellow nationalist best known as director of the city museum and editor of the local humanities journal, at which they had discussed the 'exalted Italian symbolism' and allegorical significance of a mosaic in the right nave of the cathedral.[52] Authorities in the Free Territory, who co-operated in the conversion of the castle and the courtyard, did not, in their renovations, emphasise the political importance it held for Italian nationalists. Rather, they concentrated on its importance as a meeting place for Triestines. The castle on the hill accommodated a wine cellar restaurant and outdoor entertainment space for film festivals, dances and exhibitions. This use of the space reflected the post-war desire to erase the traces of occupation by German and Nazi forces and to eradicate the memory of the part played by the castle in prolonging the Germans' final stand against Yugoslav and New Zealand forces.

After the return to Italian sovereignty in 1954, civic architecture was seen to emphasise Trieste's role as the 'product of an illuminated culture that developed in Milan and in Vienna'. Commercial influences were credited with the development of the cityscape. The dating of neoclassical local architecture reflected the city's 'casual, however continuous' affiliation with Venetian culture.[53] The compromise between Vienna and Trieste continued to be evident in 'the architecture of the banks built around the Exchange Square'. The 'gigantic Lloyd building facing the Adriatic' on Piazza Unità was described as 'largely of the Viennese neoclassical style if mixed with the tradition of Venetian and Florentine palaces of the sixteenth and seventeenth centuries'.[54] In 1955 Miramare became a state historical museum. Efforts to restore the palace to its Habsburg splendour testified to its continued importance to the local cultural landscape.

Literature and Art

In literature and art, as in architecture, the mixture of cultural influences remained. In the 1880s Roman-born architect Camillo Boito asked, 'Why do

---

[51] Comitato ordinatore del convegno regionale per la ricostruzione edilizia, 19 Aug. 1946, and president of the Mostra, 1 July 1949, CCIA, cat. XXVIII, discuss participation.

[52] Tamaro to Benco, 18 Aug. 1946, Benco papers.

[53] S. Tintori, 'Neoclassicismo e civiltà europea nella Trieste mercantile', *Casabella: rivista internzationale di architettura* ccxix (15 May 1958), 36.

[54] B. Michel, *Banques et banquiers en Autriche au début de XXe siècle*, Paris 1976, quoted in Sapelli, *Trieste italiana*, 27.

I come to this city, dear to Mercury, to write of the fine arts?'[55] In 1910 Silvio Benco lamented the fate of Triestines and their art: 'Given their ambiguous geographical and political position', the Adriatic provinces were 'not a suitable place from which to make the world feel the presence of a great living artist'.[56] Contemporary writers and scholars, including Sandra Arosio, Claudio Magris and Angelo Ara, have labelled Triestines 'writers of the frontier'.[57] Arosio noted Triestine fears that they constituted 'strangers in the fatherland'.[58] In the late 1980s Claudio Magris referred to the 'Habsburg myth' of a golden and secure *Mitteleuropa*, a recurrent allusion in Triestine works.[59] He also portrayed the commercial influences on Trieste as the 'Triestine Mephistopheles', 'a bourgeois and prudent demon'.[60]

After 1918 the survival and development of Italian cultural influences alongside Habsburg cultural traditions set the tone for an ambivalent acceptance of Triestines as cultural figures in Italy. Italo Svevo, perhaps Trieste's most acclaimed writer, exemplified the spirit of the 'frontier' and the mixture of Central European and Italian elements in Triestine literary life. Born Ettore Schmitz in the Adriatic city in 1861, the writer's given name as well as the pen name he chose, Italo Svevo or 'Italus the Swabian', reflected the influence of his mother's ethnic Italian heritage and his father's family's origin in Germany. Svevo achieved fame for his work late in life, only a few years prior to his death in 1928. His fame did not spread from Italy, but rather by way of England and France where James Joyce promoted his works. For most of his life, Svevo lived as a businessman, working first as a bank clerk and then later for his father-in-law's firm. Clearly, he drew inspiration from his commercial experiences. The basis for his in-laws' fortune lay, literally, at the foundation of Triestine commercial interests; it rested on the production and marketing of a specially formulated anti-corrosive paint to protect ship keels.

Nilini, the quintessential businessman in Svevo's *Confessions of Zeno*, embodied the author's views as a member of Trieste's commercial society. Nilini remained convinced that one learned more at the *Bourse* than at the university. He 'spoke of the Bourse as if it were an individual . . . giving people lessons in industry and temperance'. Nilini flattered himself that only 'crafty and capable people could hope to do business' there. To further demonstrate the narrowness of commercial circles, Svevo injected an element of irony into Nilini's discourses on the relationship of politics to

---

55 Boito, *Gite*, quoted in Gasparini, *Impressioni*, 101.
56 Benco referred to the failure of the music world to recognise the talents of composer Antonio Smareglia, who chose to stay in Habsburg Trieste rather than enter the musical world in the Germanic states: quoted in McCourt, *Years of Bloom*, 252.
57 See A. Ara and C. Magris, *Trieste: un identità di frontiera*, Turin 1987, and Arosio, *Scrittori di frontiera*.
58 Arosio, *Scrittori di frontiera*, 148.
59 C. Magris, *Il mito absburgico nella letteratura austriaca moderna*, Turin 1996, 13, 27.
60 Idem, *I luoghi del disincanto*, Trieste 1987, 9.

commercial ventures. His character's excessive concern with social position derived from small successes or failures of personal business ventures. Svevo's portrayal of Nilini testified to the ambiguity of national affiliations in Trieste. The fictitious broker was 'not wholeheartedly Italian, from the fact that he thought Trieste had better remain Austrian'. He also 'adored Germany, and above all the German trains, which arrived with such marvellous punctuality'.[61]

Literary debates regarding Svevo's work reflect the confusion of influences that composed Triestine identity. Questions of whether or not the acclaimed writer ever mastered written Italian testify to the controversy over ethnic influences. Svevo grew up speaking the Triestine dialect and, like many Triestines educated in Vienna, studied German. Scipio Slataper once lamented that '[Svevo's] misfortune was to write in Italian and read German books'. Slataper claimed that Svevo's 'spiritual world [was] . . . more German than Italian'.[62] Defenders of Svevo's Italianness attributed his 'eccentric' use of Italian, peculiar cadence and odd use of idiom to expressive genius, seeing it as a mark of his individual style, reflective of the 'cosmopolitan' nature of life in Trieste. Still others saw his perspective as linked to the 'enigma' of his Jewishness, his conversion to Catholicism and rather cavalier attitude toward organised religion.[63] Whatever the source, Svevo's choice of Italian peppered with foreign grammatical constructions demonstrated the marginality of Triestine literature, developed between Italy and Habsburg Central Europe and in the nationalist and economic cross currents of Europe.

The work of other twentieth-century Triestine writers reflected the borderland mixture as well. Roberto (Bobi) Bazlen, born in Trieste in 1902, was noted as a writer among Triestines, but better known in Italy for his consulting work done for the Einaudi publishing house in Turin. Bazlen wrote some of his major works, including *The captain of long voyages*, in German.[64] Giani Stuparich's writings demonstrated his profound loyalty to Italy while, at the same time, they gave voice to his frustrations with the political realities of annexation. *Colloquy with my brother*, published in 1925 as a memorial to his brother Carlo, who volunteered in the Italian army and was killed in action on Monte Cengio in May 1916, expressed the disillusionment common to many of the post-World War I generation throughout Europe. It also recounted the isolation and discomfort particular to Triestines, who felt that Italy ignored Triestine prominence and underestimated the pull and importance of local 'cosmopolitanness'. It blamed Italy for taking for granted the efforts of local nationalists who had made sacrifices to bring Trieste into the Italian nation.

[61] I. Svevo, *Confessions of Zeno*, trans. B. de Zoete, New York 1989, 336, 339–40.
[62] This is quoted by A. Spaini (ed.), 'Vita culturale a Trieste: le influenze mitteleuropee', RAI Radiotelevisione Italiana centro di produzione, Rome, 15 Nov. 1960 (transcript).
[63] E. Schächter, 'The enigma of Svevo's Jewishness: Trieste and the Jewish cultural tradition', *Italian Studies* i (1995), 34–7.
[64] Bazlen, *Scritti*, 20.

The commitment to commercial interests and the influence of 'foreign' cultural currents of the borderland was also evident in the life of Marcello Dudovich, perhaps Trieste's most noted artist of the interwar period. Dudovich became famous not for his studies of pure art, but as a graphic artist for *La Rinascente*, creating renderings for the commercial fashion world. He spent the bulk of his career in Milan, but was always associated with the Adriatic provinces and his early career in the Habsburg empire. Critics traced the formulation of his pan-European viewpoint and the eclectic mixture of Middle European, Venetian, Italian and Secessionist currents in his work to his childhood in Habsburg Europe. Formative years spent in Trieste accounted for his eccentricities with regard to nationalist affiliation and justified a mercurial, artistic temperament. All was chalked up to his disposition as 'the Triestino', 'above all a European . . . in temperament, character, and spirit'.[65] In a catalogue prepared for a retrospective exhibition of his work, critic Leonardo Borghese felt it necessary to undertake a spirited defence of Dudovich's, and by implication Trieste's, Italianness. He dismissed the artist's Slavic surname as a testament to the humble origins of Dudovich's grandfather, a fisherman in Dalmatia whose name had been 'evidently Slavic or Slavicised'. Borghese attributed the artist's inability to learn any German, despite his years of experience in Munich, to latent nationalism, a commitment to Italianness. The critic justified Dudovich's failure to fight for the Italian cause 'except with his pen' in the First World War on the grounds that he had been mistakenly suspected to be a German agent.[66]

Until the late 1930s intellectual currents associated with Central Europe, particularly an interest in psychoanalysis, pervaded the work of Triestine writers. Psychoanalysis spread across the continent in the first several decades of the twentieth century. Trieste's position in the empire and the relative weakness of the influence of Catholic politics on the commercially oriented and heavily Jewish intellectual circles in Trieste allowed for the early infiltration and spread of ideas from Vienna. The link between Triestine literature and psychoanalytic currents was not a chance one. Leading psychoanalysts, including Edoardo Weiss and Federico Levi, shared the social networks of writers.[67] Psychoanalytic passages permeate Svevo's works. Bobi Bazlen also flirted with the theories of psychoanalysis. Guido Voghera, a medical practi-

[65] R. Curci, *Marcello Dudovich, cartellonista, 1878–1962*, Trieste 1976, 9–16.

[66] M. Dudovich and R. Curci, *Marcello Dudovich, 1878–1962: i 100 bozzetti e manifesti per la rinascente, 18 marzo-20 aprile 1985*, Milan 1985, n.p.

[67] Saba, *Lettere*, and Bazlen, *Scritti*, demonstrate ties to the psychoanalytic circle. Edoardo Weiss, a student of Sigmund Freud, joined the staff of the provincial psychiatric hospital of Trieste in 1918. In 1931 he moved to Rome and the next year founded the Italian psychoanalytical society. In 1939 Weiss emigrated from Rome to the United States, settling in Chicago: Saba, *Lettere*, 92. Federico Levi became one of the editors of the Triestine daily *Il Piccolo*. He fled to Palestine after the passing of the racial laws but returned to Trieste after the Second World War: G. Voghera, *Gli anni della psicanalisi*, Pordenone 1980, 9–15.

tioner, straddled the literary and medical worlds as author of *Il segreto* published under the pen name 'Anonymous Triestine'. Voghera's choice of this alias testified to the psychoanalytic bent of his work. It also captured the Triestines' reluctance to be categorised or to categorise their work in the Italian literary framework.[68]

By the late 1930s the turn back toward Central Europe and alignment with Germany destroyed literary networks in Trieste influenced by psychoanalytic currents now considered degenerate and Jewish. The about-face in Italian foreign policy in the late 1930s exacerbated Triestine writers' sense of marginalisation and disappointment. Alignment with Germany and the weight of the Italian racial laws introduced in 1938 decimated literary circles. Writers who were Jewish or of mixed ancestry abandoned public pursuits. Umberto Saba's poems demonstrate the Jewish poet's contradictory sentiments regarding Italy and Italian nationalism. He decried persecution after 1938 and resented Italy's abandonment of Trieste to the Nazis in 1943. In the end, his devotion to Italy remained. Trieste was 'a lovely city, set between the jagged mountains and the gleaming sea', a city 'married to Italy in song'. '[T]he fascist wretch and the German pig' permitted Nazi occupation.[69] Foreign intervention had despoiled his pristine environment.

After the Second World War, in tones that echoed the words of Slataper three decades earlier, Silvio Benco called the city an 'Italian exemplar'.[70] However, even after Trieste's return to Italy in 1954, cultural production was associated with foreign influence. In 1960 a special segment produced by RAI national radio and television concluded that Triestine writers had 'their true roots buried in a fertile soil [that was] spiritually foreign'.[71]

Alberto Spaini, the Triestine-born editor of *Resto del Carlino*, summed up the trepidation Triestines felt in the post-war cultural world in his *Triestine self portrait* published in 1963. He identified the root of Trieste's distinct and Italian character as the city's defensiveness: 'Representatives of all nations run through [Trieste's] port to enrich themselves and employ their diverse talents; but having arrived there, they are imprisoned by the wall that makes Trieste a city besieged – besieged by a thousand enemies (Austria, Pan-Germanism, the nascent expansion of the Slavs).' The city was forced to 'ferociously defend its Italianness'.[72]

---

[68] Voghera, *Gli anni*, 20–5. For a recent discussion in English of the ambiguities and ambivalences evident in the works of Triestine writers see E. Coda, 'Between borders: the writing of illness in Trieste', unpubl. PhD diss. UCLA 1998, 189–247.

[69] U. Saba, 'I had', in *Umberto Saba: thirty-one poems*, New Rochelle, NY 1978, 43–4.

[70] S. Benco, *La contemplazione del disordine*, quoted in E. Pellegrini, *Trieste dentro Trieste: sessant'anni di storia letteraria triestina attraverso gli scritti di Silvio Benco (1890–1949)*, Florence 1985, 321.

[71] Spaini, 'Vita culturale'.

[72] Idem, *Autoritratto triestino*, excerpted in C. Bo (ed.), *Scrittori triestini del novecento*, Trieste 1991, 956. Spaini, born in Trieste in 1892, studied in Florence, Berlin and Rome.

The academy and local institutions

The defence of Trieste's Italianness began even before annexation to Italy. The predominance of Italian elements in the city council and the bias of Italian intellectuals and professionals permeated cultural institutions and suffused local cultural initiatives. The pattern of development of institutions of higher education in Trieste testified to the struggle of Italian interests. Prior to the First World War, the Superior School of Commerce, founded in 1877 with a bequest from the commercial leader Pasquale Revoltella, was the most noted educational institution in the city. Local attention focused on promotion of the economic role of the city in the Habsburg empire. At the turn of the century, a demand for the establishment of an Italian university in Trieste united the Italian Front in the Vienna parliament, but the initiative received little support outside pro-Italian circles. In the city itself, it did not appear to constitute a high priority. Commercial leaders concentrated on quotidian economic concerns. Assertions of local cosmopolitanism, based on ties to the international commercial traditions of the port, furnished an excuse for the lack of commitment to education in the Italian humanist tradition.

On annexation to Italy, the ascendancy of Italian professionals and the extension of the influence of Rome shifted attention to the model of higher education favoured on the Italian peninsula. In 1924 the School of Commerce was transformed into the University of Economic and Commercial Studies associated with faculties being formed to promote higher education in the humanities.[73] By 1927 the association of humanism with Italian academic traditions and the Fascist desire to 'shine the light of Italian culture and civilization' over lands to the east led to the establishment of the University of Trieste on a hill in the eastern portion of the city.[74] The university became a guardian of Italian interests and a bastion for supporters of the Italian nationalist cause.

Under the guise of academic freedom, the university promoted pro-Italian agendas even through the period of ostensibly neutral Allied military government rule. Italian nationalists representing the institution clashed openly with Allied military officials. The university was the only public institution that dared to fly the Italian flag. In April 1947 Colonel Bowman attempted to replace the university rector, Angelo Cammarata, over the assignment of a master's thesis to prove Italy's uninterrupted sovereignty over the city. Bowman interpreted this politically-charged theme as an unnecessary provocation and a challenge to the legitimacy of the Allied military government, and promptly dismissed Cammarata. Student riots erupted and local intellec-

[73] 'Trieste', in G. Treccani (ed.), *Enciclopedia italiana di scienze, lettere ed arti*, Rome 1937, 334.
[74] See Sluga, *The problem of Trieste*, 55, quoting Morpugo [sic].

tuals decried Allied interference in academic freedom.[75] The outcome of the dispute testified to the strength of the pro-Italian element. Cammarata, exalted as a protector of the sanctity of the university, returned to his post and Bowman was transferred from the Free Territory.

Other public institutions inculcated an Italian spirit. The City Museum of the History of the Fatherland and of Italian Unification housed collections emphasising the private life of the city, in particular records and memorabilia relating to local military exploits undertaken in the name of Italy during the Austrian and the First World War eras.[76] By 1925 the museum included an exhibition hall dedicated to 'the national struggle against Austria and the men who directed it'.[77]

Trieste's maritime museum, founded during the Habsburg period and 'the only one of its kind in Italy', reinforced ideas of Italian cultural attachment through emphasis on maritime culture associated with Italy. At the same time, the museum upheld the importance of the sea and markets abroad as fundamental to the survival of the city. In 1922 the museum of fishing, featuring exhibits of flora and fauna characteristic of the upper Adriatic region, opened its doors. It promoted Trieste's association with the Italian Adriatic and demonstrated the integrated nature of upper Adriatic lands, within and outside Italian borders. While clearly in line with irredentist claims and Fascist imperial visions, the museum also recalled associations with international Habsburg commercial networks.

Local exhibitions in Trieste articulated and disseminated visions of the city's Italianness. After annexation, Italian political commemorations subsumed local festivities. The National Trieste–Trent Society, an organisation founded in 1903 to promote pro-Italian sentiment in provinces remaining outside Italian state borders, sponsored various events 'of a patriotic character'.[78] Annual celebrations dedicated to the city's patron, San Giusto, coincided with festivities marking the anniversary of Italian 'salvation', the landing of Italian troops in November 1918.

Fascist exhibitions in Trieste echoed the national trope. An annual book fair promoted links to Italian culture and language. Mobile libraries, choral societies and local dramatic societies organised under the auspices of the national *Dopolavoro*, the Fascist organisation promoting leisure time activities, emphasised Italian culture in the borderland. Exhibitions took on overtly political themes in support of Italian culture. The Minerva Society, an organisation formed in the early nineteenth century to encourage the study of the Italian history and culture of Trieste, merged with the Triestine Literary Circle in 1931 and together, in 1932, they sponsored a conference on

---

[75] Sluga, 'Liberating Trieste', 145–6.
[76] 'Trieste', in Treccani, *Enciclopedia*, 334.
[77] Bertarelli, *Le Tre Venezie*, 245.
[78] 'Schema d'attività dell'ufficio di Trieste dell'Associazione nazionale Trento-Trieste', n.d., CGCVG (ag), busta 51.

Roman Trieste, mimicking the 1800s Rome celebration held in the capital.[79] In 1933, the Festa dell'Uva (grape festival), under the direction of the local chapter of the *Dopolavoro*, combined the harvest festival with a nostalgic exhibition and celebration of Trieste in the 1300s.[80] The exhibition self-consciously highlighted medieval Trieste, a city associated with autonomy and linked to Venice rather than Vienna.

Small local maritime festivals traditionally sponsored by the Maritime League grew into major events as part of Fascist efforts to mobilise and nationalise the population. In 1926 the Triestine festival commemorated naval battles of the First World War and honoured the 'glorious Italian navy' and 'heroic acts of men'. Major public attractions included fireworks and boat races. By 1927 Triestines dedicated the second Sunday in June to the Festa di Premuda commemorating the famed Italian sinking of the Szent Istvan (San Stefano), counted a First World War naval victory. Festivities focused on commemorations of those fallen at sea.[81] The national exhibition of maritime art, organised by the National League at the grand exhibition hall in Rome from 1926 to 1929, advertised Italy's role in the Mediterranean. Similar events in Trieste highlighted the city's attachment to the sea and role in the Adriatic and Central Europe. Exhibitions of marine art included Triestine and Italian works from the seventeenth century onwards, including oil paintings, watercolours, pastels, lithographs, prints and sculptures to present visions of the sea and affirm Triestine ties to the Italian maritime tradition. By 1931 the Triestine maritime festival was incorporated into the 'Giugno triestino' or Triestine June, a nationally sponsored event including sporting competitions, folklore festivals, lyric opera, fireworks and guided excursions to draw tourists to the area.

Tourist initiatives developed from a popular willingness to support the aims of the regime and also from a desire to dispel notions that the culture of Trieste was inferior to that of the rest of Italy. Two exhibitions held in Rome, the 1932 Exhibition of the Fascist Revolution, celebrating a decade of Fascist rule, and the 1937 Augustan Exhibit of the Roman Spirit, commemorating the 2,000th anniversary of the birth of Augustus, provided the quintessential examples of Fascist diversions. The 1932 Mostra provided the formula to guide the organisation of Fascist political exhibitions throughout Italy, including the Giugno triestino held from 1932 to 1936.[82] Triestines suggested that in each major centre in Italy a festival honoured the region's contribution to the Italian nation. Milan drew attention for technical achievements; Turin for fashion; Florence and Venice for art and culture; and Bari for

---

79 G. Secoli, *Il terzo cinquantennio della 'Minerva', 1910–1960*, Trieste 1965, 26–8.

80 'Oggi festa dell'uva', *Il Piccolo*, 1 Oct. 1933, 5.

81 *Il Piccolo* described the Triestine marine festivals throughout the 1920s and 1930s.

82 M. Stone, 'The politics of cultural production: the exhibition in Fascist Italy', unpubl. PhD diss. Princeton 1990, 227, 319.

commerce with the east.[83] The development of maritime exhibitions reflected the Fascist association of Trieste with the national port culture and the sea.[84]

The Triestine chamber of commerce's monthly review suggested that the Giugno triestino demonstrated for all Italians that Trieste 'at the head of the Adriatic, a few kilometres from the border, pulsed with strong Italian life'.[85] Trieste's cultural contributions related to the city's role as a guardian of Italianness on the margins of the nation. The city showed its allegiance through 'the economic and moral power of generations wishing to develop a great national Italian entity on the historical frontiers of Italy' and in the presentation of 'itself as a rich, modern city with the decorative palaces, model schools, quays, wharfs, piers, and commercial warehouses of a great world port'.[86] The local paper reported the success of Trieste's effort, publishing a comment purportedly made by Mussolini calling the maritime exhibition 'the highest expression of seafaring Trieste and the pride of the nation'.[87]

The intermingling of cultural Italianness and internationally oriented economic aspirations in exhibitions continued even under the Allied military government after the Second World War. Allied authorities did not officially support local Italian nationalist campaigns but, motivated by the desire to combat communism, they tacitly approved pro-Italian efforts. Nourished by Italian sympathies in favour of the 'redemption' of Trieste and the apparent favourable disposition of Allied officials in the city, the National League, the most prominent irredentist organisation of the Habsburg era, re-entered the scene. Although the league's programme, to support the cultural and social promotion of Italian language, tradition and culture, appeared benign, the association actually functioned as a rallying point for pro-Italian forces across the political spectrum. A cultural exhibition held early in 1948, which featured Italian books and printing, set the tone for printed materials. The 'cultural' designation of the display allowed organisers to proceed with a thinly-veiled Italian propaganda effort to reinforce the primacy of Italian language and literature.

Business concerns participated in pro-Italian political displays. Lloyd Triestino donated a tricolour flag, dating from 1848 and bearing the stamp of the firm, to a 1949 National League exhibition. Italian nationalists paraded the banner through the streets. The exhibition included mementoes of the Risorgimento era and irredentist struggles of the late nineteenth century; the First World War and annexation; Italian entry into Trieste in 1918; and the

---

[83] 'La mostra di Trieste marinara', *Il Piccolo*, 28 June 1934, 4.

[84] On the maritime exhibitions held during the Fascist period in Trieste see M. Hametz, 'Excellent citizens, perfect Italians: the Triestines and the fairs, 1920–1954', unpubl. PhD diss. Brandeis 1995, 118–213.

[85] 'Il Giugno triestino', *RMCT* v/6 (1932), 245.

[86] 'Il bilancio d'un initiativa: l'esperimento del "giugno" ', ibid. iv/7 (1931), 14.

[87] 'Il Duce riceve gli esponenti del giugno triestino e fissa le direttive per la III° mostra del mare', *Il Piccolo*, 1 Feb. 1935, 3.

birth of a 'new Trieste' in Italy. Letters from Garibaldi to the Triestines, photographs of Italian buildings dating from Roman times and pictures of victims of local ethnic strife, testified to the sacrifices of Italians in the region and highlighted 'Triestine struggles against powerful empires of the past'. They provided a non-too-subtle encouragement to Triestines engaged in the struggle against the 'foreign domination' of Allied troops. A display of documents in an exhibition of 1948 entitled 'Trieste Italiana: yesterday, today, and tomorrow' was particularly provocative. It included a room full of photographs affirming the 'unmistakable Latin features of the city and of its Istrian provinces from Duino to Pola'. This territory was included in the disputed lands of the Free Territory and much of it, including nearly the entire coast of Istria, was in Zone B, in Yugoslav hands.

Exhibits targeted Yugoslavia as an oppressor nation, emphasising the Latin heritage of Istria. One collection of photographs and documents entitled 'The Nightmare of the Forty Days' presented images of refugees, of victims in the streets and *foibes*, and of documents calling for the retreat of the Slav forces on 12 June 1945.[88] This material was hardly in keeping with the spirit of maintaining a neutral Free Territory. The occupation government justified allowing the National League to proceed with the 1949 exhibition by suggesting that it was consistent with the Allied commitment to freedom of speech and political action.

Allied allowances for nationalist Italian demonstrations stood in stark contrast to strict controls exercised over Slavic-influenced events. Allied officials considered Slavic and communist groups as participants in a concerted plan to undermine western-style government. At the trade fair held in Trieste in 1947, fair committee members rebuffed Yugoslav requests for a large exhibition space. Authorities reprimanded a Yugoslav industrial firm whose company logo bore a red hammer. The Allied military government supported fair committee members' insistence that the sign be removed or modified to properly demonstrate the 'purely economic character of the exhibit'.[89]

By 1954, despite nine years of Allied occupation and supposed neutrality, the situation for Slavs had not improved. The Slavic press charged that the Triestine fair organisation had failed to distribute flyers printed in Slovenian in an effort 'to impede trade between the hinterlands and overseas'. The Slavic paper *Primorski Dnevik* blamed political machinations in Rome for the lack of international participation in the fair. The only foreign exhibitors present in 1954 hailed from Austria, Yugoslavia and other small countries.

[88] *Mostra documentaria Trieste italiana: ieri, oggi, sempre della Lega Nazionale* (Galleria Trieste, 1949), Trieste 1949, 3ff.

[89] Allied military government, industry and utilities division, 8 Nov. 1947, and general regulations for the fiera di Trieste campionaria internazionale, regulation 6; consulta economica camerale, sezione industriale, 9 Oct. 1947; comitato camerale per la mostra di Trieste, 30 Sept. 1947, CCIA, cat. XXVIII.

An extensive display by RAI Italian television occupied centre stage at the international pavilion. Its prominence testified to the Allied military government's willingness to overlook links to Italy, but its location did not necessarily reflect an Allied effort to promote Italian presence. More likely, as non-Yugoslavs who opposed Trieste's fair suggested, members of the fair committee and Allied officials encouraged RAI's presence to mask the pointed failure of local recovery efforts and attempts to lure international traders back to the city.

In addition to economically oriented initiatives, the Allied military officials allowed festivals to continue that appeared to have deep roots but, in fact, had been invented or at least enhanced by the Fascists. The local version of the Festa dell'Uva purportedly celebrated local viticulture. In fact it had developed under the direction of the provincial chapter of the *Dopolavoro* in the early 1930s. Parades marking the occasion in Trieste in the 1950s included floats bearing Triestines in Roman costume, promoting mythical ties to Roman traditions.[90]

The construction of Triestine history

Even before Trieste was annexed to Italy, irredentist intellectuals used Trieste's history and supposed establishment by ancient Rome as a basis for their political platform. Through participation in local institutions, including the Minerva Society, they promoted the irredentist view. Such institutions attempted to monopolise public intellectual discourse and to muzzle those proposing visions inconsistent with the Italian national programme. In the early twentieth century, the works of the historian Pietro Kandler came under fire for his emphasis on the city's mission in Central Europe. Although his was largely an economic interpretation, and his archaeological work had done much to uncover Italian influence in the region, he was denounced as a Germanophile and blamed for influencing later 'anti-Italian' positions.

Angelo Vivante, who followed in Kandler's footsteps with the publication of his *Irredentismo Adriatico* in 1912, became a pariah in academic circles.[91] In his book, Vivante, a committed socialist of a well-known Triestine bourgeois family, rejected the notion that Trieste's future lay in annexation to Italy. He contended that irredentism was an outgrowth of cultural opposition to the Habsburg state and not an intrinsic trait of the Triestine populace.[92] He traced the foundations of Slav-Italian opposition to the Italian Risorgimento

---

[90] P. Spirito, *Trieste a stelle e strisce*, Trieste 1995, photograph.
[91] C. Daneo, *Il fantasma di Angelo Vivante*, Udine1988, assesses Vivante's life, writings and impact.
[92] A. Millo, *Storia di una borghesia: la famiglia Vivante a Trieste dall'emporio alla guerra mondiale*, Gorizia 1998, 215ff.

and the rise of irredentist ambitions.[93] Although Vivante committed suicide in 1915, he would be vilified for decades by irredentist historians who cast their nationalist histories in response to his claims in *Irredentismo Adriatico*.

After 1918, and during the Fascist period in particular, scholars systematically rewrote the history of the relationship between Trieste and neighbouring lands. Two local periodicals aimed at an intellectual audience *La Porta Orientale* and *Archaeografo Triestino* published articles reinforcing regional ties to Italy. *La Porta Orientale*, a cultural and literary forum, by its name confirmed Trieste's role within the Italian nation, as a guardian of Italianness along the border. The periodical featured scholarly articles, poetry and short stories supporting Fascist Italianisation and modernisation campaigns. Denunciations of Austria and Germanic culture stood alongside poetry glorifying the new cranes erected to facilitate movement of goods in the port.[94] *Archaeografo Triestino*, founded by the Minerva Society, provided a forum for pro-Italian scholarship in the humanities. Edited by such nationalists as Attilio Hortis, it provided an outlet for historians like Attilio Tamaro.

Tamaro was in the vanguard of nationalist historians. In conscious attempts to 'continue to write the history of the fatherland and to rectify errors of the Austrianized history', Tamaro published selected vignettes from the city's history to support notions that Trieste had remained committed to Italy or had been deliberately harmed by Austria.[95] His description of Trieste's role in the sixteenth- and early seventeenth-century conflict between the Habsburgs and Venice over a salt monopoly contained a typical distortion. Tamaro painted the Habsburgs as villains; their self-interest and greed forced the Venetians, who sought peacefully to expand their commercial markets along 'natural routes', to blockade Trieste. The blockade ended with the abolition of the salt monopoly in 1610, but contributed to war between Austria and Venice in 1615.[96] This allusion to Habsburg interference with the city's trade and the natural Italian interest in the Adriatic provided a timeless moral.

Tamaro's account of Trieste's request for protection from Leopold of Austria in 1382 provided a nationalist reassessment of the city's affiliation to Austria. Pietro Kandler had presented the dedication to Austria as an act of defiance against Venice: Trieste had sought Austrian protection to ward off Venetian domination. The Habsburgs had developed Trieste along lines suggested by the city's medieval political and economic orientation. Tamaro aggressively challenged Kandler's view. He cast the incorporation into Austrian lands as the result of Leopold's aggression and desire to usurp local powers. His reinterpretation helped to justify Trieste's detachment from

---

[93] Sluga, *The problem of Trieste*, 22.
[94] E. Chersi, 'Irredentismo e fascismo', *La Porta Orientale* iii/iv (1939), 94–9.
[95] Tamaro to G. Pitacco, 5 Dec. 1932, Tamaro papers.
[96] A. Tamaro, 'La "Saliera" del 1609', *Archaeografo Triestino* xvii (1932), 241–72.

Vienna and reorientation toward Rome.[97] The influence of Tamaro and his cohorts continued after the Second World War. With its fanatical defence of Italianness Tamaro's *Trieste: history of one city and one faith*, published in 1946, set the tone for post-Second World War historical literature.[98]

The nationalist attack on 'renegade' historian Fabio Cusin after the Second World War was comparable to the denunciation of Vivante prior to the First World War. Cusin's irreverent history of Trieste, *Venti secoli di bora*, aimed to debunk nationalist myths surrounding the development of Trieste. Although his account ended at about 1600 with what Cusin portrayed as the last Venetian attempt at dominance over the region, the anti-Italian implications of his text and the accompanying caricatures were clear. For example, the irony of his description of Roman settlement in the region in a chapter entitled 'How Rome succeeded in sticking its nose in among us' was not lost on locals promoting Italian nationalist interests. In a sarcastic tone, he linked disdain for the unbridled influence of commercial interests in Triestine civic life to political folly associated with nationalist aspirations.[99] The publication of the text, combined with his sometimes caustic demeanour and personal rivalries with other scholars whose work reflected the pro-Italian political tenor of the academy, cost Cusin his academic post.[100]

Throughout the period from 1918 to 1954, the 'invented traditions' of Trieste combined urban Italianness with what might be termed Central European cosmopolitanness and spiritual affinities related to the international orientation of the Habsburg port.[101] Mario Suban of the Trattoria Suban summed up the cultural enigma presented by Trieste in his description of the thin pancake-like delicacies typical of the Adriatic city. 'Palacinche are palacinche. They are not crepes nor are they English pancakes or omelettes'.[102] Palacinche, made from a mixture of eggs, flour, butter, milk and salt, and served either in a savoury fashion filled with meat or as sweets filled with jam or chocolate, are 'palaziche' for the Triestines, 'palatschinke' for the Austrians, 'palacinka' for the Croatians, 'palacsinta' for the Hungarians and 'placinta' for the Romanians.[103] At the same time, they can be associated with Latin traditions. The word 'palacinca' originated with the Latin 'placentula', which in the third century AD referred to their mode of preparation.[104] The palacinche of the twentieth century, however, hardly resemble those of centuries past nor could they be considered purely Italian. Like the Triestines, these delicacies incorporated influences of a Central Europe that transcended the borders of twentieth-century Europe.

---

97 B. Lonza, *La dedicazione di Trieste all'Austria*, Trieste 1973, 63–72.

98 A. Tamaro, *Trieste: storia di una città e di una fede*, Milan 1946.

99 Cusin, *Venti secoli*, 49–54, 201.

100 Sluga, *The problem of Trieste*, 158–60, offers a sympathetic portrait of Cusin's struggles.

101 Hobsbawm, 'Introduction', 2, on the construction of traditions.

102 Author's interview with Mario and Federica Suban, 14 Apr. 2000.

103 Fast, *I dolci*, 92–3.

104 Fonda, *Sapori nostrani*, 377.

Conclusion and Epilogue

For Italy, Trieste continues to be the 'great unknown'. If someone shows himself to have an ephemeral curiosity, it is to ask (without malice, only out of ignorance) 'What is the language they speak there – German or Slovenian?' The Triestines who have contributed writers and poets of great fame to Italian culture – it is enough to cite Italo Svevo, Umberto Saba, Scipio Slataper, Giani and Carlo Stuparich, Silvio Benco – feel betrayed and offended. Having dreamed of the Italy of Dante, of Leonardo, of Tician, of Benedetto Croce, with the first annexation they found themselves in Italy of the Fascist squads, with the second they had to recognise that for Italy, they represented only an encumbrance.[1]

Prior to the First World War, Angelo Vivante suggested that Habsburg Trieste was a 'ring of conjunction of divergent ethnic and economic currents'.[2] After 1918 a tide of loyalty to the Italian state and association with Italianness swept the city with the extension of Rome's control to the new borderland. Although nationalists portrayed Trieste's annexation to Italy as the redemption of Italian patrimony, absorption of the city into the state framework did not depend on Triestine acceptance of and adherence to a standard of Italianness set in Rome. Rather, it relied on Triestines' readiness and ability to interpret the needs of Italy, to compromise with national agendas and to balance local desires with Italian expectations. Eddies of the divergent ethnic and economic currents persisted. They formed the basis of the Triestine struggle to fit into the Italian national framework and, at the same time, provided a meeting point for local Triestine and broader Italian interests.

Trieste was an expensive acquisition for Italy. By the end of the First World War, developments in technology, finance and communication had decreased the importance of ports as centres of commerce worldwide. Trieste's markets were destroyed by changes in the system of global economic exchange, the dislocations of the First World War and the dictates of the Peace of Paris. Italy had no need for an additional outlet on the Adriatic Sea; Trieste could not compete effectively with Italian ports for traffic headed for the peninsula, and it could be easily bypassed on international routes. Without the special privileges afforded by the Habsburg empire, the port fell into decline. The port and its facilities were 'an encumbrance' from the time of annexation, but Italy had not hoped for an economic payoff.

The political significance of the cosmopolitan Habsburg maritime capital

---

1   M. Cecovini, 'Trieste, questa sconosciuta, nelle vicende della frontiera orientale d'Italia', in *Marginalités*, 22.
2   Vivante, *Irredentismo*, 259.

and its economic ties and reputation attracted Rome. The overtones of Habsburg Trieste's ethnic Italianness piqued Rome's interest and justified the extension of Italian sovereignty over the city. But, it was Rome's foreign policy ambition that lay at the foundation of calls for control of the city. Through the annexation of Trieste, Rome hoped to extend Italy's involvement in Danubian and Balkan affairs and expand Italy's power and influence in Europe. After the Second World War, the legacy of Fascism and the sharp divide between eastern and western Europe curtailed Trieste's effectiveness in supporting Rome's ambitions for Italian expansion to the north and east, but the city's situation at the western fringe of the iron curtain and on the border with Yugoslavia made it useful as a symbol of western resolve in the Cold War struggle for mastery of Europe. In Italy, over the course of the four decades following annexation, the thriving Habsburg commercial centre was forgotten. In its stead, the Italian border city of Trieste was born.

Accounts of Trieste's fate in the twentieth century generally remember best the border city separating the Italian and Slavic (read western and eastern) worlds. Ethnic and nationalist associations emerge as the determining factor in Triestine self-definition and association with the Italian state. Literature discussing the history of the city echoes with the triumphal air of the victory of Italy over Yugoslavia, or in the broader context of west over east. Italy, even under Fascism, played the role of defender of the civilised west against the barbaric, uncivilised, communist or socialist Slavs. 'Successful negotiation' of the post-Second World War crisis over the Free Territory of Trieste emerged as a case study of western skill in mediation and conflict resolution.[3]

Conventional wisdom sees Italy and Italians as the winners and Yugoslavia and Slavs as the losers in competing claims to Trieste. Yet Slavs too find their champions. Sympathetic accounts temper the picture of Yugoslavia as the host of communist villains. Slavs appear as 'under privileged' victims, misunderstood champions of freedom, heroes of the Second World War or persecuted members of minority communities trapped within 'illegitimate' Italian borders. Forgotten entirely is the Germanic influence on the city, lost with the disappearance of Central Europe and the rush to explain bi-polar post-Second World War arrangements emerging with the Cold War.

Emphasis on ethnic identity as a determining factor and on Trieste as a bulwark or sentry guarding western interests ignored the continuing influence of overlapping associations. No doubt after 1918 Trieste and Venezia Giulia became 'the proving grounds for the worst sort of political nationalism'.[4] Ethno-nationalist tensions affected community life, but nationalist politicians intent on achieving irredentist goals and international negotiators bent on using principles of ethnic self-determination to resolve territorial disputes exaggerated their importance. The position of Trieste in the

[3] See Campbell, *Successful negotiation*.
[4] Contessi, *Umberto Nordio*, 11.

169

Habsburg empire, the circumstances of annexation to Italy in 1918, introduction into the Liberal Italian state and the experience of Fascism provide necessary context for analysing the fate of the region. Champions of Trieste's Central European commercial orientation upheld cultural, political and social influences reflective of the cosmopolitan attitude and customs of the Habsburg port throughout the period of adjustment to Italian rule. Trieste continued to function, at least in Italian and local perceptions, as a bridge city, a gateway or a doorway to the east.

Emphasis on the continuing importance of Trieste's economic heritage after political ties to Vienna were severed, through the Fascist *ventennio* (twenty years), and even into the period in which 'east' and 'west' were most clearly at loggerheads, opens up the possibility for a reassessment of international involvement in the lands at the head of the Adriatic. It helps to explain the mercurial nature of relations between ethnic groups in the region by exposing links between economic and political factors and ethnic identity and state affiliation. If the peace after the First World War eliminated the Habsburg political entity and the peace after the Second World War eradicated the structures and networks that had framed nineteenth-century Habsburg Central Europe, tinges of 'foreignness' remained, influencing national and international perceptions of Trieste and Triestines. Ties to lands outside of Italy did not pose obstacles to integration into Italy. They were not simply harmless and overlooked vestiges of the Habsburg past. They formed the bases, or at least the perceived foundations, for Italian involvement with Trieste and intervention in Danubian and Balkan Europe.

Settlement of the territorial dispute in 1954 arose less as a result of brilliant mediation than in response to the changed circumstances of Trieste in the international arena. In February 1947 the internationalisation of Trieste was an unsatisfactory compromise foisted upon Italy and Yugoslavia by Allied authorities representing the four major victorious states, Great Britain, France, the United States and the Soviet Union, who were eager to avoid direct confrontation in the area. After 1948 Tito's split from the Stalinist Soviet Union became clear, and Yugoslavia occupied the peculiar position of a communist country outside the Soviet orbit. In addition, the attentions of Cold War superpowers shifted away from Europe to emerging hot spots in Asia, eliminating Trieste's usefulness as a pawn in the Cold War game. In Trieste, ethno-nationalist tensions were not eliminated but the international security threat had subsided. Feuds over territory and minority rights were relegated to the level of local disputes. By 1954 the Memorandum of Understanding afforded welcome relief for Allied authorities seeking an excuse for disengagement. Triestines living in the once prominent international port found themselves inhabiting an Italian border city with an unstable and complicated relationship to Rome.

The avowed Italian nationalist and novelist Pier Antonio Quarantotti Gambini noted the exuberance and gaiety of Trieste at the return to Italian sovereignty. But, he warned, the city was 'serious, bitter, and troubled below.

. . . Trieste knows that something quite difficult (much more difficult than Rome believed) . . . begins right now'.[5] His admonition referred specifically to the separation of Istria and the eastern hinterlands from the city of Trieste and Italy, but it captured well the mood of uncertainty and insecurity aroused by recurrent redrawing of the eastern border. From their position on the geographic periphery of Italy, Triestines realised that national identification entailed the creation and articulation of a local identity that fitted within the skeletal national framework.[6] At the same time, the city's 'foreignness' and 'cosmopolitanness' were its fibre.

The 1954 Memorandum of Understanding proved to be the penultimate chapter in the resolution of the conflict between Yugoslavia and Italy over lands in the upper Adriatic region. In 1974 disagreement erupted over Yugoslavia's placing of new border markers identifying the former line between Zone A and Zone B of the Free Territory as the edge of the 'Slovenian Republic of the Yugoslav State'. An angry note from Rome dated 11 March objected to Yugoslavia's 'extension of national sovereignty' over areas still under contention.[7] The nasty diplomatic exchange that ensued threatened to shatter the twenty-year 'temporary' peace. But, by the 1970s, the dispute was lack-lustre beyond Italian and Yugoslav diplomatic circles. A *New York Times* editorial blasted both the Yugoslav and Italian governments for fomenting dissension for 'an artificial reinforcement of unity among Yugoslavia's diverse republics or a temporary bolstering of Italy's shaky-center-left coalition government'.[8] It predicted that 'practical relations [were] likely to remain unchanged', and later on reported that, despite the tension, Yugoslavs continued to flood to Trieste to shop, spending 'up to $1–million dollars in Trieste every week'.[9]

In October 1975, after a year of diplomatic squabbling, representatives of Yugoslavia and Italy initialed the Osimo Accords, by which the parties accepted the 1954 provisional agreement as the final settlement of the border question. Osimo confirmed the frontier lines drawn by the Memorandum of Understanding and officially replaced zonal boundaries with national borders. Outstanding cultural and economic disputes were acknowledged, and both parties pledged co-operation on issues affecting the border area. Inhabitants of the region gained citizenship of the country in which they

[5] P. A. Quarantotti Gambini, 'Il cuore di Trieste', in *Primavera*, 348–9. The author, of Istrian origin, is best known for this passionately anti-Slav account of the 'forty days' in May and June 1945.

[6] A. Lyttelton, 'Shifting identities: nation, region, city', in Levy, *Italian regionalism*, 45, describes the national framework as skeletal.

[7] 'Yugoslavs and Italians rekindle Trieste dispute', *New York Times*, 27 Mar. 1974, 2.

[8] 'Senseless quarrel', ibid. 31 Mar. 1974, 16.

[9] 'Yugoslavs and Italians rekindle Trieste dispute', ibid. 27 Mar. 1974, 2, and 'Trieste, caught in old dispute sees Suez boom ahead', ibid. 7 Apr. 1974, 18.

resided upon enactment of the accord. Ceremonies in Belgrade and Ancona on 10 November 1975 affirmed mutual acceptance of the agreement.[10]

As the iron curtain lifted in the late 1980s and early 1990s, Trieste's position in the borderland and links to and affinities with *Mitteleuropa* took on new significance. Overlapping associations with Italianness, Habsburg Central Europeanness and Slavic identification held potential, but they also posed liabilities in the city no longer a dead end at the edge of the western Europe, but at the 'beginning of Europe'.[11] This vision of Trieste as a conduit concurs with much current scholarship focusing on the ineluctable trend toward globalisation, a world made smaller by economic interdependence and political integration spurred by technological advances in communication and transportation. However, despite the impact of technological advances that have changed the contours of relations between states and speeded up the pace of interactions, recent changes are not the first to have altered political relations, nor are interdependence and integration entirely new phenomena in Europe.

A pamphlet written in 1987 to commemorate the renovation and restoration of the first-floor coffee house at Trieste's Piazza Tommaseo 4 testified to an emerging spirit of co-operation between Slavs and Italians. This, whether real or imagined, was traced back to joint action against Habsburg domination. The renovation project formed part of the Assicurazione Generali's attempts to 'restore many Triestine public buildings to the ordered and mysterious beauty of the flourishing bourgeois city of an earlier time'. It honoured the memory of Nicolò Tommaseo who 'with the addition of an 'm' and an 'e' to his name Tomaso' was transformed to 'a great patriot of the Italian Risorgimento'. Tommaseo was lauded too as an 'Italo-Slav and a champion of the reawakening of the Slavic peoples'.[12]

The altered political circumstances prompted by the birth of independent Slovenia and Croatia and the politics of expansion of the European Union formed a countercurrent to this new spirit of co-operation. Increased possibilities for cross-border co-operation sparked conservative reaction, exacerbating nationalist, ethnic-based tensions between Italians and Slavs.[13] Italian press campaigns of 1992 and 1995 stirred anti-Slav sentiment with articles renewing accusations of ethnic violence that were linked to memories of the

---

[10] Bowman, *Zones*, 155. All parties to the 1947 treaty should have been consulted in 1975, but Yugoslavia and Italy were the only interested parties, so the settlement between them was regarded as permanent in nature. The break-up of Yugoslavia in 1991 did not affect the placement of the eastern boundary of Italy.

[11] T. Kezich, 'L'Europa comincia qui: Trieste, città del passato irrepetibile, ora deve inventare il suo futuro', *Bell'Italia* iii/22 (1988), 99–107.

[12] Magris, *I luoghi*, 8–12.

[13] E. Giuricin and L. Giuricin, 'La communità italiana in Croazia e Slovenia: il percorso storico, la situazione, le prospettive di cooperazione', and E. Greco, 'L'evoluzione delle relazioni politiche dell'Italia con la Slovenia e la Croazia dopo la dissoluzione della Jugoslavia', in Favaretto and Greco, *Il confine*, 107, 43–9.

foibe victims in the Carso following the Second World War. In the border hamlet of Bassovizza, a memorial site was erected in the victims' memory.[14] Scholars, spurred by recent debates, have begun to examine these incidents and their memory anew.[15]

In 1995 and 1996 scholarly debate spilled over into the public sphere. Italy sparred with Slovenia over issues of minority treatment. In July 1995 the Slovene foreign minister, Zoran Thaler, raised the spectre of Italian persecution of Slavs when he used the occasion of the seventy-fifth anniversary of the burning of the Narodni Dom as the setting for the presentation of Slovenia's 'White Book' on plans for accession to the European Union. By the spring of 1996 Rome and Ljubljana were involved in a nasty exchange, precipitated by Slovenia's proposals for joining the European Union. At issue, in particular, was Slovenian compliance with European trade standards and an article in the Slovene constitution of 1991 that barred foreign ownership of property. From the Italian perspective, such a prohibition flew in the face of European policy and had prejudicial ramifications for Italian nationals, including many 'displaced' Istrians living in Trieste. The dispute served as a nationalist distraction to whip up support for conservatives in Rome. It also testified to Italy's propensity to parade Trieste and the eastern borderland across the international stage as a launching pad for involvement in greater European issues. However, at this juncture, the local spat did not resonate with the concerns of other European powers. In April 1996 the triumph of the Uliva coalition in Italy dampened the spirits of Italian nationalists. At the same time, Slovenia agreed to relax the property restrictions in question, giving Italian 'exiles' preferential treatment in the purchase of ancestral lands.[16] Italian objections to Slovenia's entry into the EEC evaporated and attention to Trieste faded.

Less visible, but equally complicated for Italy, have been Trieste's affiliations with Germanic Central Europe. The Second World War experiences of the eastern border territory of Trieste and Venezia Giulia, separated from Italy and occupied by the Nazis, has provided Italy with an opportunity to distance Italian Fascism from German Nazism in historical memory and to play up stereotypes of Italians' innate humanitarianism. In August 1997, at the height of the firestorm surrounding the reluctance of Swiss banks to release information regarding the property of victims of the Nazis, Italy chose to return several crates of property taken from Jews in Trieste during the Nazi occupation. In a widely publicised public ceremony the president of the Italian Jewish community spelled out Italy's intentions quite clearly. Although the commercial value of the items was negligible, the ceremony

---

[14] Cernigoi, *Operazione foibe*, explores the impact of the memory of the *foibe* on the national psyche, its place in the national myth and its role in the promotion of Italianness.

[15] See, in particular, Ballinger, *History in exile*, and Cernigoi, *Operazione foibe*.

[16] *Il Piccolo* followed the dispute in great detail. The contours of the arguments were gleaned from articles dating from 14 July 1995 to 30 June 1996.

and the act of turning them over had 'a symbolic value and acts as a warning and an invitation to other European countries to likewise search out and return property to those who lost it'.[17]

A private venture in a similar vein, sponsored by Assicurazioni Generali (which has its headquarters in Trieste), followed closely on the heels of the government initiative. The firm announced that it had set aside twelve million dollars 'in honor of Generali policyholders who perished in the Holocaust'. Monies were to be used in efforts 'dedicated to the eternalisation of the memory of the Holocaust' and 'to the assistance of Holocaust victims and their families'.[18] The firm, founded by Jewish merchants in Trieste in 1831, and with extensive interests in Israel, found itself open to recrimination for its handling of assets and policies dating back to the interwar and Second World War eras.[19]

With respect to Triestine involvement in the atrocities of the Second World War, Italy has had to contend with the painful memory of the San Sabba extermination camp. Recently refurbished as a memorial and museum, San Sabba displays evidence of warehouses for confiscated property, a prison equipped with instruments of torture and a crematorium, all on territory claimed as Italian. San Sabba reminds Trieste and Italy of Italian quiescence, if not collaboration, in the Nazi occupation and of atrocities committed in the north-eastern borderlands.

Italian Trieste has been moulded in opposition to the Slavic and Germanic worlds, not in contrast to experiences of the peninsula. Scholars contend that Italian identity has been shaped 'by comparison' or in contrast to other identities. This argument is linked to debates regarding the Italian state's 'failure' to form a cohesive national community and the persistence of regional identities to the present day.[20] The south, the *Mezzogiorno*, traditionally figures most prominently in discussions that centre on historical developments including the inability to construct stable and enduring central political institutions after the Risorgimento and uneven modernisation and industrialisation. Recently, the burgeoning of separatist movements in northern Italy has resulted in a shift of analyses to attempt to explain northern support for devolution. The geographical contours of the debate have changed, but the impact of modernisation and disparate economic development remain at the core of explanations of persistent regionalism.

Despite the commonalities of experience of Triestines and other northern Italians subject to the Habsburg monarchy during the nineteenth century,

---

17 *Boston Globe*, 5 Aug. 1997, 7, quoting the president of the Italian Jewish community's remarks, only one of many international articles about the ceremony.

18 Assicurazioni Generali, 'An open letter to the families of Holocaust victims', *Moment* (Oct. 1997), 19.

19 See, for example, 'Generali's nightmare continues', *The Economist*, 9 Jan. 1999, 70.

20 D. Forgacs and R. Lumley (eds), *Italian cultural studies: an introduction*, Oxford 1996, 72, discuss understandings of national identity as derived by comparison.

modern-day separatist groups find little sympathy among Triestines. Trieste exhibits hints of cultural foreignness mingled with strong loyalty to and reliance on the national framework. While Triestine nationalism is sometimes attributed to Rome's recognition of the territory's special status and the privileges enjoyed in the border region, its roots run deeper. It is not merely indicative of pecuniary interest in the Italian state but is reflective of memories of the historical struggle for Trieste to remain a part of Italy and to be seen as Italian. Triestines' situation on the border has prompted them to seek national acceptance by promoting the city's usefulness to the nation in its ties abroad. Historical experiences have formed links that encompass cultural, social, economic and political influences that are not simply vestiges of Germanic Habsburg control, but constitute the fibre of Triestine society inspired by a 500–year history of Habsburg protection and sovereignty. Rome has recognised the value of the maintenance of extra-statal ties, not for their economic utility, but for their political currency.

At the dawn of the twenty-first century, few would challenge Trieste's position within Italian borders, but the city's Italianness, albeit vaguely constructed, remains open to interpretation. In Trieste, the confluence of loyalties to former Central Europe and associations with Germanic Europe as well as Italy has peculiar effects. The resurrection in 1998 of a statue of 'Sissy', the Habsburg empress Elizabeth, in its former position of honour in the piazza in front of the main train station, testifies to the effects of the overlap of associations. The statue sits in the centre of the Piazza della Libertà, so named in 1919 in celebration of liberation from Habsburg Austria.[21]

Historically constructed identities mix elements of fact and fiction. The granddaughter of a soldier long ago emigrated to the United States wrote to the Triestine state archive in June 1997 requesting information about her grandfather's Italian service record. The woman's widowed grandmother needed to document that her husband has been an Italian veteran, fighting on the same side as the Americans in the First World War. A delicately worded response from the staff of the archives accompanied a copy of the man's service record showing that he had fought, instead, for the enemy, Austria. He had been a loyal Triestine.[22]

Trieste continues to lie at a distance from Rome, both in geographical and spiritual terms. Historically, the distance from Rome lay in the gulf between the Italian rhetoric of irredentism and willingness to act in Trieste. It also arose from the conviction on the part of many Italians and westerners that Triestine political life remained 'fixed on the principles of the past century of the time of Franz Joseph and the grand commercial and financial bourgeoisie'. Visions of a city caught up in nostalgia for Trieste's past prominence in

---

[21] Prior to 1919 the square was known as the Piazza della Stazione: Trampus, *Vie e piazze*, 339.

[22] A member of the archive staff consulted the author on how to word the response to the letter.

European economic and political circles are no more realistic than literary accounts that have tended to harp on this 'medley repeating all the old songs' of the imagined grandeur of the turn of the century.[23] Literary fantasies see Trieste as 'nowhere', or searching,[24] or as lost in its 'timelessness', due to its position 'at the sunset of the old Europe that always waits for its time to come'.[25]

Yet, current trends toward increased cross-border co-operation make Central European associations an important component of contemporary Triestine identity. Association with Slavs to the east can be construed as useful for Rome as it tries to navigate political and economic changes in post-Cold War Europe. At some level a sense of 'municipalism' and local exceptionalism prevails in Trieste. Some Triestines feel that political manipulation interfered with the development of a city that, left to its own natural devices, would occupy a position of leadership beneficial to Italy and Europe. A recent study that aimed to inject a geographically-centred approach into local historical studies unconsciously supports this view. Scholars used geographical data presented in maps and charts to confirm the region's importance in the 'new' Europe.[26] The unstated assumption that Trieste's fate rested in the city's geography echoes geographical essentialism framed in arguments of the central role of Trieste's 'natural' port and the city's autonomy.

Trieste aspires to be a leading centre in the European community. The painting of a 10,368 square metre mural on the Piazza Unità as part of the centennial and millenial celebrations in the year 2000 demonstrated Trieste's commitment to the European project. Its design included a rising sun ascending from the face of the moon, symbolic of Trieste's historic role as a gateway to the East. Yellow stars in a field of blue were reminiscent of the flag of the European Union. The central figure, a woman armed with the halberd of Trieste, astride a mythically inspired depiction of a bull, rode off toward the open end of the square along the sea.[27] While the display of support for European ties was very public, the ephemeral nature of the painting, executed in watercolors, testified to a deeper reluctance on the part of Triestines. Even in the symbolic realm, they hesitate to record, in a public and permanent arena, ambitions and affiliations that might shift with a change in prevailing political winds.

The emphasis on Trieste as an integral part of the New Europe exists alongside visions of Trieste as a thoroughly Italian border city. An article in

23 B. Schacherl, 'Trieste frontierà di cultura', *Rinascita* xlii/28 (27 July 1985), 12.
24 J. Morris, *Trieste and the meaning of nowhere*, New York 2001, and K. Pizzi, *A city in search of an author: the literary identity of Trieste*, London 2001.
25 C. Magris quoted in Pellegrini, *Trieste dentro Trieste*, 320.
26 Istituto regionale per la storia del movimento di liberazione nel Friuli-Venezia Giulia, *Il confine mobile: atlante storico dell'alto adriatico, 1866–1992*, Trieste 1995.
27 The city of Trieste division of culture and sport posted a sign board with an aerial photograph and description of the painting in the square.

the *confini* (borders) column of a recent issue of *Sapori d'Italia e dintorni* [Tastes of Italy and its surroundings] located Trieste's cuisine in a 'cosmopolitan culture . . . in which the Mediterranean and *Mitteleuropa* harmonise in the knowledge of fine dining and in many other aspects of civil life'. Yet, in its conclusion, the article brought the city back into the national fold. Regional specialities originating in the mingling of diverse strands of local cultural life came together to form simply a variant of local Italian cuisine . . . 'that forms a world in and of itself'.[28]

The city's Italianness entices Rome; her foreign ties promise greater influence in European affairs. Seen as a guardian on the frontier of culture when Italian relations with the east are troubled, the city appears as a centre of cosmopolitanism as co-operation across national borders in the upper Adriatic region becomes a priority. Trieste's affiliations with the Italian state rest on its relationship with foreign states and on Italian ambitions for the future of Europe. At the same time, Trieste's plays a domestic role in defining the parameters of Italianness in the eastern borderland.

---

[28] B. Ulcigrai, 'Trieste, Carso e oltre', *Sapori d'Italia e dintorni* vi (1999), 6, 11.

Bibliography

Unpublished primary sources

Trieste, Archivio di stato

Archivio Igino Brocchi, 1914–31

Commissariato generale civile per la Venezia Giulia, 1919–22
atti di gabinetto
atti generali

Prefettura della provincia di Trieste
divisione I: riduzione cognomi, 1926–43

Trieste, Biblioteca civica

Archivio diplomatico
RP, MS Misc. 58 papers and correspondence of Silvio Benco
RP, MS Misc. 152 papers and correspondence of Attilio Tamaro
Raccolta patria

Trieste, Camera di commercio, industria e artigianato
busta 4065.19 (1919–22)
gruppo 16–18 (1922–42)
categoria XXVIII (1947–57)

Trieste, Musei civici
Archivio Morpurgo
Collezione fotografica

Trieste, Museo Ente Portuale
uncatalogued photographs

Washington DC, National Archives

George C. Marshall Foundation
Drawer 1600, xeroxes

Published primary sources

Astori, H. and B. Astori, *La passione di Trieste: diario di vita triestina (luglio 1914–novembre 1918)*, Florence [1920]
Bazlen, R., *Scritti*, Milan 1984

Bebler, A., *Equilibrium or justice? Speech delivered, September 3, 1946 in the political and territorial commission of the peace conference*, New York 1949

Borsa, G., 'What Trieste means to Italy', *The Listener* (BBC), 15 Oct. 1953, 619–20

Bowman, A. C., *Zones of strain*, Stanford 1982

Cannadine, D. (ed.), *Blood, toil, tears, and sweat: the speeches of Winston Churchill*, Boston 1989

Cusin, F., *La liberazione di Trieste*, Trieste 1946

De'Stefani, A., *Documenti sulla condizione finanziaria ed economica dell'Italia*, Rome 1923

Eden, A., *Full circle: the memoirs of Anthony Eden*, Boston 1960

Galli, C., *Diarii e lettere: Tripoli 1911, Trieste 1918*, Florence 1951

Gasparini, L. (ed.), *Impressioni su Trieste, 1793–1887*, Trieste 1951

Il diritto d'Italia su Trieste e L'Istria, Milan 1915

Kandler, P., *Albo storico topografico della città e territorio di Trieste*, ed. S. Zorzon, Trieste 1989

Ludwig, E., *Colloqui con Mussolini*, Verona 1950

Mosconi, A., *I primi anni di governo italiano nella Venezia Giulia, Trieste 1919–1922*, Bologna 1924

Mussolini, B., *Opera omnia*, XXIX: *1 ottobre 1937–10 giugno 1940*, ed. E. Susmel and D. Susmel, Florence 1959

Pitacco, G., *Avvenimenti di vita Triestina: discorsi podestarili, 1923–1933*, Rome 1935

Quarantotti Gambini, P. A., *Primavera a Trieste e altri scritti* [Italy] 1985

Saba, U., *Trieste et un poète*, Paris 1977

────── *Umberto Saba: thirty-one poems*, New Rochelle, NY 1978

────── *Lettere sulla psicoanalisi*, Milan 1991

────── *The dark of the sun: selected poems of Umberto Saba*, Lanham, MD 1994

Santin, A., *Trieste, 1943–1945: scritti, discorsi, appunti, lettere*, Udine 1963

Schiffrer, C., *Antifascista a Trieste: scritti editi e inediti, 1944–1955*, Udine 1996

Segrè, D. V., *Memoirs of a fortunate Jew: an Italian story*, Northvale, NJ 1995

Sforza, C., *Cinque anni a palazzo Chigi*, Florence 1952

Slataper, S., *Scritti politici*, ed. G. Stuparich, Verona 1954

────── *Lettere triestine: col seguito di altri scritti vociani di polemica su Trieste*, Trieste 1988

Sleeping car to Trieste, 96 min. videocassette distributed by Evergreen Entertainment, Los Angeles 1997 [video release of feature film Eagle-Lion, Two Cities, UK, 1949]

Staderini, T. (ed.), *Legislazione per la difesa della razza*, Rome 1940

Svevo, I., *Confessions of Zeno*, trans. B. de Zoete, New York 1989

Tamaro, A., *Trieste: storia di una città e di una fede*, Milan 1946

Trieste 18–19 settembre XVI – Mussolini, Trieste 1938

Wilson, W., 'The fourteen points', www.lib.byu.edu/~rdh/wwi/1918/1points.html, accessed Dec. 2000

Official documents and publications

Airey, General T. S., *Report on the administration of the British-US zone of the Free Territory of Trieste*, i–xi, Trieste 1947–51.

Allied military government British/United States zone, Free Territory of Trieste, *Trieste handbook*, Trieste 1950

Army map service, 'The frontiers of the Free Territory of Trieste', no. 10612 (US Department of State, map division, Dec. 1946) (1:100,000)

Atti del XIII° congresso nazionale fra commercianti-industriali-esercenti [Trieste, 11–15 Sept. 1921, Trieste], Trieste 1921

Azienda autonoma di soggiorno e turismo Trieste, *Das Triest der Touristen*, Trieste 1938

Camera di commercio e industria Trieste, *L'economia triestina nel quinquennio, 1919–1923*, Trieste 1924

———— *Relazione annuale 1947: sull'andamento economico nella provincia di Trieste*, Trieste 1947

Carnegie Endowment for International Peace, *The treaties of the peace, 1919–1923*, New York 1924

Comitato triestino dei traffici, *Esame della nuova situazione dell'Europa centro-orientale, in relazione agli interessi italo-germanici, con particolare riguardo ai porti di Trieste e di Fiume*, Trieste 1940

Consiglio provinciale dell'economica corporativa Trieste, *Relazione sull'andamento economico della provincia di Trieste negli anni 1933 e 1934*, Trieste n.d.

Economic Co-operation Administration, *Trieste: country study, European recovery program*, Washington, DC 1949

Federazione provinciale fascista del commercio di Trieste, *I commerci di Trieste nel 1931: relazioni dei presidenti di gruppo*, Trieste 1932

Fiera campionaria internazionale Trieste, *Catalogo ufficiale 1920*, Trieste 1920

———— *Catalogo ufficiale degli espositori alla fiera campionaria internazionale Trieste, 9–24 ottobre 1920*, Trieste 1920

———— *Catalogo degli espositori alla fiera campionaria internazionale di Trieste, 3–18 settembre 1922*, Trieste 1922

———— *Statistiche della seconda fiera campionaria internazionale Trieste, 3–24 settembre 1922*, Trieste 1922

Fiera di Trieste, *Discorso inaugurale della II fiera campionaria internazionale di Trieste pronunciato il giorno 26 agosto 1950 dal presidente dell'ente dott. ing. Ernesto Sospisio*, Trieste 1950

———— *Fiera di Trieste campionaria internazionale, 27 agosto–10 settembre 1950*, Trieste 1950

———— *Catalogo ufficiale fiera di Trieste campionarie internazionale: 17 giugno–4 luglio 1954*, Trieste 1954

Giugno triestino, *III° mostra nazionale del mare: giugno triestino 1935–XIII*, Trieste 1935

Mostra di Trieste, *Mostra di Trieste 1947, stazione marittima, 11–26 ottobre*, Trieste 1947

Ordine dei lavori e regolamento del congresso nazionale per l'espansione economica e commerciale all'estero, Trieste [4–8 Nov. 1923], Naples 1923.

Results of the preliminary investigations by the Italian authorities on the events of
Trieste, n.p. 1954
www.retecivica.trieste.it. accessed Sept. 2000

Newspapers and periodicals

The Blue Devil, Apr.–Oct. 1954 (published for TRUST [Trieste United States
Troops])
Bollettino della Camera di Commercio e Industria di Trieste
Bollettino Mensile del Lloyd Triestino, later Bollettino Mensile del Gruppo Armatoriali
Italia-Cosulich-Lloyd Triestino
The Economist (London), 2000–1
L'Emancipazione: settimanale repubblicano della Venezia Giulia, 1920–25 (biweekly
after Dec. 1921)
L'Era Nuova, 1920–2
Fiera Campionaria Internazionale di Trieste
Fiera di Trieste
Gazzetta Ufficiale del Regno d'Italia: parte prima: leggi e decreti (Rome)
Il Giornale di Trieste, 1948–54
L'Idea Liberale, 1945–51
Il Lavoratore, 1947–55
Il Lavoratore: organo della federazione socialista della Venezia Giulia, 1920–1
Il Lavoratore: organo del partito comunista d'Italia, 1921–3
Il Lavoratore socialista, 1921–2
L'Illustrazione italiana, 1882
Il Mare: informatore economico finanziario, 1949
La Nazione, 1919–22
La Nazione della Domenica, 1920–1
Notiziario Industriale, 1947–54
L'Ora Socialista, 1945–9
Il Piccolo, 1919–43, 1954–5
Il Popolo di Trieste, 1933–6
La Porta Orientale
Rassegna Stampa Slava: servizio quotidiano 6 June 1954–30 Oct. 1954,
Astra-Trieste. Trieste, Serv. 132 – 249 (Italian translations of select articles
appearing in the Slavic press)
Rivista Mensile della Città di Trieste
Sul Mare: rivista di viaggi del Lloyd Triestino
Le Tre Venezie: rivista mensile edita sotto gli auspici della federazione veneziana dei
fasci di combattimento
Tribuna dei Lavoratori
Trieste Libera, 1945–50
Trieste: rivista politica/ rivista politica giuliana/ rivista politica della regione, etc.
[subtitle varies]
Trieste Sera, 1946–52
La Voce Libera, 1947–9
Yearbook of the United Nations, 1953–4

Contemporary books and articles

Babudri, F., 'La fiera campionaria internazionale di Trieste del 1920', in Suttora, *La fiera campionaria*, 11–23
—— 'L'arte e la fiera triestina', *Fiera Campionaria Internazionale di Trieste* (May 1922), 19–22
Bachi, R., *L'Italia economica nell'anno 1919: annuario della vita commerciale, industriale, agraria, bancaria, finanziaria e della politica*, Città di Castello 1920
Benco, S., 'Trieste', *Illustrazione Italiana: Numero Speciale Trento e Trieste* (1919), 23–40
Bernardi, R., *I grandi progetti per lo sviluppo del porto di Trieste*, Trieste 1945
Bertarelli, L.V. (ed.), *Le Tre Venézie*, Milan 1925
Budinich, P., 'Il porto di Trieste', *Le Vie d'Italia: rivista mensile del Touring Club Italiano* (Feb. 1923), 164–70
Camera di commercio, industria e agricoltura, Trieste, 'I caratteri economici del territorio libero di Trieste zona anglo-americana', *Sintesi Economici* lxxxix (Sept. 1949), 1–25
Caprin, G., *Trieste e l'Italia*, Milan 1915
Castellini, G., *Trento e Trieste: l'irredentismo e il problema adriatico*, Milan 1918
Centro sviluppo economico Trieste, *Appunti sull'economia di Trieste: funzione e particolarità della VI fiera campionaria internazionale*, Trieste 1954
Chersi, E., 'Irredentismo e fascismo', *La Porta Orientale* iii/iv (1939), 94–9
Cobolli-Gigli, G., *Opere pubbliche: panorama di vita fascista*, Milan 1938
Comitato austriaco di liberazione, *Trieste: porto dell'Austria e del bacino danubiano*, Trieste 1945
Committee of emigrant Jugoslavs in London, *The South Slav programme*, London 1915
Comune di Trieste, *Trieste, 1945–1955*, Trieste 1956
Cusin, F., *Venti secoli di bora sul carso e sul golfo*, Trieste 1952
De' Stefani, P., 'Trieste e Roma', *Il Borghese* ix (20 Mar. 1958), 506
Digovic, P., *La Dalmatie et le problèmes de L'Adriatique*, Lausanne 1944
Ente fiera campionaria internazionale, *Trieste e il Levante: un binomio economico*, Trieste 1955
Ente per il turismo, *Trieste*, Trieste 1953
Ente per il turismo di Trieste, *Trieste*, Trieste 1950
Ermacora, C., *Vino all'ombra: le Tre Venezie*, Pordenone 1942
Farolfi, F., 'L'arco romano detto "di Riccardo" a Trieste', *Archeografo Triestino* xxi (1936), 135–69
Franchini, V., 'Aspetti e momenti della funzione del porto di Trieste: a traverso i tempi', *Rivista di Cultura Marinara* (Nov./Dec. 1932), supplement
Furlani, L., 'I commerci di Trieste e la concorrenza nordica', *La Porta Orientale* iii (1933), 388–96
Gabronsek, F., *Jugoslavia's frontier with Italy: Trieste and its hinterlands*, New York 1942
Gaeta, G., *Trieste ed il colonialismo italiano*, Trieste 1943
Gayda, V., *Modern Austria: her racial and social problems*, New York 1915
Gregorin, G., *La Question de l'Adriatique*, Paris 1919
Griffini, M., 'Fiume integratrice di Trieste', *Congresso nazionale per l'espansione*

economica e commerciale all'estero: ordine dei lavori e regolamento del congresso, [Trieste, 4–8 Nov. 1923], Trieste 1923

Guida di Trieste e della Venezia Giulia, Trieste 1937

Guida pratica illustrata di Trieste, Trieste 1919

Jangakis, C., *Le Port de Trieste: avant et après la dissolution de la monarchie austro-hongroise*, Lausanne 1923

Jones, S., *Boundary-making: a handbook for statesmen, treaty editors and boundary commissioners*, Washington, DC 1945

Kane, H., 'Trieste – side door to Europe', *National Geographic Magazine* cix (June 1956), 824–57

Lloyd Triestino, *Appunti per lo studio delle sovvenzioni nelle linee dell'Adriatico*, Trieste 1922

Magazzini generali di Trieste, *The port of Trieste restored to its former technical efficiency*, Trieste 1947

Martin-Chauffier, J., *Trieste: libération de la Vénétie Julienne: conférences de Londres et de Paris: le problème de l'internationalisation*, Paris 1947

Mihovilovic, I., *Trieste et son port*, Susak 1945

Montemuliano, G., *Venezia Giulia: italiana ed europea*, Rome 1945

'Monumenti nazionale della nuova Italia: il tempio maggiore israelitico di Trieste', *La Grande Illustrazione d'Italia* iii (Oct. 1926), 13–16

Moravec, Z., *Italie et les Yougoslaves*, Paris 1919

Moschitti, C., 'Per il disciplinamento delle fiere campionarie in Italia', *Congresso nazionale per l'espansione, economica e commerciale all'estero*, [Trieste, 4–8 Nov. 1923], Naples 1923, 3–18

Mostra del centenario del Lloyd Triestino: catalogo 1936 – XIV, Trieste 1936

Mostra documentaria Trieste italiana: ieri, oggi, sempre della Lega Nazionale (Galleria Trieste, 30 May 1912), Trieste 1949

Muratti, S. 'Parte I', in Partito democratico di Trieste, *Per il portofranco a Trieste*, Trieste n.d., 5–11

Museo commerciale della camera di commercio ed industria, *Guida per il commercio col Levante*, Trieste 1925

Pattini, G., *L'Italia irredenta*, Milan n.d.

Peterlin, G., *Guida di Trieste e dei luoghi più notevoli della Venezia Giulia*, Trieste 1925

Pizzagalli, A., *Per l'italianità dei cognomi nella provincia di Trieste*, Trieste 1929

Polidori, P., 'Le origini della fiera campionaria internazionale di Trieste', in Suttora, *La fiera campionaria*, 7–10

Ragusin, L., 'L'avvenire del porto di Trieste', *Esteri: quindicinale di politica estera* (Rome) iv/23 (15 Dec. 1953), 33–40

Ragusin-Righi, L., *Interessi e problemi Adriatici*, Bologna 1929

Relazione presentata alla VIII riunione della società italiana di demografia e statistica tenutasi in Milano, 10–11 Jan. 1942

Roletto, G., 'Funzione imperiale dei porti italiani: Trieste', *Commerciale Imperiale* ii/12 (Oct. 1937), 8–12

—— *Il porto di Trieste*, Bologna 1941

Romersa, L., 'Storia dell'italianità di Trieste', *Tempo* (Milan) xiv/18 (26 Apr. 1952), 24–9

Rziha, F., *Sull'importanza del porto di Trieste per l'Austria: relazione letta il 2 maggio 1873 nel consorzio politecnico in Praga*, Trieste 1874

Salvemini, G., *Racial minorities under Fascism in Italy*, Chicago 1934

Sanzin, L., *Aspetti, carattere e funzione della espansione assicurativa italiana all'estero: relazione presentata alla viii riunione della Società italiana demografia e statistica tenutasi in Milano*, [10–11 Jan. 1942], n.p. 1942

['Sator'], *La populazione della Venezia Giulia*, Rome 1945

Scala, C., *Dei commerci di Trieste nel 1928*, Trieste 1929

Schaerf, S., *I cognomi degli ebrei d'Italia*, Florence 1925

Schiffrer, C., *Venezia Giulia: study of a map of the Italo-Yugoslav national borders*, Rome 1946

Scocchi, A., 'I nomi pagani slavi e l'onomastica romana', *La Porta Orientale* (1932), 275–83

Segrè, V., *Il problema nazionale del porto di Trieste*, Trieste 1927

Selb, A. and A. Tischbein (eds), *Memorie viaggio pittorio littorale austriaco*, Trieste 1842

Sestan, E., *Venezia Giulia: lineamenti di storia etnica e culturale*, Rome 1947

Squinabol, S. and V. Furlani, *Venezia Giulia*, Turin 1928

Suttora, A. (ed.), *La fiera campionaria internazionale di Trieste, 3–18 settembre 1922*, Trieste 1922

Tamaro, A., *Trieste et son rôle antigermanique*, Paris 1917

———— 'La "Saliera" del 1609', *Archeografo Triestino* xvii (1932), 241–72

———— *Storia di Trieste*, 1st edn, Rome 1924, repr. Trieste 1974

Treccani, G. (ed.), *Enciclopedia italiana*, lxxii, Rome 1929

———— (ed.), *Enciclopedia italiana di scienze, lettere ed arti*, Rome 1937

Unione antifascista italo-slovena, *Trieste nella lotta per la democrazia*, Trieste 1945

Vivante, A., *Irredentismo adriatico*, 1st edn, Florence 1912, repr. Trieste 1984

Zanetti, S., *Trieste e l'economia nazionale*, Trieste 1934

Secondary sources

Adelman, J. and S. Aron. 'From borderlands to borders: empires, nation-states, and the people in between in North American history', *American Historical Review* civ (1999), 814–41

Albrecht-Carrié, R., *Italy at the Paris Peace Conference*, New York, 1938, repr. Hamden, Conn. 1966

Anderson, B., *Imagined communities: reflections on the origin and spread of nationalism*, London 1983

Anderson, M., *Frontiers: territory and state formation in the modern world*, Cambridge 1996

Andri, A., 'I cambiamenti di cognome nel 1928 e la scuola triestina', *Qualestoria* xi (Feb. 1983), 9–16

Apih, E., 'Fascism in Trieste', *Trieste: Political Review* vii (May/June 1955), 9–14

———— *Dal regime alla resistenza: Venezia Giulia, 1922–1943*, Udine 1960

———— *Italia fascismo e antifascismo nella Venezia Giulia (1918–1943)*, Bari 1966

Appadurai, A., 'How to make a national cuisine: cookbooks in contemporary India', *Comparative Studies in Society and History* xxx (1988), 3–24

Apple, R. W., 'The crossroads cooking of Trieste', *Saveur* lxii (2002), 54–67

Ara, A. and C. Magris, *Trieste: un identità di frontiera*, Turin 1987

Arosio, S., *Scrittori di frontiera: Scipio Slataper, Giani e Carlo Stuparich*, Milan 1996

Ascoli, A. and K. von Henneberg (eds.), *Making and remaking Italy*, Oxford 2001

Ash, T. Garton, 'Does Central Europe exist?, *New York Review of Books*, 9 Oct. 1986, 45–52

Assicurazioni Generali, 'An open letter to the families of Holocaust victims', *Moment* (Oct. 1997), 19

Associazione caffè Trieste, *Cent'anni di caffè, 1891–1991*, Trieste 1991

Azienda autonomo di soggiorno e turismo, *Dudovich & C.: i triestini nel cartellonismo italiano*, Trieste 1977

Balakrishnan, G. (ed.), *Mapping the nation*, London 1996

Balibar, E., 'The borders of Europe', in Cheah and Robbins, *Cosmopolitics*, 216–29

Ballinger, P., *History in exile: memory and identity at the borders of the Balkans*, Princeton 2003

Barnes, T. and J. Duncan (eds), *Writing worlds: discourse, text and metaphor in the representation of landscape*, London 1992

—— and J. Duncan, 'Introduction: writing worlds', in Barnes and Duncan, *Writing worlds*, 1–17

Bartolini, E., L. Menegazzi and R. Curci, *150 manifesti del Friuli-Venezia Giulia: vita e costume di una regione, 1895–1940*, Padua 1982

Basch, A., *The Danube basin and the German economic sphere*, New York 1943

Bauer, O., 'The nation', in Balakrishnan, *Mapping the nation*, 39–77

Belci, C., *Quel confine mancato: la linea Wilson (1919–1945)*, Brescia 1996

—— *Gli uomini di De Gasperi a Trieste*, Brescia 1998

Ben-Ghiat, R., *Fascist modernities: Italy, 1922–1945*, Berkeley 2001

Benvenisti, M., *Sacred landscape: the buried history of the holy land since 1948*, Berkeley 2000

Berezin, M., *Making the Fascist self: political culture of interwar Italy*, Ithaca 1997

Berghold, J., *Italien-Austria: von der Erbfeindschaft zur Europäischen öffnung*, Vienna 1997

Biagini, F., *Mussolini e il sionismo*, Milan 1998

Blanchard, W. O., *Economic geography of Europe*, New York 1931

Bo, C. (ed.), *Scrittori triestini del novecento*, Trieste 1991

Bon, S., *La persecuzione antiebraica a Trieste (1938–1945)*, Udine 1972

—— 'Un campo di sterminio in Italia', *Il Ponte* xxxiv/11–12 (1978), 1440–53

—— *Gli ebrei a Trieste, 1930–1945: identità, persecuzione, risposte*, Gorizia 2000

Bonelli, F., 'L'intervento statale e il mercato nell'esperienza del Lloyd triestino', in Lloyd Triestino, *Il Lloyd Triestino*, 241–304

Bosetti, G., 'La Jeune Nation italienne entre "ethnos" e "demos" ', in *Marginalités*, 47–61

Bosworth, R. J. B., *Italy, the least of the great powers: Italian foreign policy before the First World War*, Cambridge 1979

Botteri, G., *Il Caffè degli specchi*, Trieste 1985

—— 'L'attività editoriali del Lloyd triestino nel primo dopoguerra: "Il Bollettino" e la rivista "Sul Mare" ', in Lloyd Triestino, *Il Lloyd Triestino*, 409–40

Bracco, B., *Carlo Sforza e la questione adriatica: politica estera e opinione pubblica nell'ultimo governo Giolitti*, Milan 1998

Braudel, F., *The Mediterranean and the Mediterranean world in the age of Philip II*, Berkeley 1995

Breuilly, J., 'Approaches to nationalism', in Balakrishnan, *Mapping the nation*, 146–74

Buci-Glucksmann, C., 'Hegemony and consent: a political strategy', in Showstack Sassoon, *Approaches to Gramsci*, 116–26

Butlin, R., *Historical geography through the gates of space and time*, London 1993

Camera di commercio, industria, artigianato ed agricoltura, *Cinquant'anni di vita economica a Trieste, 1918–1968*, Trieste 1968

Campbell, J. (ed.), *Successful negotiation: Trieste 1954: an appraisal by the five participants*, Princeton 1976

Cannistraro, P. (ed.), *Historical dictionary of Fascist Italy*, Westport, Conn. 1982

Capuzzo, E., 'Sull'introduzione dell'amministrazione italiana a Trento e a Trieste (1918–1919)', *Clio* xxiii (1987), 231–79

Cassels, A., *Mussolini's early diplomacy*, Princeton 1970

Catalan, T., *La comunità ebraica di Trieste (1781–1914): politica, società, e cultura*, Trieste 2000

Cattaruzza, M., 'Slovenes and Italians in Trieste, 1850–1914', in Max Engman (ed.), *Ethnic identity in urban Europe*, New York 1992, 189–219

—— (ed.), *Trieste, Austria, Italia tra settecento e novecento*, Udine 1996

Cecovini, M., *Del patriottismo di Trieste*, Milan 1968

—— *Cinquant'anni di storia: il Rotary a Trieste, 1924–1974*, Trieste 1974

—— 'Trieste, questa sconosciuta, nelle vicende della frontiera orientale d'Italia', in *Marginalités*, 13–31

Cergoly, C., *Il complesso dell'imperatore: collages di fantasie e memorie di un mitteleuropeo*, Milan 1979

Cernigoi, C., *Operazione foibe a Trieste: come si crea una mistificazione storica: dalla propaganda nazifascista attraverso la guerra fredda fino al neoirredentismo*, Udine 1997

Cervani, G. (ed.), *Nazionalità e stato di diritto per Trieste nel pensiero di Pietro Kandler*, Udine 1975

Cheah, P. and B. Robbins (eds), *Cosmopolitics: thinking and feeling beyond the nation*, Minneapolis 1998

Ciana, A., *Trieste scomparsa: demolizioni e rinnovamenti, 1932–1939*, Trieste 1982

Cirrincione, S., 'Il contributo della marina mercantile giuliana all'economia nazionale', in Camera di commercio, *Cinquant'anni*, 163–285

Clifford, J., 'Mixed feelings', in Cheah and Robbins, *Cosmopolitics*, 362–70

Coceani, B., *Mussolini, Hitler, Tito alle porte orientali d'Italia*, Bologna 1948

—— 'L'acesa industriale', in Camera di commercio, *Cinquant'anni*, 287–368

Collotti, E., 'Sui compiti repressivi degli Einsatzkommandos della polizia di sicurezza tedesca nei territori occupati', *Il movimento di liberazione in Italia* xxiii/103 (1971), 79–97

—— *Il litorale adriatico nel nuovo ordine europeo, 1943–1945*, Milan 1974

Confino, A., *The nation as a local metaphor: Württemberg, imperial Germany, and national memory, 1871–1918*, Chapel Hill 1997

Contessi, G., *Umberto Nordio: architettura a Trieste, 1926–1943*, Milan 1981

Coslovich, M., *I percorsi della sopravvivenza*, Milan 1994

Cox, G., *The road to Trieste*, London 1947

—— *The race for Trieste*, London 1977

Curci, R., *Marcello Dudovich, cartellonista, 1878–1962*, Trieste 1976

Daneo, C., *Il fantasma di Angelo Vivante*, Udine 1988

De Castro, D., *Il problema di Trieste: genesi e sviluppi della questione giuliana in relazione agli avvenimenti internazionali*, Bologna 1952

———— 'Trieste and the Italian economy', in P. Thorneycroft (ed.), *Italy: an economic survey*, *The Statist* [supplement] 25 Oct. 1952, 36–8

De Felice, R., *Storia degli ebrei italiani sotto il fascismo*, Turin 1993

De Grand, A., *The Italian Nationalist Association*, Lincoln, Nebr. 1978

De Grazia, V., *How Fascism ruled women: Italy, 1922–1945*, Berkeley 1992

Delanty, G., 'L'identità europea come costruzione sociale', in L. Passerini (ed.), *Identità culturale europea: idee, sentimenti, relazioni*, Florence 1998

Della Pergola, S., *Anatomia dell'ebraismo italiano: caratteristiche demografiche, economiche, sociali, religiose e politiche di una minoranza*, Assisi 1976

De'Stefani, P., 'Trieste e Roma', *Il Borghese* ix/13 (20 Mar. 1958), 498–506

Dinardo, R., 'Glimpse of an old world order? Reconsidering the Trieste crisis of 1945', *Diplomatic History* xxi (1997), 365–81

Donnan, H. and T. Wilson, *Borders: frontiers of identity, nation and state*, Oxford 1999

Dubin, L., *The port Jews of Habsburg Trieste*, Stanford 1999

Dudovich, M., *Mostra delle opere di Marcello Dudovich*, Milan 1969

———— and R. Curci, *Marcello Dudovich, 1878–1962: i 100 bozzetti e manifesti per la rinascente: 18 marzo–20 aprile 1985*, Milan 1985

Duggan, C., 'Italy in the Cold War years and the legacy of Fascism', in Duggan and Wagstaff, *Italy in the Cold War*, 1–24

———— and C. Wagstaff (eds), *Italy in the Cold War: politics, culture and society, 1948–58*, Oxford 1995

Duroselle, J., *Le Conflît de Trieste, 1943–1954*, Brussels 1966

Ellwood, D. W., 'Italy, Europe and the Cold War: the politics and economics of limited sovereignty', in Duggan and Wagstaff, *Italy in the Cold War*, 25–46

Fabi, L., *Trieste, 1914–1918: una città in guerra*, Trieste 1996

Fast, M., *I dolci a Trieste: punto d'incontro di civiltà*, Trieste 1989

Favaretto, T. and E. Greco (eds), *Il confine riscoperto: beni degli esuli, minoranze e cooperazione economica nei rapporti dell'Italia con Slovenia e Croazia*, Milan 1997

Fiera di Trieste, *40 anni di fiera, 40 anni di vita a Trieste*, Trieste 1988

Fink, C., A. Frohn and J. Heideking (eds), *Genoa, Rapallo, and European reconstruction in 1922*, Cambridge 1991

Fölkel, F., *La risiera di San Sabba: Trieste e il Litorale Adriatico durante l'occupazione nazista*, Milan 1979

Fonda, C., *Sapori nostrani: manuale completo della cucina triestina, istriana, e isontina*, Trieste 1993

Forgacs, D. and R. Lumley (eds), *Italian cultural studies: an introduction*, Oxford 1996

Forsyth, D., 'The peculiarities of Italo-American relations in historical perspective', *Journal of Modern Italian Studies* iii (1998), 1–21

Galli della Loggia, E., *L'identità italiana*, Bologna 1998

Gentile, E., *The sacralization of politics in Fascist Italy*, Cambridge 1996

Giuricin, E. and L. Giurcin, 'La comunità italiana in Croazia e Slovenia: il percorso storico, la situazione, le prospettive di cooperazione', in Favaretto and Greco, *Il confine*, 92–125

Greco, E., 'L'evoluzione delle relazioni politiche dell'Italia con la Slovenia e la

Croazia dopo la dissoluzione della Jugoslavia', in Favaretto and Greco, *Il confine*, 25–50

Hametz, M., 'Friuli-Venezia Giulia and Italian foreign policy: local identity as a centripetal force', *Italian Politics and Society: Review of the Conference Group on Italian Politics and Society* xlix (1998), 63–70

——— 'The ambivalence of Italian antisemitism: Fascism, nationalism, and racism in Trieste', *Holocaust and Genocide Studies* xvi (2002), 376–401

Harper, J., *America and the reconstruction of Italy, 1945–1948*, Cambridge 1986

Hearder, H., *Italy: a short history*, Cambridge 1990

Heuser, B., *Western 'containment' policies in the Cold War: the Yugoslav case, 1948–1953*, London 1989

Hobsbawm, E. and T. Ranger (eds), *Inventing traditions*, Cambridge 1983

Ipsen, C., *Dictating demography: the problem of population in Fascist Italy*, Cambridge 1996

Isnenghi, M., *L'Italia in piazza: i luoghi della vita pubblica dal 1848 ai giorni nostri*, Milan 1994

Istituto regionale per la storia del movimento di liberazione nel Friuli-Venezia Giulia, *Il confine mobile: atlante storico dell'alto adriatico, 1866–1992*, Trieste 1995

Istituto di sociologia internazionale, *Confini e regioni: il potenziale di sviluppo e di pace delle periferie: problemi e prospettive delle regioni di frontiera* [Gorizia, 24 March 1972], Trieste 1973

Kezich, T., 'L'Europe comincia qui: Trieste, città del passato irrepetibile, ore deve inventare il suo futuro', *Bell'Italia* iii/22 (1988), 99–107

Kollmann, R., *Trieste, millenovecento cinquanta 5, cronache dei poveri amanti*, Trieste 1956

Konvitz, J., 'The crises of Atlantic port cities, 1880– 1920', *Comparative Studies in Society and History* xxxvi (1994), 293–318

Lattimore, O., *Studies in frontier history: collected papers, 1928–1958*, London 1962

Ledeen, M., *D'Annunzio: the first duce*, New Brunswick 2002

Lederer, I., *Yugoslavia at the Paris Peace Conference*, New Haven 1963

Levy, C. (ed.), *Italian regionalism*, Oxford 1996

Lloyd Triestino, *Il Lloyd Triestino, 1836–1986: contributi alla storia del cinquantennio*, Trieste 1986

Lonza, B., *La dedicazione di Trieste all'Austria*, Trieste 1973

Loseri, L., *Guida di Trieste : la città nella storia, nella cultura e nell'arte*, Trieste 1985

Lundestad, G., 'Empire by invitation? The United States and western Europe, 1945–1952', in C. Maier (ed.), *The Cold War in Europe*, New York 1991, 143–65

Lyttelton, A., *The seizure of power: Fascism in Italy, 1919–1929*, Princeton 1987

——— 'Creating a national past: history, myth and image in the Risorgimento', in Ascoli and von Henneberg, *Making and remaking Italy*, 27–74

——— 'Shifting identities: nation, region and city', in Levy, *Italian regionalism*, 33–52

Macartney, M. and P. Cremona, *Italy's foreign and colonial policy, 1914–1937*, New York 1938, repr. New York 1972

McCourt, J., *The years of Bloom: James Joyce in Trieste*, Madison 2000

Maffioli, G., *Cucina e vini delle Tre Venezie con 638 ricette*, Milan 1972

Magris, C., *I luoghi del disincanto*, Trieste 1987

————— *Danube*, New York 1989

————— *Il mito absburgico nella letteratura austriaca moderna*, Turin 1996

Maiden, M., *A linguistic history of Italy*, London 1995

Marginalités: frontières, nations et minorités, Grenoble 1994

Maserati, E., 'Simbolismo e rituale nell'irredentismo adriatico', in Salimbeni, *Dal litorale austriaco*, 125–50

Mayda, G., *Ebrei sotto Salò*, Milan 1978

Michaelis, M., *Mussolini and the Jews: German-Italian relations and the Jewish question in Italy, 1922–1945*, Oxford 1978

Migliorino, E. Ginzburg, 'Jewish emigration from Trieste to the United States after 1938, with special reference to New York, Philadelphia, and Wilmington', *Studi Emigrazione* xxviii (1991), 369–78

Mihelic, D., *The political element in the port geography of Trieste*, Chicago 1969

Millo, A., *L'élite del potere a Trieste: una biografia collettiva, 1891–1938*, Milan 1989

————— *Storia di una borghesia: la famiglia Vivante a Trieste dall'emporio alla guerra mondiale*, Gorizia 1998

Morris, J., *Trieste and the meaning of nowhere*, New York 2001

Morris W. (ed.), *The American heritage dictionary of the English language*, Boston 1981

Novak, B., *Trieste, 1941–1954: the ethnic, political, and ideological struggle*, Chicago 1970

Pagnini, C., *I giornali di Trieste dalle origini al 1959*, Milan 1960

Palladini, G., 'Il commercio triestino con l'estero', in Camera di commercio, *Cinquant'anni*, 435–86

Parovel, P., *L'identità cancellata: l'italianizzazione forzata dei cognomi, nomi e toponomi nella 'Venezia Giulia' dal 1919 al 1945, con gli elenchi delle provincie di Trieste, Gorizia, Istria ed i dati dei primi 5,300 decreti*, Trieste 1985

Patriarca, S., 'National identity or national character? New vocabularies and old paradigms', in Ascoli and von Henneberg, *Making and remaking Italy*, 299–319

Pellegrini, E., *Trieste dentro Trieste: sessant'anni di storia letteraria triestina attraverso gli scritti di Silvio Benco (1890–1949)*, Florence 1985

Petracchi, P., 'Italy at the Genoa Conference: Italian-Soviet commercial relations', in Fink, Frohn and Heideking, *Genoa*, 159–70

Pilastro, G., *Miramare: the castle of Maximillian and Charlotte*, Trieste 1984

Piovene, G., *Viaggio in Italia*, Milan 1957

Pizzi, K., *A city in search of an author: the literary identity of Trieste*, London 2001

Pupo, R., *Fra Italia e Iugoslavia – Saggi sulla questione di Trieste (1945–1954)*, Udine 1989

————— *Guerra e dopoguerra al confine orientale d'Italia, 1938–1956*, Udine 1999

Queirazza, G., C. Marcato and others (eds), *Dizionario dei nomi geografici italiani: origine e significato dei nomi di regione, città, paesi, mari, laghi, fiume, e isole*, Milan 1992

Rabel, R., *Trieste, the United States and the Cold War, 1941–1954*, Durham, NC 1988

Ranchi, S. and M. Rossi, *Il Lavoratore: richerche e testimonianze su novantanni di storia di un giornale*, Trieste 1986

Ranki, G., *Economy and foreign policy: the struggle of the great powers for hegemony in the Danube valley, 1919–1939*, Boulder, Colo. 1983

Reitlinger, G., *The final solution: the attempt to exterminate the Jews of Europe, 1939–1945*, London, 1968, repr. Northvale, NJ 1987

Riccardi, L., *Francesco Salata tra storia, politica e diplomazia*, Udine 2001

Rokkan, S. and D. Urwin, *Economy, territory, identity: politics of west European peripheries*, London 1983

Rosignoli, G., *Uniformi e distintivi della polizia civile del governo militare alleato Venezia-Giulia* [sic], *1943–1945 e del governo militare alleato territorio libero di Trieste 1947/54*, Castelbolognese 1986

Ruppin, A., *The Jews in the modern world*, New York 1973

Rusinow, D., *Italy's Austrian heritage, 1919–1946*, Oxford 1969

Rutteri, S., *Trieste: storia ed arte tra vie e piazze*, Trieste 1981

Sahlins, P., *Boundaries: the making of France and Spain in the Pyrenees*, Berkeley 1989

Salimbeni, F., 'Tra Vienna e Venezia: Trieste', in G. Romanelli (ed.), *Venezia Vienna*, Milan 1983, 227–42

—— (ed.), *Dal litorale austriaco alla Venezia Giulia: miscellanea di studi giuliani*, Udine 1991

Sapelli, G., 'Il Lloyd nel contesto dell'economia triestina e del suo hinterland', in Lloyd Triestino, *Il Lloyd Triestino*, 121–92

—— *Trieste italiana: mito e destino economico*, Milan 1990

—— 'Riflettendo sulla "presenza ebraica" nel ceto dirigente della Riunione Adriatica di Sicurtà', in Todeschini, *Il mondo ebraico*, 491–515

Schacherl, B., 'Trieste frontiera di cultura', *Rinascita (Rome)* xlii/28 (27 July 1985), 12–14

Schächter, E., 'The enigma of Svevo's Jewishness: Trieste and the Jewish cultural tradition', *Italian Studies* i (1995), 24–47

Schama, S., *Landscape and memory*, New York 1995

Schöpflin, G. and N. Wood (eds), *In search of Central Europe*, Cambridge 1989

Schwarz, E., 'What Central Europe is and what it is not', in Schöpflin and Wood, *Central Europe*, 143–56

Scrinari, V., G. Furlan and B. Favetta, *Piazza Unità d'Italia a Trieste*, Trieste 1990

Scroccaro, M., *Dall'aquila bicipite alla croce uncinata: l'Italia e le opzioni nelle nuove provincie Trentino, Sudtirolo, Val Canale, 1919–1939*, Trent 2000

Secoli, G., *Il terzo cinquantennio della 'Minerva', 1910–1960*, Trieste 1965

Seri, A., P. Covre and L. Grassi, *Le insegne dell'ospitalità: due secoli di esercizi pubblici a Trieste*, Trieste 1988

Serra, E., 'Il ruolo internazionale della società e la politica estera italiana', in Lloyd Triestino, *Il Lloyd Triestino*, 65–120

Seton-Watson, C., *Italy from Liberalism to Fascism, 1870–1925*, London 1967

Showstack Sassoon, A. (ed.), *Approaches to Gramsci*, London 1982

Silvestri, C., *Dalla redenzione al fascismo: Trieste, 1918–1922*, Udine 1959

Sluga, G., 'The risiera at San Sabba: Fascism, anti-Fascism, and Italian nationalism', *Journal of Modern Italian Studies* i (1996), 401–12

—— *The problem of Trieste and the Italo-Yugoslav border: difference, identity, and sovereignty in twentieth-century Europe*, Albany 2001

Sondhaus, L., *The Habsburg empire and the sea: Austrian naval policy, 1797–1866*, West Lafayette 1989

———— *In the service of the emperor: Italians in the Austrian armed forces 1814–1918*, Boulder, Col. 1990

Spazzali, R., *Epurazione di frontiera: le ambigue sanzioni contro il fascismo nella Venezia Giulia, 1945–1948*, Gorizia 2000

Spirito, P., *Trieste a stelle e strisce*, Trieste 1995

Stone, M., *The patron state: culture and politics in Fascist Italy*, Princeton 1998

Strasser, K. and H. Waitzbauer, *Über die Grenzen nach Triest: Wanderungen zwischen Karnischen Alpen und Adriatischem Meer*, Vienna 1999

Taylor, G., *Environment and nation: geographical factors in the cultural and political history of Europe*, Chicago 1936

Tintori, S., 'Neoclassicismo e civiltà europea nella Trieste mercantile', *Casabella: Rivista internazionale di architettura* ccxix (15 May 1958), 36–45

Todeschini, G. (ed.), *Il mondo ebraico: gli ebrei tra Italia nord-orientale e impero asburgico dal medioevo all'età contemporanea*, Pordenone 1991

Todorova, M., *Imagining the Balkans*, New York 1997

Trampus, A., *Vie e piazze di Trieste moderna: toponomastica stradale e topografia storica*, Trieste 1989

Trieste, 1900–1999: cent'anni di storia, Trieste 1999

Tuathail, G., 'Foreign policy and the hyperreal: the Reagan administration and the scripting of "South Africa"', in Barnes and Duncan, *Writing worlds*, 155–75

Tucci, U., 'Il manuale cucina di Katharina Prato e Trieste', in Cattaruzza, *Trieste, Austria, Italia*, 131–50

Ulcigrai, B., 'Trieste, Carso e oltre', *Sapori d'Italia e Dintorni* vi (1999), 6–11

Ulmer, C. and G. D'Affara, *The castles of Friuli: history and civilization*, Cologne 1999

Università degli studi di Trieste, *La scuola media ebraica di Trieste negli anni 1938–1943: storia e memorie*, Trieste 1999

Valdevit, G., *La questione di Trieste, 1941–1954: politica internazionale e contesto locale*, Milan 1986

Valussi, G., 'Caratteri e funzioni del nuovo confine italo-jugoslavo', in *Confini e regioni: il potenziale di sviluppo e di pace delle periferie: problemi e prospettive delle regioni di frontiera Gorizia*, Istituto di Sociologia Internazionale [Gorizia, 24 Mar. 1972], Trieste 1973

Viatori, D., 'Il commercio a Trieste nell'arco dell'ultimo cinquantennio', in Camera di commercio, *Cinquant'anni*, 395–434

Vinci, E. and S. Vinci, 'La storia del Caffè San Marco', in S. Vinci (ed.), *Al Caffè San Marco: storia, arte, e lettere di un caffè triestino*, Trieste 1995, 31–73

Visintin, A., *L'Italia a Trieste: l'operatore del governo militare italiano nella Venezia Giulia, 1918–19*, Gorizia 2000

Voghera, G., *Gli anni della psicanalisi*, Pordenone 1980

Wagnleitner, R., *Coca-colonization and the Cold War: the cultural mission of the United States in Austria after the Second World War*, Chapel Hill 1994

Weinberg, L. Stock, *L'Anello: the link between past and present*, Trieste 1988

White, R., *The middle ground: Indians, empires, and republics in the Great Lakes region, 1650–1815*, Cambridge 1991

Wilson, R., 'A new cosmopolitanism is in the air: some dialectical twists and turns', in Cheah and Robbins, *Cosmopolitics*, 351–61

Winkler, E., *Wahlrechtsreformen und Wahlen in Triest, 1905–1909: eine Analyse der politischen Partizipation in einer multinationalen Stadtregion der Habsburgermonarchie*, Munich 2000

Wolff, L., *Inventing eastern Europe*, Berkeley 1994

Wörsdörfer, R., 'Zwischen Karst und Adria', in R. Streibel (ed.), *Flucht und Vertreibung: zwischen Aufrechnung und Verdrängung*, Vienna 1994, 92–133.

Zamagni, V., 'American influence on the Italian economy, 1948–1958', in Duggan and Wagstaff, *Italy in the Cold War*, 77–88

———— *The economic history of Italy 1860–1990*, Oxford 1993

Ziller, P., 'Le nuove provincie nell'immediato dopoguerra: tra ricostruzione e autonomie amministrative (1918–1922)', in Salimbeni, *Dal litorale austriaco*, 243–74

Zuccotti, S., *Under his very windows: the Vatican and the Holocaust in Italy*, New Haven 2000

Unpublished material

Andreotti, L., 'Art and politics in Fascist Italy: the exhibition of the Fascist revolution (1932)', unpubl. PhD diss. MIT 1989

Coda, E., 'Between borders: the writing of illness in Trieste', unpubl. PhD diss. UCLA 1998

Day, D., 'The shaping of postwar Italy', unpubl. PhD diss. Chicago 1982

Hametz, M., 'Excellent citizens, perfect Italians: the Triestines and the fairs, 1920–1954', unpubl. PhD diss. Brandeis 1995

Sarti, R., 'We have made Italy', response to H-Italy query by P. Cannistraro, 8 Feb. 1997, http://www.h-net.msu.edu

Sluga, G., 'Liberating Trieste, 1945–1954: nation, history and the Cold War', unpubl. PhD diss. Sussex 1993

Spaini, A. (ed.), 'Vita culturale a Trieste: le influenze mitteleuropee', RAI Radiotelevisione Italiana centro di produzione, Rome, 15 Nov. 1960 (transcript)

Stone, M., 'The politics of cultural production: the exhibition in Fascist Italy', unpubl. PhD diss. Princeton 1990

Index